W9-AFG-952

Speaking of HILLARY

A Reader's Guide to the Most Controversial Woman in America

White Cloud Press
Ashland, Oregon

Speaking of HILLARY

edited by SUSAN K. FLINN

 Inquiries should be addressed to: White Cloud Press, PO Box 3400, Ashland, Oregon 97520. Web site: www.whitecloudpress.com

Printed in the United States

9 8 7 6 5 4 3 2 1

First Edition: 2000

Cover design: David Rupee, Impact Publications
Cover photograph by: The Oregonian
Photograph of Susan K. Flinn: Adam Shannon

Library of Congress Cataloging in Publication Data

Speaking of Hillary : a reader's guide to the most controversial woman in America / edited by Susan K. Flinn.--1st ed.
p. cm.
Includes bibliographical references
ISBN 1-883991-34-X
1. Clinton, Hillary Rodham. 2. Clinton, Hillary Rodham--Miscellanea. 3. Presidents' spouses--United States--Biography. I. Flinn, Susan K.

E887.C55.S66 2000
973.929'092--dc21
[B]

00-043233

Notice of previously published materials: see citations at the end of each selection for sources.

Table of Contents

Profiles and Background

1992 Election

The Role of the First Lady

Health Care

Religion & Spirituality

1994 Elections

IT TAKES A VILLAGE & CHILDREN'S DEVELOPMENT

MONICA & MARRIAGE

1998 ELECTIONS

SENATE RACE

Profiles & Background

THE ARTICLES COLLECTED IN THIS BOOK present a largely chronological survey of Hillary Rodham Clinton's impact and influence. Beginning with these overview articles, which set the stage and provide a general introduction to the First Lady, the essays parallel her public life from the 1992 presidential election through her current New York Senate campaign.

People today are very interested in how an individual's earliest experiences shape their life. ROGER MORRIS describes Hillary Rodham's formative years in the conservative Park Ridge suburb of Chicago. Morris touches on her tenaciousness, strong Methodist faith and commitment to social change — all key components of Mrs. Clinton's personality and her activities as First Lady.

WALTER SHAPIRO provides a profile dating from the beginning of the public's relationship with the First Lady and debunks some of the more pervasive myths about her. Along the way, he also introduces the reader to Mrs. Clinton's (by all accounts) wicked sense of humor. As early as 1993, Hillary Clinton describes herself as a Rorschach test, and Shapiro notes that "she entered the national consciousness as a caricature and became a cartoon." Not much changes in the years to come.

CAMILLE PAGLIA's psychological assessment of Mrs. Clinton's childhood, personality and marriage touches on her "excesses, heartbreaks, torments and comebacks." Paglia explores the effect of the 1960s on Hillary Rodham's views and her development into a role model for other women. Hillary Rodham Clinton, she says, is "a bewitching symbol of professional women's sometimes-confused search for identity in this era of unlimited options."

These pieces address three major questions that feed popular curiosity about Mrs. Clinton: what is she really like, how did she get to be who she is, and what is going on in her marriage? Throughout the ups and downs of the two Clinton Administrations and into the New York Senate run, these questions lie at the center of most assessments of the First Lady.

Park Ridge
She Had to Put up with Him

Roger Morris

IN THEIR OWN WAYS, they were casualties of their America and refugees from the depression, much as Virginia Cassidy and Bill Blythe had been.

Dorothy Howell was of Welsh-Scottish descent with French and Native American ancestry as well. She was born in 1919 into the blue-collar tenements of South Chicago, the daughter of a fireman and of a half-Canadian mother who was all but illiterate. Part of the vast migration of the era, the family later moved to southern California, where Dorothy grew up in the sunlit but bittersweet promise of the Los Angeles basin. At high school in Alhambra, she was a member of the scholarship society, an admired athlete, and an energetic organizer of student activities. She left the West Coast almost as soon as she graduated, never looking back "too fondly," as one account put it, on a seemingly painful, unreconciled childhood and adolescence. Intelligent and pretty, with a compelling smile and an abiding sense of independence, eighteen-year-old Dorothy was back in Chicago in 1937, applying for a job as a secretary with the Columbia Lace Company, when she met a witty yet severe and begrudging young curtain salesman named Hugh Rodham.

He was seven years older and had been raised amid English working-class sternness and privation. His own father was brought from the bleak miners' slums of Northumberland to Pennsylvania at the age of three and, while still a child, was put out to work at the Scranton Lace Company, later to marry another English immigrant who had been a winder in a silk-mill sweatshop since her teens. Theirs was an unsparing household, bound by the evangelical Methodism of their origins and the hard-bitten lunch-pail Republicanism of the time. One of three boys and his father's namesake, Hugh managed to attend Penn State on a football scholarship, majoring in physical education. But out of college during the depression, he found himself back in the lace factory himself, a second generation now "lifting boxes for lousy money," as one account put it. He soon fled, laboring for a time in the grim Pennsylvania coal mines, restlessly looking for jobs in New York, then Chicago, where he ended up in the fabric business after all, though in a more respectable, white-collar job as a salesman. He was still engaged to a woman in Scranton, and they had even taken out a marriage license. Then he noticed smiling Dorothy Howell at the office.

Their courtship went on for five years, with "much romantic back and forth," as friends described it. In his late twenties, he already foreshadowed the stinting, harsh husband and father he would become. Dorothy Howell was sadly ahead of her time, enjoying a brief relative independence during the depression and war years and ever after yearning for an equity and opportunity painfully denied in her married life. Proud, quietly ambitious, she had fallen in love with a "Mr. Impossible," as one chronicler of the family wrote. When Pearl Harbor came she was still a working girl, seeing Rodham but with hopes for higher education. She now put off college indefinitely, and they were finally married in 1942.

During the war, Hugh Rodham, with his college degree in physical education, supervised young recruits in the navy's Gene Tunney program, a regimen of conditioning and self-defense named for the former heavyweight boxing champion. In naval stations around the country, instructors like Rodham were expected to be stringently rigorous, austere, and aloof — tight-jawed calisthenics leaders equally free of emotion and flab, withholding praise, unconsoling, mocking of the slightest failure. Believed to harden the erstwhile civilians to a new toughness and resolve, it was all an unsentimental hazing for the warfare waiting outside the gate.

After 1945, the Rodhams were very much a part of the postwar generation of resumed hopes, intent on stability after years of uncertainty. "They wanted secure jobs, secure homes, and secure marriages in a secure country," Elaine Tyler May wrote of anxious millions like them. Just as traveling salesman Bill Blythe dreamed of owning an auto-parts franchise, Hugh Rodham would start his own drapery business. He began to sell custom work to major purchasers like hotels, corporations, and airlines, buying, printing, and sewing the fabric himself, even hanging the curtains. He usually had only one employee — whom he generally treated as a slack navy recruit, with an irascibility those around him struggled vainly to gloss. "Although he badgered his help inordinately," said one account of the business, "there was an undercurrent of good humor in his manner — and nobody took Hugh at face value."

When he came home from the service he and Dorothy lived for a time in a one-bedroom apartment in an area of Chicago only miles from the house Bill Blythe had purchased. In January 1947 she gave birth to a placid 8½-pound girl, "a good-natured, nice little baby," she would say, who was "very mature upon birth." In a small act of unconventionality, she called her Hillary, a family name she saw as "exotic and unusual."

Three years later the family left the city for the new space and status — what many saw as the refuge — of the suburbs, a sedate place comfortably northwest of Chicago on the wooded moraine that gave it its fashionable name, Park Ridge. Taking in a wave of postwar migrants, it was no dusty subdivision of tract houses hammered up on a treeless grid but an established community of shade and character. The locale had been one of the older settlements adjoining Chicago's city limits, the site of a nineteenth-century brickyard that eventually exhausted its clay deposits. With the arrival of the Chicago & Northwestern tracks, the old industrial village gave way to a commuting suburb, suitably changing its name from Brickton to Park Ridge. By the 1950s a neat little town center had thriving small businesses and solid, respectable public buildings. To many this was the prize, the way life in America was supposed to be. "We could have been a Frank Capra set without changing a thing," one resident would say. "Park Ridge was where Dick and Jane lived with their perfect parents and their little dog, Spot," another resident remarked.

When Hillary Rodham grew up there in the 1950s and 1960s, the streets and yards were teeming with the children of the postwar baby boom and suburban exodus, literally hundreds of them in the blocks around her house. Over the decade after her family moved, the population of Chicago proper grew by some 20 percent, but the near suburbs exploded, Park Ridge itself almost tripling to nearly forty thousand residents.

They were hardly a dozen miles from Chicago's Loop, yet Park Ridge was a world apart from the city and even from more diverse suburbs like Skokie, blocks away to the east. Park Ridge was on the rural outskirts of the metropolis. A few miles to the southwest, the area that would become O'Hare Airport, the world's busiest, there was still an apple orchard with cornfields beyond. Nearby were also Chicago's distinct communities of Italians, Poles, Mexican Americans, and Appalachian refugees, even Native American ghettos, and the largest single Jewish population in the metropolitan area. From all that, however, Park Ridge and similar suburbs were cordoned off by discreet but towering barriers of class and ethnicity. Here as elsewhere in the nation, sharply defined, exclusive enclaves of affluent, white Anglo-Saxon Protestants were segregated from unwanted minorities by racist real estate covenants and sub-rosa mortgage discrimination, as well as by income and economic privilege.

For the most part, it was a society of the educated upper middle class, among whom Hugh Rodham, even with a lucrative drapery business and his own new Cadillacs year after year, could seem déclassé. Away from his sewing machine and curtain hanging, he did not socialize with suburbia's "doctors, lawyers, and Indian chiefs," according to his daughter. "I never knew any professionals growing up," she would make a point of telling a reporter a quarter century later. In the social life the family did have, Dorothy Rodham herself would feel sharply the lack in her own background and forfeited education, "so unsure of her knowledge that she would drop out of conversations," wrote Judith Warner, "or simply play supportive audience to her husband's stronger voice." In their prescribed role, the mothers of Park Ridge stayed home to care for their houses and children. "Independent women, admired during the1930s and the war," wrote one historian, "were now looked upon as neurotic freaks."

"It was a lily-white area," remembered Sherry Heiden, a childhood friend of Hillary Rodham. "I think finally by our senior year there was one black kid in the whole school." They all went diligently to Sunday school and services in lovely brick churches with the requisite steeples and stained glass — and sometimes grew into adults without realizing they were all so numbingly alike. "I was in college before it hit me that everybody and everything was in the same mold," said one. Only in the consolidated high school, enrolling students from neighboring Skokie and elsewhere, did many of them have their first social contacts with Catholics, Jews, or simply children from blue-collar families.

Invariably the politics of Park Ridge followed its social and economic contours, finding expression and lead in the newspaper and broadcast empire of Chicago's legendary reactionary, Colonel Robert R. McCormack. The area was "white-collar country," as a group of political analysts once described it, "where the Chicago *Tribune* is a staple and where children are brought up to despise and fear the city [Democratic] machine." In a larger suburban district known for conservative sentiment, Park Ridge itself could be uniquely dogmatic and rigid, a contrast even to wealthier but more politically mixed and socially secure suburbs north along the Chicago lakeshore. A fiercely and unctuously dry community while liquor was sold just a township away, Park Ridge elected local, state, and national representatives known almost uniformly as *Tribune* Republicans for their right-wing extremism.

In a familiar pattern of class reaction, many in the town seemed all the more jealous of their exclusivity for having recently emerged themselves from poor or working-class origins. In the 1950s the picturesque community was an early center of the ultrarightist, conspiracy-minded John Birch Society, assailing President Dwight Eisenhower as a "Communist dupe," if not a Soviet agent, and equating Democrats in general with outright treason. So powerful was the reactionary fear taking root in Park Ridge and nearby suburbs that right-wing Republicans won the district's congressional seat in the early 1950s and never let go. Harold Collier, a former match company personnel manager and a colorless creature of Colonel McCormack's, served nine terms and was succeeded in 1966 by a rotund state assembly politician and affable ideologue, Henry Hyde, who over ten more terms — until his embroilment in a banking scandal in the mid-1990s — would be known as "defender of the suburbs" and the GOP right's "most effective partisan weapon" on Capitol Hill.

In exclusive enclaves around Chicago — as in the Arkansas subdivisions — there were formidable social forces arrayed against honesty and revelation, both within and outside the family. Added to the prevailing cultural images of parents and children and to the postdepression, postwar drive for stability and security were vast corporate powers fastening on the happy new suburban family in its roles as advertising icon and lucrative market. Not least, there were the deeper politics of the moment. In many respects mirroring cold war reaction and conformity on the outside, the conservative male-dominated family regime and ideology of the 1950s and early 1960s abhorred and checked rebellion in the home almost as national policy contained revolt abroad — and often with similar means of reward and punishment. Just as Arkansas folk wisdom taught resignation to the fixity of local power, suburban orthodoxy in Park Ridge posed all the implicit contracts of the new postwar affluence and stability — the approved credentials and paths to success, the cost of dissent or mere nonconformity, the seeming disappearance of the old basic divisions of class and wealth, the manifest superiority of the American system at home and abroad. "Domestic containment," as historian Elaine Tyler May called the ethos of postwar life in the suburbs, "was bolstered by a powerful political culture that rewarded its adherents and marginalized its detractors."

In the same suburbs, it was true, there were warning signs dating from the early 1950s — a growing and affecting literature chronicling discontent and the emptiness of materiality, a six-fold increase in psychiatrists and untold additional patients, and what sociologist Todd Gitlin called "generational cleavage in the making" among the young. There had been all that and more. But behind most closed doors in Park Ridge and its replicas, women and children in particular learned somehow to cope, to go on — perhaps even to feel better about their predicament, to reconcile themselves, though seldom to change the deeper pattern or to question the connections between their own despair or disillusionment and the larger social, economic, and political framework.

America's most powerful First Lady was to come from that crucible and those confines as markedly — and in some ways as painfully — as a future president emerged from his landscapes of Hope and Hot Springs.

THE RODHAMS LIVED IN A GRACEFUL two-story stone-brick Georgian house built before the war at the corner of Elm and Wisner. Hillary was soon joined by two younger brothers, Hugh, Jr., and Tony. As the only daughter she had her own bedroom, a cheery yellow with polished oak floors and a sundeck looking out on the pleasant neighborhood. There she grew into an obviously bright, determined, accomplished girl whose experiences were so stamped with the people and cultural setting as to seem now almost apocryphal.

"There's no room in this house for cowards," her mother remembered scolding her about confronting the neighborhood bully. "You're going to have to stand up to her. The next time she hits you, I want you to hit her back." According to the family story, the Rodhams' little girl did just that and won with her own fists a precious male acceptance and a coveted chance to play with the boys in the neighborhood. "Boys responded well to Hillary," Dorothy would say proudly. "She just took charge, and they let her." She also played avid ping-pong, took music and ballet lessons, organized neighborhood "Olympics" and circuses, competed gamely with her athletic brothers, and amused everyone with a biting gift for mimicry that she would carry into her political adulthood. At Eugene Field Grammar School and Ralph Waldo Emerson Junior High, she was "a chronic teacher's pet," by one account. After school, she faithfully went on to the Brownies and Girl Scouts, earning a sash "so loaded with badges and dazzling little pins," thought Martha Sherrill, "that it's amazing she didn't walk with a stoop." On Sundays she was devoutly at the First United Methodist Church. Despite what one recollection called "the burden of that ceaseless public do-gooding," little Hillary Rodham seemed "to love it all." It was what growing up in Park Ridge was supposed to be.

How she reacted to the rest of her childhood was never part of the public myth. In the house at 236 Wisner, Dorothy Rodham was the town's conventional "stay-at-home mother" and child's "chauffeur," as Judith Warner described her. "I spent all my time in the car then," she herself would say. "The mother is the encourager and the helper, and the father brings news from the outside world" is how her daughter later benignly described what she called the family's "classic parenting situation." In that sense, however, the "news" from the world was often harsh, and the solicitous mother could not help her children with what writer Carolyn Susman saw as "a looming presence in all their lives" — the implacably judgmental and exacting Hugh Rodham. "Kind of like the glue that held the family together. But not the way you would think," Hugh, Jr., would say of him after his death. "My father was confrontational, completely and utterly so."

Most of the public memories of the man and his impact were cast after his daughter became famous — and with so much political and personal discretion as to be distorted. Nevertheless, the essence is unmistakable. "The suburban Hugh Rodham was tightfisted, hard to please, and always in command," concluded Norman King. "Though it is not fashionable to be macho today, Hugh fit the pattern perfectly then." There would be ostensibly fond recollections of the father's spending time with his children, devoting himself in a sense — though always with the drillmaster's mania for performance, endurance, proof of worth. One spring, Martha Sherrill noted, the entire family went to a local park and stood watching the man "pitch and pitch and pitch until his daughter Hillary learned to belt a curveball." She became an accomplished shortstop and hitter and applied her categorical intelligence to baseball lore, treating less knowledgeable young fans in the neighborhood with the impatience, if not contempt, her father had shown his children. "She knew everything about the Cubs and everybody else, and really showed it off," said a childhood friend.

In the same way, friends remembered, Hugh Rodham had drilled his daughter on stock prices, requiring her to pore over quotes on the *Tribune*'s stock market page for "good investments" and then praising her sparingly or upbraiding her with his usual rigor, depending on her "success." "You actually got tongue-lashed or sanctioned for losing money in that little game they had, and she learned the ropes fast," one recalled. "Making money like that was always very important to Mr. Rodham, very important," said another, "and it was something he tried to instill in her like everything else. No matter what you did, you weren't worth very much if you couldn't make money."

"Mr. Reality Check," Hillary would call him in the more neutral language of another generation. "I used to go to my father and say: 'Dad, I *really* need a new pair of shoes. My shoes have holes in them,' and he'd say, 'Have you done your chores? Have you done this? Have you done that?'" There were constant reminders of how fortunate — and precarious — their situation was, of what bitter hardships their father had suffered during the depression. He took them to an old coal mine in Pennsylvania to show them the grimy, spectral setting in which he once worked, however briefly. "The youngsters got the point," thought Norman King. "We were probably the only kids in the whole suburb who didn't get an allowance," Tony Rodham recalled vividly. "We'd rake the leaves, cut the grass, pull weeds, shovel snow. All your friends would be going to a movie. After your errands you'd walk in and say, 'Gee, Dad, I could use two or three dollars.' He'd flop another potato on your dinner plate and say, 'That's your reward.'" His approach to avoiding "spoiled" children, according to his wife, was straightforward: "'They eat and sleep for free! We're not going to pay them for it as well!'"

For misbehavior they were "spanked on occasion or deprived of privileges," as one account put it. Neighbors and friends saw Hugh, Jr., as the family rebel — "a kind of rascal, a roustabout," a local minister would say — but his sister as the obedient, amenable "perfect child." "I was a quick learner," Hillary told Marian Burros. "I didn't run afoul of my parents very often. They were strict about my respecting authority, and not just parental authority. My father's favorite saying was: 'You get in trouble at school, you get in trouble at home.'"

But in Hugh Rodham's family boot camp, the even harsher response was reserved for conformity and success. When his proud little girl came home with straight As, he said to her dismissively, "It must be a very easy school you go to." Later, when she excelled in college prep courses, as Hugh, Jr., remembered, "He would say, 'It must be a pretty small college.'" " At his sons' football games, Rodham disdained the bleachers and other parents, carrying a folding lawn chair in order to sit out on the sidelines, nearer the action, alone. After Hugh, Jr., who would go on to play at Penn State, quarterbacked a 42–0 championship victory and completed ten of eleven passes, he came back to Wisner Street to find his father lying on the sofa, ready with the familiar reproach. "I got nothing to say to you," he told the boy, "except you should have completed the other one."

Decades afterward, family and friends tried to interpret the elder Hugh Rodham's motives more gently. "With all of those things, he was not being mean or tactless. . . . He was trying in his own way to show us that we could be better," a son offered. "It's hard out there," Hillary quoted her father, explaining to an interviewer that his "encouragement was tempered by realism." The deeper cost of that tempering, however, no tactful language could conceal. Among both relatives and friends, many thought Hugh Rodham's treatment of his daughter and sons amounted to the kind of psychological abuse and adversity that might have crushed some children — and came close to doing so in Park Ridge. It was not the episodic, detonating, often bloody abuse her future husband suffered in Hope and Hot Springs but a slightly more subtle oppression. The

Rodhams were not like the Clintons, with a "crisis every four minutes," Hillary would later tell her future mother-in-law. In a sense, she was right. The quieter, more discreet abuse of Park Ridge had known no intervals. "Her spirit, though, was unbreakable," biographer Judith Warner concluded. Others disagreed. "I don't think there's any question that the real little Hillary was broken," said a longtime observer. "The point is how she got mended, and the person put in her place."

Family and friends adopted Rodham's own pretense — that it was all good for them, however hurtful. Victims themselves, her mother and brothers came to rationalize what had happened to Hillary, arguing that the relationship with the father fortified her and bred her famously fierce determination and endurance. The family story of how she resolved at the age of nine to keep her maiden name when she married was the sort that proved how well she coped and survived and was stronger than most. Yet there was no real hiding the quiet cruelty and pain. The sense of stinted or denied love, a resort to refuge outside the family, the alternating warmth and vitriol, compassion and sarcasm, the tightly controlled yet seething perpetual anger not far beneath the impenetrable shell — all would be visible in the independent but camouflaged woman she became. "She loves talking about ideas. She loves asking questions," Jan Piercy would say of the Hillary Rodham she knew well in the years just after childhood and adolescence. "Ask her about herself and I think you'll find she shuts down. Oh, she may answer your question, but I don't think you'll see much energy behind it." The same verdict would come from the other woman who had watched it all and felt her own wounds. "Maybe that's why she's such an accepting person," Dorothy Rodham said in a moment of candor about her outwardly strong but long-suffering daughter. "She had to put up with him."

The parents "made no distinction between her and her two brothers," one observer wrote later, but the old shadings were in fact always there. With Hugh Rodham's approval, Hillary might take jobs as a babysitter, wading-pool lifeguard, or recreation counselor, but never in the drapery business, where her brothers worked often. At the same time, friends remembered the mother's steady, conscious effort to spur her daughter to succeed in academic and career terms, albeit terms still defined by men. "I've always spoken to Hillary as you would to an adult," Dorothy once recalled, with echoes of Virginia Clinton. The girl growing up in Park Ridge was to be what her mother had never been free to be in Alhambra, Chicago, or the suburbs — above all, a presence, even a power, in the competitive, image-conscious, male-run outside world. That, in some ways, was more important than the trappings of marriage and family, which the mother had without fulfillment. "I was determined that no daughter of mine was going to have to go through the agony of being afraid to say what she had on her mind," Dorothy would say later. "Just because she was a girl didn't mean she should be limited."

One of her fellow students recalled that in the early 1960s their high school was "a big factory but also a really snobby place in its own way. The kids were just like their well-off parents, and everybody seemed headed for college with good jobs for boys, marriage for girls, and big homes and cars just like their folks." Utterly composed, a serious, busy young woman, Hillary Rodham seemed easily a part of that world, those expectations, yet in some ways deliberately separate. Through three years at Maine East, then a final year among some four thousand students attending the huge new Maine South, she continued to excel academically. At the same time, she played field hockey and volleyball, debated, acted in school plays, sang in the variety show. Asked years afterward if she and her friends had ever cut classes or openly challenged school authority, a close friend could only gasp, "Are you *kidding*?"

She dressed conventionally, wearing her society's familiar box-pleated skirts, blouses with Peter Pan collars, kneesocks and loafers, though she remained relatively oblivious to clothes and pointedly spurned cosmetics and hairstyling. "She rejected offers to have her ears pierced . . . didn't smoke in the bathroom, didn't make out with the boys in 'the Pit' at Maine South's library, didn't even wear black turtlenecks," recorded Martha Sherrill. "She was totally unconcerned about how she appeared to people," thought Jennie Snodgrass, a classmate, "and she was loved for that."

Dorothy Rodham was less certain. "When she was fifteen or sixteen, and other kids were starting to use makeup and fix their hair, she wasn't interested," the mother recalled. "That used to annoy me a little bit; I used to think, 'Why can't she put on a little makeup?'" There were moments when Hillary might look like the rest, dressed for the 1964 junior prom, for example, in gown and long white gloves, with lipstick and short, specially cut, slightly teased hair. But it was almost as if she were wearing a bizarre, slightly disagreeable costume, and after Maine South she would not return to its like for fifteen years, until the 1980s, when she appeared as the deliberately "made-over" wife of a comeback candidate for governor of Arkansas.

Defiantly unadorned and blithely uninterested in boys, she had little social life beyond her extracurricular activities and almost no dates, taking an old childhood friend to "girl's choice" dances and preferring a college boy from Princeton to her callow peers, though seeing little of him either. Like the makeup and clothes, sexuality was one of the rites of suburban passage for which she had neither time nor enthusiasm. "She wouldn't let some young man dominate meetings if he had nothing to say," said one of her teachers. "She wasn't going to be demure and spend a lot of time looking cute to attract people." To others, however, there was already an air of something more, an edge about her relations with young men. With no patience for her intellectual inferiors, she seemed to seek out intelligent boys, then coolly compete with them, establishing her dominance. It was not a matter of finding equality, some came to think, but a matter of maintaining a respectable superiority. "She was strong and secure and graceful, almost aloof," said Bob Stenson, a classmate who made even better grades. "I always felt a little funny around her. She was a tough competitor and formidable. I was always hoping she'd stumble a little bit."

The high school paper at one point predicted that Hillary Diane Rodham would become a nun, to be known caustically as Sister Frigidaire.

THE POLITICS OF THE RODHAMS were as fixed as their demands on their children. "Hugh always voted Republican," said a friend, "and not just voted, but could be downright righteous and rabid about it." At home they seldom discussed political topics when their daughter and sons were younger. But there were summer gatherings of the larger Rodham clan around lakes in northeastern Pennsylvania, where staunch Republican relatives deplored the Democrats, convinced that John Kennedy had stolen the 1960 presidential election from Richard Nixon by the connivance, among others, of Mayor Daley's notorious Cook County Democratic machine in Chicago.

Meanwhile, there arrived in Park Ridge a gentle, energetic young minister who would change Hillary's life. The Rodhams' red-brick First United Methodist Church was a stronghold of the town's fearful right-wing reaction well into the 1960s. In the wake of the Kennedy murder in

Dallas and initial publicity about foreign conspiracies by Fidel Castro or the Soviets, the parish director of Christian education felt compelled to send a calming, cautionary letter to the entire membership of three thousand, "hoping that they wouldn't begin finding Communists under every rock," as one account put it. "There were a lot of John Birchers in that church," one of its pastors said later. The year of the Kennedy-Nixon race, when Hillary Rodham was thirteen, Donald Jones, a new youth minister, was appointed to the church. A thirty-year-old recent graduate of the Drew University Seminary, he brought to the suburb a professorial passion to give his sheltered young Methodists a broader sensibility.

As a seminarian, Jones had been deeply influenced by Paul Tillich, and it was Tillich's robust, socially active, and redemptive Protestantism that now shaped Jones's ministry in Park Ridge. Against the backdrop of the early 1960s — the civil rights movement, the fashion of the Kennedy administration, the first stirrings of a youth rebellion — his Thursday night class for a handful of teenagers became what they called with some awe the University of Life. His group was "not just about personal salvation and pious escapism," Jones would explain, "but about an authentic and deep quest for God and life's meaning in the midst of worldly existence."

He rented a projector to show Francois Truffaut's classic *Four Hundred Blows*, Rod Serling's *Requiem for a Heavyweight*, and similar films. On his own guitar, he strummed the songs of Bob Dylan and had his pupils analyze the lyrics. There were lively discussions of Picasso prints, readings from Stephen Crane and e. e. cummings, a debate between an atheist and a Christian — all to make real "the feelings of others," as one remembered him telling them, and to enliven the "practical conscience and content" of their faith. "I was used to relating theology to pop culture, theology to art, theology to the world," Jones said later. "By the time I got to Park Ridge, I had read all kinds of things. I got them reading too."

They went on the usual group retreats, swimming and skiing. But Jones's more remarkable outings took them into a different world. He now led them on a startling series of visits to Chicago's inner city, taking them to recreation centers and other churches to meet black and Hispanic youth, even gang leaders. At one point, he carried along a large reproduction of *Guernica*, set it before a ghetto gang and his suburban teenagers, and asked them to relate to their own lives Picasso's portrayal of anguish and suffering in the Spanish civil war. The session, he well remembered, evoked far more candor and feeling among the poorer, supposedly less educated young people of the city than from their more privileged visitors. Eventually they also met the legendary social activist and organizer Saul Alinsky. Proselytizing among affluent church groups like Jones's young people as well as among Chicago's poor, the flamboyant, irreverent, profane, and hard-drinking Alinsky was at the height of his now acerbic, now raucous challenges to the domestic power structure. Typically, he had once staged a "fart-in" among protesters at a corporate headquarters and, to wring concessions from the Chicago city council, had threatened a demonstration that would flush all the toilets simultaneously at the new O'Hare Airport. He was another unique encounter for the Park Ridge teenagers. However brief, the meeting would have an interesting sequel. In a college thesis a few years later, Hillary Rodham would reveal much of herself in writing about Alinsky and his strategies, and the crusty organizer himself would offer her a coveted job as a virtual protégé.

Most of the inner-city encounters would be genuine revelations for the Park Ridge group, not least for the earnest, impressionable Hillary Rodham. "I was in junior high and high school and got a sense of what people were up against, and how lucky I had been," she once told an interviewer, still remembering the visits to Chicago with obvious emotion. "I don't think those kids had seen poverty before," Jones recalled, "don't think they had interacted with kids that weren't like themselves." On April 15, 1962, he took the class to Chicago's Orchestra Hall to hear Martin Luther King, Jr., preach a sermon entitled "Remaining Awake through a Revolution." After the address he spirited them down to meet the already famous civil rights leader. Thirty years later, Jones himself and most of the others had forgotten the details of that night, but Hillary Rodham remembered it vividly, recalling that Jones had introduced them one by one and that she had personally shaken hands with King. "To accuse her of taking this message literally would not be going too far," one thought of her response to King's admonitions.

Eventually a Thursday evening discussion of teenage pregnancy filtered back to parents and stirred the inevitable controversy and outrage at United Methodist. Still, Jones mollified his superiors and managed to continue the youth group. By 1962–63 his pupils were busily organizing food drives for the poor and even a baby-sitting pool for the children of migrant farm workers camped amid wretched hovels and open sewage in fields west of the city. Small acts of virtual charity, the efforts touched no real power or politics yet in spirit and sensibility were extraordinary for Park Ridge. The imbued and shared idealism of Jones's young Methodists was plain — if bitterly poignant in terms of so much that followed. "We believed in the incredible social changes that can happen," said Sherry Heiden, "if you change your perspective."

Hillary Rodham began dropping by Jones's church office after school or on summer afternoons, eager to talk more about the new ideas and insights from the class. Responding warmly, he gave her a first taste of modern Protestant theology, in excerpts from Tillich, Søren Kierkegaard, Dietrich Bonhoeffer, Reinhold Niebuhr, and others, and they carried on long, increasingly serious discussions. "She was curious, open to what life had to bring," the young minister would say. "She was just insatiable."

When she was in high school he gave her his copy of J. D. Salinger's *Catcher in the Rye*. "I didn't tell you at the time, but when you had me read *Catcher in the Rye*, I didn't like it, and, moreover, I thought it was a little too advanced for me," she wrote Jones her sophomore year in college. "But now that I've read it a second time, I realize, I think, why you gave it to me. I don't think it was too advanced, as a matter of fact."

The minister introduced her to the larger social-political implications of Tillich's reformism, the quest to subdue with Christian idealism what many theologians saw as the postwar's social alienation and secular loss of values. They talked as well, he remembered, about Kierkegaard's "leap of faith" in the face of rational cynicism, about Bonhoeffer's "religionless Christianity" of public morality and ethics, and especially about Niebuhr's more tragic, unsentimental view of history and human nature and of the necessary force of civil governance. "She realizes absolutely the truth of the human condition. . . . . She is very much the sort of Christian who understands that the use of power to achieve social good is legitimate," Jones would say. Yet much of that was in retrospect, when the inquisitive girl of the youth group had become a famously powerful First Lady and when the politics of Hillary Rodham had been shaped by her experience in Arkansas as much as by theology.

At the time, in Jones's small church office, their quiet afternoon talks were less a matter of political tutelage than the tentative discoveries and questions, the first fitful awakenings of critical intellect and sensibility in a spiritually minded young woman. She was at heart, he knew, a cautious, carefully contained, and self-protective girl whose judgments about herself and the world, like her perception of *Catcher in the Rye*, were still forming. "Unlike some people who at a particular age land on a cause and become concerned," Jones said later about what would be a gradual, almost lifelong process, "with Hillary I think of a continuous textured development."

Jones was to leave students like Hillary with the habit of carrying small Methodist devotionals with them for comfort. The warm and ultimately loving personal relationship with him, unique in Hillary Rodham's life, was obviously crucial at the time. Jones was not only intellectually exciting and nurturing but fondly approving and accepting. A "world beyond . . . growling Hugh Rodham," Martha Sherrill called it. "Boys liked her," Reverend Jones once said, defending his favorite student to a reporter questioning her lack of social life in high school. "And not because she was flirtatious. She was not — she wasn't a raving beauty, but she was pretty enough. What attracted guys around her was her personality, her willingness to talk to them, at parity with them." It was a memory, some thought, that mirrored more accurately the maturity and affection of the thirty-year-old minister than the common attitude of suburban teenage males in the 1960s.

To Don Jones, as to no one else, she would continue to bring her questions and reflections. "I wonder if it's possible to be a mental conservative and a heart liberal?" she wrote at one point, charting the inner division that began in her adolescence. Before she finished high school the minister was gone, assigned to another church after little more than four years in Park Ridge. (He would eventually go back to Drew for a PhD and a teaching career free of rancorous congregations like First United Methodist.) She was elected vice president of her junior class at Maine East but in the spring of 1964 ran for senior class president at Maine South and lost, producing a rambling, "philosophical" letter to Jones about reconciling herself to defeat. "Hillary," the pastor remembered clearly, "hated to lose." The letter was only the beginning of her correspondence, usually single-spaced and crowded onto both sides of the page, sent faithfully to him over the next three decades from Park Ridge, college, law school, Washington, Arkansas, and finally the White House.

Not long after he left Chicago in 1964, she wrote about the disapproval she felt from the new minister who had taken his job. "He thinks

I'm a radical," she told her confidant and mentor with some exasperation. It was, after all, an irony they both understood.

IN THE AUTUMN OF 1964 Park Ridge backed with unusual enthusiasm the conservative Republican candidate for president, Senator Barry Goldwater of Arizona. "AuH_2O '64" bumper stickers seemed to fill the driveways, and Hillary Rodham, to the delight of her parents, joined the campaign as an official Goldwater Girl, wearing her straw boater and sash to rallies, briskly canvassing the already solidly Republican neighborhoods, and "[speaking] out for the right wing," according to Judith Warner, "with all the passion of a teenager." Elected to the student council as a senior the same fall, she organized around the national election an elaborate mock political convention in the new Maine South gym, showing her appreciation of the rituals of politics and even planning political demonstrations in the aisles. In November Lyndon Johnson crushed Goldwater by some sixteen million votes, though Park Ridge was unreconciled, its bumper stickers unremoved, fading irreconcilably in the midwestern sun over the years to come. That December Hillary Rodham wrote one of the ritual senior self-portraits in the Maine South paper. She chose to recount her high school experience in terms of a prosecuting attorney pursuing a case that has gone on "literally for years." To the routine question about her ambitions she answered pertly and, to some, a bit unexpectedly, "To marry a senator and settle down in Georgetown."

She graduated fifteenth out of a thousand in the class of 1965. Most of her affluent friends were bound for college, although many young men from lower-income suburbs were soon destined for Vietnam. Some saw their class as a last charmed moment before the upheaval of the rest of the 1960s. Hillary Rodham was voted the girl most likely to succeed. The boy named for the same honor killed himself with a drug overdose before the end of the decade.

She had been a National Merit Scholarship finalist and National Honor Society and student council leader, known almost uniformly for her toughness, competitiveness, and strong convictions. Fellow students said she spoke out for things that she believed in, took unpopular stances, reconciled conflicting positions, and never exhibited a rebellious nature.

Like her future husband's, Hillary Rodham's high school poise and achievements shrouded a deeper loneliness and hurt — and decisive influence — few saw at the time. If Bill Clinton's models had been Roger Clinton and Virginia, hers were no less the long-suffering Dorothy Rodham and her stringent husband. But unlike Bill, she also had a genuine intellectual mentor and an exposure to ideas and to the diversity of American life otherwise as uncommon to Park Ridge as to Hot Springs. The essential contrast in their experiences was in many ways the difference between Uncle Raymond Clinton and the Reverend Don Jones.

Yet she seemed to take away nothing so much as the mark of her childhood place and time. "What people don't seem to realize is that Hillary's so conventional, so traditional, so midwestern, so middle class," her friend Sara Ehrman once said with unintended irony. "Her taste in art is middle class. Her taste in music is middle class. Her clothes. . . . She's very simple, brilliant, a nice person, and a product of her upbringing."

At the urging of two young Maine South teachers, she considered some of the most prestigious women's colleges in the East, including Radcliffe and Smith. "She was set on going to an all-girls' school," her mother said later. She had chosen Wellesley, as she told the story the moment she saw pictures of its bucolic Gothic campus outside Boston: "the lake in the middle, the quaint Victorian classrooms, the tiny surrounding town."

Her parents drove her to Massachusetts in the fall of 1965 in Hugh Rodham's Cadillac. Saying good-bye, the mother, at least, realized how insular, how much within the sustaining, punishing family her daughter's life had been. "Aside from a few trips away with girlfriends, Hillary hadn't really been away from home," Dorothy remembered. "After we dropped her off, I just crawled in the back seat and cried for eight hundred miles."

— ***Richard Morris*** resigned from President Nixon's National Security Council in protest over the Vietnam War. His books include *Richard Milhaus Nixon: The Rise of an American Politician*. From: "Park Ridge" from *Partners in Power: The Clintons and Their America* by Roger Morris.

Whose Hillary is She, Anyway?

Walter Shapiro

I LAUGH POLITELY EACH TIME I hear another rendering of the classic Hillary joke: Bill and Hillary are out for a drive, and they pull into a gas station. As the attendant shambles over, Hillary turns to Bill and confesses, "I used to date that guy." Bill puffs himself up and says, "If you'd married *him,* you'd be stuck here instead of being married to the President of the United States." Hillary shakes her head. "No, if I had married him, *he'd* be President." But, in truth, I have never viewed Hillary as a power-mad string puller, the puppeteer to Bill Clinton's Howdy Doody.

Make no mistake, even among those in the administration who know her well, the name Hillary invokes a certain respect, a tiny shiver of danger, a hint of the deference that might be owed, say a Medici in sixteenth-century Florence. Chatting with a top level economic policymaker, I expressed the standard lament that the Clinton staff was too soft, too amiable, devoid of anyone to play the enforcer. "That's Hillary's role," he replied, as if reducing powerful men to quivering pools of protoplasm were inherent in the job description of a first lady. But is this conceit true or just a convenient window into the hearts of highly placed but insecure men?

The malicious Hillary-as-lesbian rumors — passed around like antipasto platters at lunches in Washington and New York — belong in the same category. I mention the innuendoes reluctantly because I don't believe a word of them. I trust views like those of a close law-school friend of Hillary's, who recalls, "She took a certain lusty pleasure in her relationship with Bill. She had an active, heterosexual existence." No, what fascinates me is the obvious psychosexual release that accompanies the Hillary slander-mongering. There is something about Hillary's role that invites nasty male put-dawns, even among liberal baby boomers who should know better. And certain women have their own problems with Hillary — the sneering "Who elected her?" question — but those, of, course, stem mostly from differing interpretations of feminism, not from gut-wrenching threats to male self-esteem.

"I'm a Rorschach test," Hillary told me during a recent interview in the White House library. She's right. Despite being one of the most treacherously overexposed figures of our time, Hillary Rodham Clinton the real person is largely unknown. We look at her visage on television and magazine covers — and we see what we want to see. A number of Hillary's friends used the hoary five-blind-men-and-an-elephant metaphor to describe their frustrations with media portraits of the First Lady — the facts may even be accurate, but the minutiae of her personality are grotesquely exaggerated. She entered the national consciousness as a caricature and has become a cartoon. Recall all the bizarre twists and odd lurches of her public persona in the last eighteen months. Most Americans first saw Hillary on "60 Minutes" in the wake of the Gennifer Flowers debacle when she came across as a tigress ridiculing the notion that she was a Tammy Wynette, "Stand by Your Man" dishrag. She was muzzled after the milk-and-cookies flap when it seemed that she was ridiculing stay-at-home moms. By the time of the Democratic Convention, the official Hillary makeover was complete — now it was all loving wife and devoted mother, as if her legal career had been just so many Little Rock Tupperware parties. With Hillary as First Lady, the media schizophrenia has reached clinical proportions. Typical was a cloying Katie Couric special that played up a bionic Hillary who worries about rug stains in the Lincoln bedroom, whether to let Chelsea pierce, and reinventing health care. This Hillary makes Katherine Hepburn in *Woman of the Year* look catatonic. Then came Hillary the Thinker, the Religious Searcher — the Protestant reincarnation of Barbara Streisand in *Yentl* — a visionary mudwrestling with Tillich and Niebuhr as she gropes to define "the politics of meaning."The apogee came with *The New York Times Magazine* portraying her as Saint Hillary (incidentally sparking a hot debate about whether the *Times* for the first time in history was being ironic) questing after "a unified field theory" of existence. And, yes, on the seventh day she rested.

Granted, it's not easy to decipher Hillary, since her handlers safeguard her privacy as if she were in the Federal Witness Protection Program. (Oh, another joke: Why does the Secret Service guard Hillary so closely? Because if anything happens to her, Bill becomes President.) She grants only the occasional interview, and there are no provisions for press to accompany her when she travels. "It's like covering Ross Perot," a newspaper reporter grumped while Hillary gave a bland commencement address at the University of Pennsylvania. "We're not restricting access," insists Lisa Caputo, Hillary's press secretary. "This is a woman who has tremendous demands on her schedule." True enough, in addition to her policy work, she insists on choosing the napkins for While House dinners. But there is also a reticence, a reserve, to Hillary, a hidden zone of privacy that may date back to her need to maintain a public face in Arkansas during the time of troubles in the Clinton marriage. "I don't think what she's labeled or called matters to Hillary," said her close friend Diane Blair, a political scientist at the University of Arkansas. "Not one thousandth of her time is spent worrying about what people think of her."

Maybe not, but what then are we to make of the First Lady? Her public virtues are genuine — intelligence, decisiveness, guts and a willingness to make the right enemies. In private, she frequently rails against Washington, using the phrase "this town" as an epithet, and you want to cheer her on in righteous indignation at Congress, lobbyists, and the preening peacocks of the press corps. At a time when the President's approval ratings resemble Woody Allen's, Hillary alone has avoided the missteps of an administration that is fast making the Carter years a metaphor for competence. If Bill Clinton is to rebound as president, then Hillary represents his last, best hope for political redemption. The health-care plan — whenever it debuts — may be the first step on the road to recovery. Hillary more than her husband, is the avatar of an era in which substance is making a surprise comeback against symbol. But the myths that make up what we know of Hillary have about as much connection to the real world as Rush Limbaugh and his femi-Nazis. To understand the real Hillary we need a crash course in debunking the myths. Only by getting rid of the rubbish, and our own mental complicity in fostering it, can we begin to see Hillary as a woman whom we, well. . . .really like.

MYTH: *Hillary has the sense of humor of Pat Nixon. . . .* By all accounts, Hillary is the Dana Carvey of the West Wing, combining artful put-downs and pranks with perfect-pitch mimicry and a true relish for self-mockery. During the campaign, for instance, she was known for routinely dispatching her staff to trash Clinton aide-de-camp Bruce Lindsey's hotel rooms before he would have a chance to settle in. And on the famed campaign bus trips, word has it that the Clintons and Gores would take peculiar pleasure in trading off-color barnyard stories. "There's a reason that Hillary's humor doesn't come out in the press," explains a top Clinton adviser "It's sardonic, even bitchy, and not at all repeatable. But it's very funny." Hillary's staff long ago decided — after the milk-and-cookies mistake — that America was not ready for a First Lady with an earthy streak, or what her chief of staff, Maggie Williams, refers to as Hillary's rowdy side.

MYTH:. . . .*And the common touch of Nancy Reagan.* Equally at odds with Hillary's austere public image is her love for the Chicago Cubs. It's as baffling as discovering that Shannen Doherty's true passion in life is the harpsichord. Hillary the single-minded workaholic, had intended to take a day off from the office to throw out the first ball at Wrigley Field. Hillary clung to that plan even after her father was felled by a devastating stroke. Often during her bedside vigil in Little Rock, Hillary would toss a baseball around with her brothers so she would not "throw like a girl" on opening day. The trip to Wrigley never came off — Hugh Rodham died just as the season opened.

I interviewed Hillary twice during the campaign, but both sessions were narrow Q-and-A's, not full CIA debriefings. As I waited for her amid the nineteenth-century formality of the White House library I fretted that our conversation might be too stiff; because of both the setting and the First Lady's natural caution. At that moment, Hillary walked into the room with a businesslike stride, wearing a pinkish suit, a pink-and-green scarf and a gold bracelet on her right wrist. The look was safe, Republican, and boring. (Hillary just doesn't care about clothes. Before the Inauguration, confidante Susan Thomases managed to force her to choose a gown by finally imploring, "Hillary treat it like a piece of history. What dress do you want in the Smithsonian?")

With an opening question about the Cubs a relaxed, chatty Hillary emerged. "I used to go to Wrigley Field, and in those days it was like going to a minor league park now. It was fun. You could wander around and see the bleacher bums. Your parents always said, 'Don't go down there, those men are drinking.' But you'd sneak down and watch them sitting there bare-chested." Her eyes grew wide, almost in reverie. In her voice there was a sense of liberation so different from her normal elocution. "We went to the great [1984] San Diego-Cubs playoff game. And I took my father and mother. Of all the things that I ever did for my father, I think that was probably the best. It was just heavenly."

MYTH: *Hillary takes her cues from Marx (and it ain't Groucho) and is at the core of a secret radical coven.* With the subtle grace that is the hallmark of Texas Republicans, Congressman Dick Armey let loose the other week that "Hillary Clinton bothers me a lot . . . She hangs around a lot of Marxists. All her friends are Marxists." Clinton strategist Paul Begala laughed. "Yeah, she studied Marxism at Sam Walton's knee." Walton, a well-known Arkansas free-market subversive, had Hillary on his WalMart board.

Liberals, for their part, also accept a version of the comrade-Hillary fantasy when they beatify her as a new-age Emma Goldman, a bleeding heart fighting to save Bill Clinton from the conservative clutches of Lloyd Bentsen and David Gergen.

The problem is that the evidence belies the left-wing image. As far back as her 1969 graduation speech at Wellesley, Hillary was talking about "a very strange conservative streak that goes through a lot of the New Left collegiate protests that I find very intriguing." Trust me, this was not standard language in manifestos from the Weathermen. During the campaign, Hillary's only ideology was forcing her always reluctant husband (*tomorrow*, as we know is his watchword) to make tough decisions — most notably putting James Carville in charge of the campaign. "She has as much contempt for fuzzy-headed traditional liberal thinking as James and I do," says Begala, Carville's partner. "That's why the War Room worked so well. She was our mentor-protector." Hillary also invented the Clinton line on abortion (it should be "safe, legal, and *rare*"), not exactly the gospel according to Faye Wattleton.

"I find Hillary to be very conservative," argues Maggie Williams. "When she talks about rights and responsibilities, it's a very big deal for her." Maggie, to be sure, is Hillary's chief image-maker, but that view is reinforced by a close adviser to the President who says, "In all the meetings I've attended with Hillary, she has never been more liberal than the consensus in the room. And often she's more conservative."

Could the First Lady be a secret soul mate of Bob Dole? I read that last quote to Hillary. Her unhesitating response: "That's probably true."

But the insidious Hillary network is discussed so often, most people assume it's on cable. Who, in truth, does Hillary talk to? Ira Magaziner, the President's health care adviser, at least three times a day. But that's work. There's Marian Wright Edelman at the Children's Defense Fund (CDF), Hillary's longtime mentor. Conspiracy buffs will have to work overtime to find a Cuban connection in Hillary's advocacy of child-immunization programs. The alleged kingpin of the Hillary network is New York corporate lawyer and freelance Clinton adviser Susan Thomases. While Thomases can be brutally direct — Hillary must secretly envy her freedom to say precisely what she thinks — it is hard to find anything more radical about Thomases than her eastside Manhattan zip code.

Okay, it's true, Hillary's friends tend to be to the left of David Gergen. How shocking that — while at Wellesley at Yale Law School, working on Nixon's impeachment, then serving on the CDF board — Hillary met and actually befriended people who were nasty liberals. And the First Lady's two top staffers have, in fact, worked for nasty liberal interest groups: CDF (Maggie Williams) and Norman Lear's People for the American Way (Deputy Chief of Staff Melanne Verveer). But the office most commonly cited as the KGB headquarters of the Hillary network is that of Secretary of Health and Human Services Donna Shalala, who is the kind of liberal who gives litmus tests a bad name. Shalala may owe her job to Hillary but that does not mean that the two are exactly Thelma and Louise.

These days, Hillary is privately so exasperated with Shalala's doctrinaire views that she won't even refer to her by name — it's always "those people at HHS" with a dismissive sweep of her hand. The rift is partly over Shalala's dogmatic insistence that the Clinton health care plan provide abortion services and full coverage for illegal aliens. In the words of an angry White House staffer, "Shalala would rather the plan go down than abortion for illegal aliens not be covered."

Without mentioning Shalala, I asked Hillary about these two issues to test precisely where she stands on the ideological spectrum. Her answers, numbingly cautious as they were, reflected nothing so much as her irresistible pull to the magnetic center. Radicals would be ashamed to talk like this. Hillary on abortion: "I don't think this is an issue that should be permitted to undermine the larger purpose of providing adequate health care to every American." The message beneath the verbiage was that she's willing to compromise with Congress. Hillary on whether illegal aliens should be covered: "I feel they should not be."

MYTH: *Hillary the virtuous — the greatest feminist role model since Joan of Arc.* Had Hillary been five years older — part of the pre-Vietnam Wellesley class of '64 rather than '69 — odds are that she would have married a neurosurgeon and be living in Evanston. Had Hillary been five years younger — graduating from Yale Law School in the late '70s — she probably would have shrieked at Bill, "Go back with you to Arkansas? What about *my* career?"

As Hillary herself tends to admit, the odd contradictions between her ambitions and her life choices reflect the confusion of early feminism. Hillary played the classic '50s wife-to-be in following Bill to Arkansas, but her dreams — and, for that matter, his — were a far cry from *The Man in the Gray Flannel Suit.*

"I have often thought of myself and my friends as transitional figures," Hillary remarked after I outlined this theory, "maybe more sure of where we were coming from than where we were going. And friends of mine have described our coming-of-age as being on the cusp of changes that fundamentally redefined the role of women."

Now, keyhole journalism is not my métier. So I tend to believe that the Clinton marriage is what it seems: two people who care about each other, who had their rough spots in the past, and who are united in their devotion to their daughter. But after all the reports, articles, and claims that have either missed the mark or just been scurrilous, there was one alarming myth about Clinton family life that I couldn't get even my best White House sources to discuss. Only my favorite newspaper, *Le Monde* of the supermarket tabloids, *Weekly World News*, dared touch the story. I reached into my briefcase near the end of the interview and brandished the paper with its screaming headline: HILLARY CLINTON ADOPTS ALIEN BABY. The First Lady gasped. "Oh my God," she cried. "You found me out." She quickly regained her composure, a little too quickly I thought, and tried to pretend that this was old news. "I was just talking with

Tipper about this," she said. "She was quite jealous that I made the cover." At last, a Hillary rumor with legs.

When it was time to go, Hillary and I still had our differences. She views rooting for the Cubs as a metaphor for hope, while I regard it as a symbol of futility. And I find her sincerity too sugary. (When she lapses into earnest autopilot, the temptation is to shake her or feel for a pulse.)

A friend of hers had said, "Hillary's a missionary. It's up to you to discover her mission." So I asked her. "My mission?" she repeated, weighing each word as if the future of the administration depended on her response. "I want to have some fun and do good along the way." We walked down the marble corridor of the White House. In the Map Room, a dozen advisers and issue mavens were anxiously waiting for Hillary to begin a meeting to plan the marketing blitz for health care reform. Turning to me, the First Lady said, "Next time, if you're really lucky, we'll let you see the nursery where we keep the alien babies."

Those politicians — always making promises.

— ***Walter Shapiro*** covers politics for *USA Today*. He has also written about politics for *Esquire* and *Slate*. He has reported on the last six presidential elections, and his books include *Ten Lessons from Election '96*. This article originally appeared in *Esquire* (vol.120, no.2, Aug. 1993), and is reprinted with the generous permission of the author.

Ice Queen, Drag Queen:
A Psychological Portrait of Hillary

Camille Paglia

SCENE 1:
December 4, 1995. Trailed by television cameras, brightly smiling Hillary Rodham Clinton graciously conducts reporters through the First Lady's annual Christmas tour of the White House. Patiently pointing out charming knickknacks on the festooned trees, she rounds a corner and sees for the first time the kitchen staff's special surprise for her: a lavishly detailed gingerbread house, an exact replica of her childhood home in Park Ridge, Illinois. As she peers into its cleverly electric-lit interior, the cameras move in for a close-up, and her face tightens. The wall has been stripped from her old bedroom, and several million people are staring over her shoulder into her most private adolescent preserve. As if to expel us into the outdoors, she eagerly exclaims at a tiny street-corner sign, then launches into a story about her home's northern exposure: snow on the Rodham front lawn lasted all winter, longer than anywhere else on the street. Their snowman was the only one that never melted till spring.

SCENE 2:
January 26, 1996. Like Roman aristocrats at the Colosseum, two wisecracking CNN correspondents lounge in deck chairs across the street from the federal court building in Washington, D.C. Behind them mill police officers and protesters holding a gigantic blue banner reading "IT'S ETHICS, STUPID!" The world is waiting for Hillary Clinton, who has become the first First Lady subpoenaed to testify before a grand jury. A limousine pulls up, and out steps not Hillary the shrewd lawyer or Hillary the happy homemaker but Hillary the radiantly glamorous movie star. Her blond hair is dramatically, seductively styled. She is wearing, quite improbably, a long black velvet coat trimmed with royalist gold brocade. Head high, she stalks grandly to the microphones and greets the press as if they were dear friends come to bid her well. Then, like Mary Queen of Scots on her way to the scaffold, she sweeps away for her grueling four-hour rendezvous with independent counsel Kenneth W. Starr.

THESE TWO SCENES, so different on the surface, contain the key to one of the most fascinating yet baffling personalities of our time. Ice queen, drag queen: the Great White Feminist Hope is a far more conflicted and self-destructive creature than either her admirers or revilers understand. Free associating under uncomfortable public scrutiny, Hillary contemplating a sugared version of her long-lost childhood home eerily resembled another embattled public figure pulled back to the past — Richard Nixon invoking his "saint" of a mother in his rambling farewell speech to the White House staff. Hillary, trying to recreate the warmth of bygone family holidays, saw only the snowman who is herself — a proud, lonely, isolated consciousness on guard and ever vigilant, a powerful presence who even in high achievement hovers at the edges of communal experience. The woman her classmates called "Sister Frigidaire" has the "mind of winter" of Wallace Stevens's poem "The Snow Man." She, too, in Stevens's words, has "been cold a long time."

This coldness is the brittle brilliance of Hillary's calculating, analytic mind, which at its most legalistic has a haughty, daunting impersonality. It is also the genderlessness of a precocious firstborn child who modeled herself on her crustily independent father and who fought a long, quiet war of stubborn resistance against a hypercritical, puritanical mother. Hillary had to learn how to be a woman; it did not come easily or naturally. What we see in the present, superbly poised First Lady is a consummate theatrical artifact whose stages of self-development from butch to femme were motivated by unalloyed political ambition. She is the drag queen of modern politics, a bewitching symbol of professional women's sometimes-confused search for identity in this era of unlimited options.

America's first two-career presidential couple represents both a modern updating of the ancient practice of political marriage and a failed feminist experiment in redefinition of the sexes. Hillary was first attracted to Bill when she heard him boasting about the size of Arkansas' watermelons in the Yale Law School lounge. In her book she speaks of the "clean plate" system of her suburban youth, when her parents forced her and her two resentful brothers to eat "a catastrophe of calories" in deference to "starving children in faraway places." Bill's exotic, rural, sensually sweet and ripe watermelons were a symbol of freedom, fruitfulness and abundance. He was Female Man, whose boyish androgyny seemed to promise Hillary's feminist generation an escape from the sexist past. The irony is that Bill's aw-shucks, Huck Finn rap is one of the most effective womanizing styles of all time, triggering the caretaking maternalism in likely marks. Among Hillary's present humiliations is that Paula Jones's largely credible sexual harassment suit against Bill exposes Hillary's own romantic misjudgments: the sensitive New Man turned out to be just another old-fashioned masher and skirt chaser.

A hostility to conventional masculinity can be detected, in both Clintons' past. Because his father died before he was born and his stepfather proved abusive, Bill had no immediate positive models of manhood. While she idolized her father and seems to have competed with her mother and siblings to be daddy's number one girl, Hillary also saw the psychic damage inflicted by his iron rule in their close-knit, secretive family. Just one brother, Hugh, has surfaced in the media, and he has the moist, pleading eyes of the son who can never cut it — like Bing Crosby's (later suicidal) sons or Fredo in *The Godfather*. Someone else had those wounded, haunted eyes: Vincent Foster, Hillary's Rose Law Firm partner who would follow the Clintons to Washington and die there.

In her book Hillary tells of an incident in grade school when an older boy from outside the area chased her, threw her to the ground and kissed her. She fled home "screaming" and washed her face "over and over again." The theme of male intrusion and contamination would recur in a pivotal public moment described by her classmates in an Arts and Entertainment Network biography. On the podium at her Wellesley

College commencement in 1969, Hillary abandoned her prepared speech to berate the invited guest, Edward Brooke, the black U.S. senator from Massachusetts. Her confidantes' rationale for this high-handed rudeness, which infuriated college officials, is that Hillary was striking a youthful blow against the establishment represented by Republican Brooke. But I have another theory: Hillary was lashing out in a visceral response to the invasion of her all-women's school by a glamorous, lordly male who, from my one passing encounter with him as he sauntered elegantly down the Capitol steps in 1972, had a distinctly roving eye.

The sexual repressions and resentments of Hillary the snow queen would have long-reaching effects on policy when the Clintons arrived in Washington. With his reputation as a draft dodger, it was critical that Bill forcefully establish himself from day one as commander in chief of the armed forces. But far from reassuring skeptics, he compromised his nascent authority with appointments that, whatever their objective merits, made his administration seem a ragtag band of the neutered and the physically stunted. The most masculine Clinton appointee was Janet Reno. A disastrous consequence of the Clintons's discomfort with masculine men was their mishandling of the gays in the military issue, which went down in flames because of their obliviousness to the historic and still vibrant codes of warrior culture.

Tensions have been reported between Hillary and the first Secret Service agents assigned to her family, as well as with the governor's security detail in Little Rock who allegedly colluded in her husband's amorous escapades. The masculine is inherently vulgar and untrustworthy for her. Nor did she bother to conceal her contempt for machoism when, during Bill's time as governor, she pulled out a book on the fifty-yard line while he cheered on the University of Arkansas football team. Vincent Foster was Hillary's poetic soulmate in Little Rock, her gallant relief from Bill's huntin', fishin', golfin' buddies. Foster was another of her failed experiments in the new male, eventually collapsing under her expectations and his inability to protect her in Washington.

The masculine may have been taboo in Hillary's family partly because her mother was born to a 15-year-old girl, whose descendants might naturally see the male as raptor, exploiter, spoiler. Groomed to excel, young Hillary the thinker would sense the danger in seeming too feminine, which meant passive and vulnerable. Photos of her in law school and early in her marriage show that she used a frumpy, owlish, bookworm persona as an ardor-quenching, defensive tool. Like many gifted, ambitious women, she had difficulty integrating her intelligence with her sexuality. This sporadic chilliness (analogous to her obsession with privacy) would play a part in her husband's infidelities. Physically, Gennifer Flowers was Hillary without the ice — a doting, compliant geisha ever on call. In the fishbowl White House, it appears, Bill has risen to his responsibilities and courageously borne his lack of bimbo access. Chelsea, who looked like a war orphan compared to the ebullient Gore children in 1992, has flourished during her parents' renewed marriage.

WHEN BILL LOST his 1980 re-election bid in Arkansas, Hillary plunged into her first big make-over. It was "as if she went to cheerleader's school," remarked a Little Rock reporter. The present charismatic First Lady, with her chameleon-like blond hairdos, was born in that politically motivated self-transformation. Out went "Rodham," along with the horn-rimmed spectacles, and Bill triumphantly regained the governorship. Good student that she is, Hillary had discovered that the masks of femininity could be learned and appropriated to rise in the world. She had become a political drag queen, a master-mistress of gender roles. But her steely soul remains, the butch substrate that can be seen in the baleful, bloodless face of lawyer Susan Thomases, the intimate with whom she repeatedly conferred the night of Foster's suicide. Thomases can be seen as Hillary's dark side, her Janus twin or alter ego, a suspicious Medusa with the cold, dead eyes of a commissar. Along the continuum of sexual personae, Hillary is pulled between the poles of cordial, yielding Gennifer Flowers and grim, lantern-jawed Susan Thomases. One is the watermelon of lush, slippery fleshiness; the other is a stonily sealed, skull-like coconut (which in her book Hillary describes trying to crack one night against the governor's driveway), harsh, ungiving, withholding the milk of human kindness.

Thomases also symbolizes the now-doctrinaire mainstream feminism that endorses government oversight and regulation to cure social and sexual ills. Arriving in college as a conservative who had campaigned for Barry Goldwater in 1964, Hillary had a conversion experience at Wellesley from which she has never recovered. Within five years of her graduation, the Wellesley Center for Research on Women was founded and soon became a propaganda mill for victim rhetoric. Among its quack theories: Peggy McIntosh's claim that women and people of color are "lateral thinkers" and Nan Stein's labeling of boys who flip girls' skirts in elementary school as "gender terrorists." The high-toned old WASP citadels of Wellesley and Yale confirmed Hillary in her sense of entitlement and moral superiority, already in place from her Methodist upbringing where, she says, "We talked with God, walked with God, ate, studied, and argued with God." That elect strain in her is still all too evident in her hammering, hectoring, sermonizing delivery of major speeches, as at last year's U.N. conference on women in Beijing. She has words but no music; she is, she admits, "tone-deaf."

THE '60S FERMENT from which Hillary's generation emerged had several distinct elements, each with its own subsequent tradition. The pro-porn, pro-pop culture wing of feminism to which I belong, for example, was defeated and has only recently enjoyed a resurgence. Hillary was on the winning side, along with Gloria Steinem and Catharine MacKinnon. All three overvalue the verbal realm and confuse good intentions with good effects. Hillary has the arrogant '60s sense of social mission, but her idealism took an authoritarian turn, a pattern William Blake and Charles Dickens divined in the philanthropists of their time. As a child advocate (a commitment dating from law school), Hillary promulgates an aggressive protectionism that nullifies the "biological rights" of birth parents and extends the period of incompetence of the young, whom she deems incapable of informed sexual choice until age 21. Hillary's career has been intricately intertwined with a heady plutocracy of lawyers, bureaucrats and special interest groups who encouraged her delusion that she and her coterie could quickly and unilaterally reform the nation's health care system. High I.Q. and despotic instincts are a dangerous combination in a democracy.

Which brings us to today, with Hillary trapped in a web of unconvincing denials and half-truths that she herself spun. She seems incapable of self-analysis or of leveling with the public. As a utilitarian, she lacks the sense of subtlety and ambiguity one gains from the study of art. Like many of her colleagues in the feminist establishment, she seems hostile to psychology and may have gravitated toward law as a way to avoid acknowledging the internecine complexities of family relationships. Her moral reasoning is deficient, since she begins with the *a priori* premise of her own virtue. Yet, with all that said, Hillary Clinton is now, and is likely to remain, a leading role model for women throughout the world. By focusing on children, her book usefully steers feminism away from sterile theory and back to basics. We are just at the start of what may be a lifelong soap opera, followed by millions. Like Judy Garland, Maria Callas or Madonna, with their excesses, heartbreaks, torments and comebacks, Hillary the man-woman and bitch-goddess has become a strange superstar whose rise and fall is already the stuff of myth.

– ***Camille Paglia*** teaches at the University of the Arts, Philadelphia. She is a frequent contributor to *Salon*, and the author of *Vamps & Tramps: New Essays* and *Sexual Personae: Art and Decadence from Nefertiti to Emily Dickinson*. Reprinted by permission of *THE NEW REPUBLIC*, © 1996 (vol. 214, no. 10, Mar. 4, 1996), The New Republic, Inc.

1992 Elections & Afterwards

THE DEMOCRATS FIELDED five candidates in the 1992 elections, and it was by no means assured that Bill Clinton would be the nominee. Many of the candidates' wives had professional careers of their own and, in that respect alone, differed from the wives of past presidential candidates. The 1992 election was probably the first in which the question of the First Lady's subsequent occupation was raised.

Among all the candidates' wives, Democrat or Republican, Hillary Clinton was the most scrutinized and criticized. This attention may have resulted from her outspokenness, marriage to the Democratic frontrunner or prominence in her husband's campaign. There were certainly commentators, however, who felt the criticism resulted from suspicion and ambivalence toward articulate and determined women. Whatever the cause, the media furor Mrs. Clinton generated was stunning. Every move she made was dissected and analyzed — from her hairstyle to her legal assessments of children's rights. Her prominence prompts WILLIAM SAFIRE to advise Mrs. Clinton how to be an effective campaigner.

Hailed as a role model for intelligent and independent women, Hillary Clinton was also criticized for being too ambitious and aggressive. ANNA QUINDLEN notes that much of this discussion addressed "how we feel about smart women, professional women, new women." Many of the issues that generated press coverage revolved around Hillary Clinton's femininity or perceived lack thereof. Enormous amounts of ink appeared on her clothes, cooking and use of her maiden name. In response, Mrs. Clinton changed her persona to meet the public's expectations, morphing from hard-boiled litigator and campaigner into devoted wife and mother.

Bill and Hillary Clinton's personal and professional partnership was also a matter of much curiosity during the campaign. ELLEN GOODMAN describes the way in which their marriage highlights the need to redefine what we mean by "partnership" and "leadership" in this country.

After the election, ANNA QUINDLEN speculates on what kind of First Lady Mrs. Clinton will become and what her position will be. She was clearly going to hold a major, possibly official, position in the Clinton Administration, leading many to hope that topics typically dismissed as "women's issues" — child care, education, health care — will be addressed as never before.

The Hillary Problem

William Safire

LYNDON JOHNSON HAD "the Bobby problem"; Bill Clinton now has "the Hillary problem."

The problem is not that Hillary Clinton, successful lawyer and feminist, is coming across as a cunning political animal, threatening to insecure male voters. On the contrary, she is coming across as a political bumbler by appearing to show contempt for women who work at home.

Her first gaffe, derogating the Tammy Wynette stand-by-your-man pose, can be excused as an unfortunate choice of words under incredible pressure.

But Mrs. Clinton's second outbreak of foot-in-mouth disease — "I suppose I could have stayed home and baked cookies and had teas" — betrayed ignorance of the fundamentals of campaigning: You do not defend yourself from a conflict-of-interest charge by insulting a large segment of the voting public.

The cookies-and-tea stereotype is elitism in action. Even the columnist Ellen Goodman, a grass-roots feminist, was moved to comment: "Ouch."

There is still time for both Clintons to solve the Hillary Problem. The six-step solution:

1. Hillary: Stop defining yourself by what you're not. Self-definition by exclusion is needlessly defensive, as is claiming to be quoted out of context when you were not.

2. Bill: Make your own victory statements or concession speeches.

After the Illinois primary, in which Hillary was so effective, the networks switched to your headquarters to hear from the candidate. What they got was an interminable introduction from your wife, with reaction shots of you looking like a hanger-on hungering for home-baked cookies. The body language of both Tom Brokaw and Peter Jennings registered amazement and amusement at this usurpation of the candidate's moment.

3. Hillary: Press your strength, which is not articulation but realism.

I ran into Mike Mansfield, the wisest living Democrat, and asked him if you were an asset or liability. He counted you as an asset because he was struck by what you said on *60 Minutes* — that if people didn't like your explanations, then don't vote for you. That was straightforward. Honest people like such realism.

4. Bill: Stop trying to have it both ways; you cannot be gallant about a feminist.

When Jerry Brown, in his $1,500 suit, accused you of steering state business to your wife's firm, you lit into him like an outraged husband for "jumping on my wife."

That may have been an effective riposte in debate, especially against a lifelong bachelor, but it dodged the issue. His target was not your wife (to slip past your inelegant phrase), requiring the sort of how-dare-you response of Ronald Reagan at any criticism of Nancy's high-style income tax evasion. On the contrary, Mr. Brown was charging you with corruption. Get mad; get even; but don't suddenly get chivalrous.

5. Hillary: You don't need "face time"; fish where the fish are.

When the paramount fear was Gennifer-with-a-G, it was necessary to stick close to your husband on tour. Now you should spend your time going after George Bush's strength: Republican women.

Read Roger Rosenblatt's new book, *Life Itself*, which takes the permit-but-discourage middleground on abortion. Many Republican women, especially youngish executives, are ready to desert Mr. Bush on this issue. You should be working professional fences in key states — Illinois, Ohio, California — but never knocking women who work at home.

6. Both of you: Get more specific about what role Hillary would play in your administration.

A pre-appointment would be presumptuous, but voters should know beforehand what sort of First Ladyship is in store. Would she work on the outside as a public-interest lawyer (children's rights, animal rights, mineral rights)? Or inside, as White House counsel with no conflict of interest, or as a Cabinet member accountable to Congress?

If we are to have a new kind of partnership at the top, reflecting generational change and the trend toward two-career couples, the candidate team should disclose more about its plans before the vote.

Only if they handle it right can the Hillary Problem become the Clinton Solution.

— ***William Safire*** is a Pulitzer Prize-winning author and journalist; his columns appear twice-weekly in *The New York Times*. He is the author of several books, including *Spread the Word* and *Scandalmonger*.

Hillary's Problem

Ellen Goodman

IT'S THE TAIL END OF A KILLER DAY and Hillary Clinton settles into a sofa at the Intercontinental, looking remarkably alert and limp free, drinking spring water straight out of a plastic bottle.

The day broke 15 hours earlier with a sheaf of headlines declaring that the campaign was manufacturing a "gentler, kinder" Hillary. *Family Circle* featured a political bakeoff between Hillary's and Barbara Bush's chocolate chip cookie recipes. More than one story talked about the "two sides" of the candidate's wife: heads up she's a lawyer, heads down she's a wife. And Republications were comparing Hillary Clinton at the stove to Mike Dukakis in a tank.

The candidate's wife had spent the day at the Texas caucus, the Emily's List luncheon, a powwow for congressional wives (dubbed "power wives" on the schedule) and eight other stops, where she offered everything from a wave to a 25-minute speech without notes. At the Women of Color reception, not surprisingly, the woman in my row offered this piece of high praise with a kicker, "Isn't she great! (Pause.) Gee, I wish she were running for the Senate."

Now, at Madison Square Garden, six female Democratic nominees for the Senate were speaking and everyone was talking about the year of the woman. Women had become the symbols of change in the political process. But what about wives?

Is it actually easier for a woman to be the candidate this year than the candidate's wife? Have we come that far? Or not so far?

Hillary answers with a knowing but cautious, "Maybe." We knew what it was to be a wife, she agrees. Over the past decades, we've learned what it is to be an independent woman. But we haven't yet figured out what it looks like to be a strong, independent and wifely — especially First Wifely — all at the same time.

"I thought I understood that before this race was under way," says Hillary Clinton, who comes across as comfortable and thoughtful. "That's what I was living. I thought that with some stops and starts and changes along the way trying to get it all straight, I was a very lucky person because I had a profession that I valued, a marriage that I through was a partnership in the best sense of the word and gave me a lot of personal satisfaction."

"I thought I understood how to walk through that minefield of defining myself and striking the balance between my own needs and family needs that we all struggle with all the time."

Now this mother, wife and lawyer finds the controversy that has followed her from conservative Arkansas to the national stage "surprising" and even "bewildering." Hillary had, to be sure, a rocky introduction to the American public. Her image was flanked by Flowers and cookies, Tammy Wynette and Betty Crocker.

But so much of the Hillary Problem is another case study about men, women, change. And this time also marriage. As Hillary says, "I thought we [women] were beginning to develop a framework for that kind of life we could lead, still married, still committed to family, still engaged in the outside world. And I've just been surprised, I guess, by the assumptions that bear little resemblance to how all of us — not just me — make our way through this uncharted terrain."

Where do we still get lost in this terrain? At the White House door? In the territory marked partnership? At the woman's caucus Tuesday morning, Bill Clinton tells the audience of women, "We have to say that building women up does not diminish men."

Harvard Business School's Rosabeth Kantor says our trouble is with teams as much as with mates. "We don't understand teams in America. We have this idea there has to be one leader, one CEO. So we can't help comparing couples. We can't see it as both/and. It's either/or."

But more acute is this disparity between our view of marriage as a merger — two people as one — and our view of what it means to be a successful individual. It's not easy for women to be seen or to feel both professional and coupled.

We have few models of "two-someness," as Sissela Bok once described it, relationships in which men and women remain two but together. As Hillary Clinton knows well, "We're all trying to work this out. We're all trying to find out way and we don't have a common language." In the era of public partnership marriages, she says, "I may be on the front line."

Frontlines are notoriously unsafe places. Cookies or not, there is no makeover in the making. A whole generation lives on these frontlines now. Hillary Clinton has just become the most visible resident.

— ***Ellen Goodman*** is Pulitzer Prize-winning journalist for *The Boston Globe*. Her books include *Making Sense* and *Value Judgments*. (July 15, 1992.)

The (New) Hillary Problem

Anna Quindlen

THERE'S JOB TALK in Little Rock, about who will be Secretary of the Treasury, Chief of Staff, Attorney General. And there's job talk across the country, too, among many women. Here's the question: Now that we have a First Woman as educated, intelligent, superachieving and policy-savvy as her husband, what do we do with her?

"Promise me she won't talk about cookies anymore," moaned a woman in Philadelphia.

"She did what she had to do to get him elected," said another in New York. "Now let's give her a real job." And a circle of professional women in San Jose, Calif., erupted at a question about what Hillary Clinton should not do in the White House:

"I don't want her to keep her mouth shut."

"Forget the photo ops."

"I don't want her to make hospital visits; I want her to make policy so that all sick kids will get good care."

"The thing is," said one finally, "we feel so strongly about it because she's one of us."

One of us. So much of the discussion about Hillary Clinton has not been about her at all. It has been about how we feel about smart women, professional women, new women. We want her to make the world safe, not only for education reform and preschool programs but for opinionated women who want to be taken seriously. To do that, she has to do something.

A week before her husband was elected, riding to an airport in the back of a sedan, she said she was keenly aware of how many women saw her as a stand-in. "That feeling has been sweeping over me," she said. "I feel the responsibility so much." When you read Hillary Clinton's clippings, the word "hard-edged" appears more than any other except "headbands." It's an interesting word, not only because it's code but because you rarely hear it applied to men. It's like "feisty," a word used only for women and short guys.

The woman I talked with was smart, intense and approachable, which is how many people describe her in Arkansas. She needlepoints, but like most women with a kid and a job, she's been working on the same project for years. She said she was collecting Eleanor Roosevelt lore, a heartening indication of how she sees her future.

"We talked, as I recall, about policy in Africa," she said of one of her first dates with Bill Clinton, a recollection so weird it must be true. He gave her advice about cases; she gave him advice about appointments. She traveled the state to study the Arkansas school system and made sweeping recommendations to reform it. Her husband proposed legislation to implement the reforms. Both of them were hissed afterward by teachers. A modern marriage to the max.

This is no Nancy Reagan, obsessed with the man. This is a woman who lives and breathes social welfare policy, who has a resume that would have put her on transition team lists had Bill Bradley just been elected president, who was a key player in her husband's campaign. Some women think she should have a Cabinet-level position, pointing out that John Kennedy made his brother Attorney General.

Others say she should try to create a more meaningful First Woman's role, cut to fit the tenor of the times. I think the most important thing is that she fashion a meaningful job in her areas of expertise, that she ignore criticism of that job and that we stop the criticism and focus on the benefits — for our schools, for our kids, for all the issues she works on. If they want to give the job a name, that's fine; just don't give it a fashion emphasis.

Breaking ground is never easy, and Hillary Clinton surely knows about the people who said they wanted to "get the pants off Eleanor and onto Franklin." (Gee, how times have not changed.) There will be people who complain that they didn't elect her. Get over it; you didn't elect James Baker, either. There will be people who wanted an older Princess Di and are quick to cast her instead as a younger, left-wing Margaret Thatcher. Get over it.

If we put her in a little pink box of old expectations, truncate her contribution because of stereotypes, cut her down to size because we feel threatened, we lose. When he was running, Bill Clinton liked to say we don't have a person to waste. Certainly not this one.

— ***Anna Quindlen*** was a Pulitzer Prize-winning columnist for *The New York Times* when this article was published; she currently writes for *Newsweek*. Her books include *One True Thing* and *Black and Blue*. (November 8, 1992.)

The Role of the First Lady

PRESIDENT CLINTON STRONGLY endorsed his smart and capable wife playing a key role in his Administration, and made it clear the First Lady was one of his most important advisors. After the election, Mrs. Clinton became the first First Lady to have her own office in the West Wing and started using her maiden name again, a gesture reminiscent of her adopting Clinton's name only after his 1980 gubernatorial loss. (A *Wall Street Journal*/NBC News poll revealed that most Americans surveyed thought she should drop "Rodham.")

While the Clintons were defining her role, Washington was awash in "Billary" jokes about Mrs. Clinton's power, rumors about her sexuality, and stories about their relationship (see chapter 9 also). The backlash against Hillary Rodham Clinton's role reflected America's continuing, evolving assessment of professional, independent women, as embodied by the "First Wife." On this subject, Joan Mondale remarked: "newness startles people. She is new. She continued her career — wives of people in politics haven't done that before. People look at something new and, at first, it frightens them."

What, exactly, is the First Lady's role? Clearly, the social requirements alone demand immense organizational talent and diplomatic skill. Aside from planning state dinners, accompanying the president and promoting favored causes, though, what *is* a First Lady supposed to do with her time?

In this chapter, KATE MUIR and the late, great MEG GREENFIELD examine First Ladyship past and present. Looking back from Abigail Adams to Rosalynn Carter, Muir points out that America has a long history of activist First Ladies, a largely ignored legacy. Greenfield describes the White House as "a household, a symbol, a source of great potential good, a place from which important values can be reflected," and encourages Mrs. Clinton to build upon the First Lady's traditional power to make an impact on her country.

Who Wears the Trousers in the White House?

Kate Muir

HITLER WAS CONVINCED that Eleanor Roosevelt, not her husband, was the real ruler of America. The new First Lady, Hillary Clinton, will obviously have a lot to live up to.

Amid all the pre-inauguration huffing and puffing about Hillary Clinton's role as the supposed "presidential partner," it has been forgotten that America's First Ladies have a long tradition of sharing the trousers, if not wearing them.

The caricature of the interferin', screamin', schemin' broad in the White House is an ancient one, and whatever the truth, decrying her is a fine route of attack for the party out of power.

Of course, some First Ladies were more in-your-face than others about influencing their presidents. As early as 1797, Abigail Adams was dubbed "Autocratrix of the United States" by the opposition, after she wrote regular letters advising her husband John on both foreign and domestic policy. Julia Tyler preferred to be called "Lady Presidentress" or "Mrs President Tyler". In 1844, she was the first president's wife to use a press agent to promote herself. But the greatest recognition was paid to Eleanor Roosevelt, whose radio shows, newspaper columns and royal-style visits led Adolf Hitler to say: "Eleanor Roosevelt is America's real ruler."

Just the idea of an unelected, unknown woman with more access to the seat of power than anyone else makes the blood of many politicians and journalists boil. As Carl Sferrazza Anthony, the author of *First Ladies The Saga of the Presidents' Wives and Their Power 1789-1961* (Quill), puts it: "The First Lady is the wild card of the American political system. There is no way to escape the reality of a wife's influence, but we are very, very uncomfortable with that."

Mrs Clinton was much given to reading biographies of other First Ladies on the interminable plane and bus journeys of the 1992 campaign. At the moment, her office says, "she is considering what sort of role she will take and has not finally decided." Perhaps she can take some hot tips from her predecessors.

Mary Lincoln, the wife of Abraham, should be of particular interest. Mrs Lincoln also followed her husband on the campaign trail, and was not afraid to describe his Democratic rival as "a very little, little giant by the side of my tall Kentuckian."

Mrs Clinton was much involved with the transition team, but has been sensibly low-key about it. Mrs Lincoln, on the other hand, wrote to a friend discussing the possible appointment of Norman Judd to the new cabinet: "Perhaps you will think it no affair of mine, yet as I see it . . . Judd would cause trouble." She also threw a tantrum when Honest Abe failed to make an appointment she wanted.

Some factions supported Mrs Lincoln's influence. *The New York Times* wrote: "The country may congratulate itself upon the fact that its president elect is a man who does not reject, even in important matters, the advice and counsel of his wife."

Rosalynn Carter's intervention in her husband's presidency was not welcomed. As she noted in her autobiography, *First Lady From Plains*, "Criticism began to mount when, in the second year of Jimmy's presidency, I started attending Cabinet meetings. In retrospect I can understand why, but at the time I couldn't. Jimmy and I had always worked side by side."

Soon it was rumoured that Mrs Carter was pretty well in charge of the future of the Western world, plus "there was a not very subtle implication that cabinet meetings were no place for a wife. I was supposed to take care of the house period."

The template for the new-style First Lady was created by Eleanor Roosevelt in the 1930s. Partly because her husband had been crippled by polio, she became his "eyes and ears" in the outside world. Her national radio show, sponsored by a cosmetics company, on which she gave her strong opinions on political and moral issues such as prohibition, made her at least as famous as her quieter husband. When she signed a contract to syndicate a daily newspaper column and commanded lecturing fees of $1,000, Congress asked to examine her tax returns. It turned out she was giving all her earnings to charity.

Her profile became the highest of any First Lady so far, apart from perhaps Jackie Kennedy, who became famous for quite different reasons. Mrs Roosevelt received up to 1,000 letters a day, and employed 12 staff to deal with her mail. Whereas before, people wrote to the First Lady in the hope that she would have influence with the president, these correspondents wrote to Mrs Roosevelt herself, asking for her advice and her help. . . .

The power of each First Lady depends almost entirely on her husband, and only he knows its extent. Some early American presidents were less vulnerable to women's arts than others. John Quincy Adams was by no means a new man. "There is something in the very nature of mental abilities which seems to be unbecoming in a female," he observed. Louisa Adams, an intellectual and a great hostess, had greatly helped his election chances by ensuring the right people attended her salons and dinners. After the election, however, Mr Adams had little use for his wife's opinions. The Adams lived apart for months, and signed their letters to each other with their full names.

Mrs Clinton is the most highly qualified of all the post-war generation of First Ladies. Coming from a position of responsibility as a lawyer and children's rights campaigner, there is no suggestion from her staff that she will even attempt to pretend that her role is just that of loving wife.

Living up to the loving wife role is tough. Mrs Reagan was pilloried for the adoring stare she put on when her husband was making speeches. Mrs Bush despite her homely tales of Millie the First Dog was a big mover behind the scenes, being instrumental in the sacking of John Sununu, the White House chief of staff. When Jackie Kennedy was told that she would have to make concessions to the First Lady role, she said: "I will. I'll wear hats."

While one extreme of First Ladyhood is becoming an extravagant fashion plate, the other is being caricatured as Lady Macbeth. Mrs Clinton will have to tread a careful path between the two, fearing that many will continue to believe what one early American feminist, Maria Chapman, wrote in 1855: "The power behind the throne is the power."

— ***Kate Muir*** is a Washington columnist for *The Times* of London. She is also the author of the novel *Suffragette City* and two non-fiction books: *The Insider's Guide to Paris* and *Arms and The Woman*.

First Ladyhood

Meg Greenfield

I AM ABOUT TO MAKE A POINT that is certainly unfashionable and conceivably also felonious by now. It is that while we are all arguing about whether Hillary Clinton should take a job inside or outside the administration and which meetings, if any, she should sit in on, she already has one job waiting for her. It is the job that goes by the rather awful, terminally quaint name of First Lady. She can do other things too. But the duties (and fantastic possibilities) involved in the job of First Lady, as it has developed over the years, are not to be underrated or despised.

Now — if anyone female and under the age of 82 is still present — let us go on to talk a little about that job in the context of attitudes toward women in general and wives in particular in Washington. In my time here I have seen those attitudes transformed. We aren't "girls" anymore, and that's not just because some of us aren't girls anymore by even the most generous standards. The whole giggly, girly, patronizing, little woman junk, the ladies'-lunch-with-party-favors-and-pink-dessert culture, if they live on at all, live on somewhere out of sight. Women work; women think; women count — as they always did, of course, but now with greater recognition of the fact and, so far as working and counting are concerned, certainly in greater numbers. Yes, there are still slights and there are still incorrigibles. But as compared with the old days? Don't get me started.

In relation to wives the change has been particularly sharp. When I came here in the 1960s and for many years thereafter, wives were widely regarded as political chattel. They were meant not only to do whatever housekeeping functions went with their husbands' jobs, but also to think what their husbands thought (at least out loud), to hold no job and engage in no activity that could in even the tiniest degree compromise their husbands' positions or create a professional awkwardness, be it ever so minuscule. This was true in my profession as well as in politics and government: it was deeply frowned on and sometimes forbidden for reporters' wives to be in jobs or on boards or involved in election campaigns that might create doubt about their husbands' detachment (there weren't enough female reporters yet to require a policy for husbands).

Well, no more. A number of bold, prophetic wives, "new age" before their time, were at work on that even before the women's movement was much of a force, and attitudes have been truly shaken. Women in general and wives in particular are now widely believed — will wonders never cease? — actually to exist, and also to be free to choose their course. The nature of the full-time work done by some — for example, diplomats' wives — in furtherance of their husbands' jobs has generated bitter disputes with traditionalists over such questions as whether they should be obliged to perform these tasks and, if so, whether they should not be paid.

Nobody, I think, argues that Hillary Clinton should go around sounding off against her husband's policies or that she should get a wage for being First Lady. But there is argument over the merit, the worthiness of the functions she will be expected to perform in the White House: chooser of visitors, provider of hospitality, emissary to and contact with worthy enterprises, setter of tone, selector of projects and so forth. These are real functions. They are also important. They are representational, political, diplomatic. They don't have to do with endless vacuuming or the concoction of cornflake-crumb-and-tuna casseroles just when one wanted to argue a case before the Supreme Court, as you might suppose they did from some of the put-downs of First Ladyhood. The flowers get arranged and the lamps get dusted and the soufflés rise without the ministrations of the president's wife. But there are other things that need doing.

VAST ENTERPRISE

THE WHITE HOUSE, in other words, is more than the Oval Office and more than a state dining room. It is, as well, a vast enterprise — a household, a symbol, a source of great potential good, a place from which important values can be reflected and in which they can be reinforced by the nature of whom the inhabitants recognize, whom they hear, whom they bring together. All of these are functions of state, of first familyhood, not strictly speaking of government. They cannot merely be contracted out or ceded to hired professionals. They are the Clintons' job.

I realize that this may sound somewhat monarchical in nature, but there is a kind of benedictory political function to be performed from the White House. You need only observe the incredible lines of tourists, day in, day out, waiting surpassingly long stretches to get into the building or witness the unbelievable pleasure people get when some good deed of their school or their project or club, whatever it is, gets recognized with a visit there, to know that this is much more than an extravagant house and that those who determine how it is used have enormous opportunities.

The paradox, of course, is that the inhabitants of the White House must combine this head-of-state, vaguely monarchical function with constant recollection that these are borrowed luxuries and temporary powers. They must not, as some have, get mixed up about that and start behaving in kingly and queenly, which is to say, obnoxiously anti-republican ways. Used properly and with a personal sense of humility and proportion, the White House as a setting and a center of activity has an incredible potential. There is no cause with which either Clinton has been identified that could not profit greatly if that potential were put in its service.

Even as it is said that Hillary Clinton will be more engaged in her husband's work than other wives of presidents have been, so I would not be surprised to find that these duties and possibilities, conventionally associated with First Ladies only, will involve her husband to an increased degree. The sorts of things they have been talking about trying to preserve once in office — contact with "real" people, an awareness of what is on minds outside the much deplored Beltway, and so forth — can depend in large part on successful, imaginative use of the White House and its magnetic powers. I'm not saying that Hillary Clinton should check her law degree and her mind at the door. I'm not even saying that she shouldn't get involved in policy, in outside projects — whatever. I'm saying she will find there's another serious job to do there as well, and she could be awfully good at it.

— ***Meg Greenfield*** was, for 20 years, the editor of *The Washington Post's* editorial page; she was also a Pulitzer Prize-winning writer for the *Post* and columnist for *Newsweek* magazine. She died in 1999. This article appeared in *Newsweek* magazine (January 18, 1993). Reprinted with permission.

Health Care Reform

In 1993, President Clinton appointed his wife to oversee the development of a health care reform plan. The shocking inadequacies of health care in the world's richest nation was a key issue in the elections, and one of the first issues the Clinton Administration addressed. The effort was enormous. Mrs. Clinton's task force employed over 500 staff members, held countless meetings with both legislators and the public, and incorporated the views of a wide range of health care professionals and organizations. *Time* magazine described it as "the largest piece of legislation attempted since Social Security, a health care plan that would affect one-seventh of the American economy."

While Hillary earned kudos for her command of the issue and her dazzling Congressional appearances, it wasn't enough. Mired in bureaucracy, besieged by competing constituencies, and attacked as radical, her plan faltered and Hillary Rodham Clinton's popularity plummeted. The health care reform proposal (running to over 1,300 pages) was presented to Congress in September, 1993 and was bitterly contested for the next year until it was removed from the legislative agenda the following fall. Any hopes for enacting reform were dashed by the Republicans' landslide electoral victory in 1994.

In this chapter, Meg Greenfield touches on the high point of the effort, describing Mrs. Clinton's first Congressional appearance as "a political 10." Ellen Goodman describes the immense strain Mrs. Clinton faced at the time, compounded by the death of her father and longtime friend Vince Foster. Leonard Larsen and Martin Walker describe the devastating loss of the Administration's first major policy battle.

In retrospect, it's hard to tell what the impact really was. While some maintain that the failure of the Administration's plan set back the cause of health care reform irreparably, the issue continues to emerge in the platforms of both congressional and presidential candidates.

Did She Take the Hill?

Meg Greenfield

I DON'T KNOW WHAT Hillary Rodham Clinton's TV ratings were on her televised testimony in Congress on health reform last week, but her political ratings, by most accounts, were off the charts. It's not just that she has an exceptional gift for mastering the head-breaking details of a hard subject and then translating them into understandable English. It was that tonally speaking she also was a political 10. The horn-helmeted Valkyrie, the wicked witch, the intellectual ax murderess of conservative Republican theology could not be assaulted because nothing even remotely resembling such a creature was present. Hillary Clinton was the model of modesty, civility, family-minded understanding and concern, willingness to listen and learn — a gaggle of virtues that made her infinitely more invulnerable to attack than any well-armed Valkyrie, witch or ax murderess ever could be. She disarmed the guys. The only thing many of them could think to do was burble on about how much they admired the work she had done on the health care project. They then half apologized and half asked permission for expressing, ever so gently, just a few doubts.

It was a hoot. I am aware that some people watching, and not all of them Republicans either, were less amused than disgusted by the obsequious manner of so many of the male interrogators. But this aspect of things was, surely, in the first instance, comic. It put me in mind of nothing so much as that dazing moment a few years back when it became plain to the legislators conducting the hearing that any hostile question or even rudeness of bearing directed at the saintly Oliver North was likely to be repaid at the polls in November with political mayhem. Part of the would-be hostile congressmen's discomfiture in going after North was no doubt due to his incredibly effective testimony; but as much, I think, was due to his special cachet as a decorated serviceman. Likewise Hillary Clinton came to the Hill with the special cachet of being the president's wife, a lady, as the gents still say, the First Lady, yet. They don't know how to sock such a person in public, any more than they could successfully jump a teary-eyed, prayerful, uniformed Marine.

I dwell on this because it should carry a bit of warning as to both the depth and the longevity of all the amity proclaimed on this matter in Washington last week. Eras of good feeling have an awfully short life expectancy here, and the very greasiness of some of the compliments suggested to me that they were not wholly premised on Clinton's command of the subject and commitment to getting something big and serious done. There was a whiff of that artificial, condescending little-ladyism that is sort of like the cockroach and the spiky horsetail plant, those life forms that have defied the odds and survived intact since remotest prehistoric times, while seemingly hardier creatures were going extinct right and left. Like them, little-ladyism will never be eliminated from the ecosystem, in this case Washington's. It will just be there. And it will always be expressed in the same patronizing way many people choose to congratulate some elderly soul, say, for being "92 years young." Thus, of a politician's wife it is invariably said, in this mode, during banquet introductions and so forth, "Now, she should be the president [or governor or senator, or whatever], of course," at which everybody present goes, "Heh, heh, heh," and after that, clap, clap, clap.

Well, naturally, this is being said about Hillary Clinton as she moves to the center of the health care reform debate. But in her case it is more than just the usual embarrassing badinage. It should be taken as an ominous sign by those in the Clinton entourage who may be dazzled by the response she got in her first week's testimony. For it says that, whatever her professional presentation, she is seen not as a working official but as a First Lady, and today's response of excessive gallantry can easily become tomorrow's response of suspicion and resentment. The fact is that Hillary

Clinton has gone well beyond all her modern predecessors in her engagement in her husband's government. She may have the independent spirit of Betty Ford, the shrewdness of Lady Bird Johnson, the seriousness of Rosalynn Carter etc., down the line, but she is something different from all of these and more than the sum of their attributes. She is a strong, separate source of power inside the administration with a mandate of authority from the president and an operational base from which to carry it out.

In fact, the proper comparison for her is not another First Lady at all, but rather Bobby Kennedy — the second most important person in government; a close relative whose relationship with the boss was thus unbreakable, only partly official and impervious to outside scrutiny or pressure; the most thoroughly trusted and thoroughly empowered agent of JFK, given many of the most sensitive and difficult tasks to be accomplished, and, finally, someone whose own vitality, skill and power managed to create within the government a kind of quasi network of workers in the agencies known as "Bobby's people." All this earned him variously admiration, adoration, respect, fear and detestation throughout the administration as well as in Congress. For better and for worse Hillary Clinton can expect about the same.

For here is one unblinkable truth. As smart and professional and hardworking as she is and whatever she may accomplish in government, Hillary Clinton is the president's wife and that fact will continuously play into the way she is perceived and treated by others in government. She is Clinton's wife as much as Bobby was Kennedy's brother. As with Bobby, when she says "we" as she did last week — "we" will look at your proposal or "we" would not prohibit that — her interlocutors are wondering just who the "we" is, the task force or the family. This is unfair because she has been so unremittingly professional about her work, but it is true because she is not Hillary Jones. Hillary Clinton is making precedents big time in her role. Many of those legislators who were so deferential last week haven't yet figured out how to deal with this. You have to believe that, caught looking like simps, they will now set about trying.

— ***Meg Greenfield*** was, for 20 years, the editor of *The Washington Post*'s editorial page; she was also a Pulitzer Prize-winning writer for the *Post*, and columnist for *Newsweek* magazine. She died in 1999. *The Washington Post* (October 4, 1993). Reprinted with permission.

Even Hillary Can't Do It All

Ellen Goodman

OK, SO YOU SHOULD have been a brain surgeon. Up in the morning, out on the job. The White House limo drops you at the hospital. You open up a few craniums and you're home for dinner.

This is the kind of health care involvement nobody would criticize. It's the kind of two-career family everybody would understand. Unless you do an accidental frontal lobotomy on a major world leader, you're home free.

If you don't want to go to the Easter Egg Roll, you can just get beeped. You don't even have to worry about what you wear. A nice scrub suit will do.

But here you are — lawyer, public policy junkie, health care honcho, full-time volunteer, first lady — stuck in the center of the Whitewater controversy. The headlines are calling Hillary to the pillory. There's a cartoon around that names you Tonya Harding Clinton.

The pundits are talking ominously — again — about the dangers of having someone in power who can't be fired, just divorced. And you have to listen to Alfonse D'Amato — *Alfonse D'Amato!* — questioning *your* ethics.

If you haven't entirely lost your sense of humor, there must be a good belly laugh in the stories about the tarnishing of the halo around your head. Just when was that hallowed halo time?

Was it back in 1992, when you answered the first questions about Whitewater by saying that you could have stayed home and baked cookies? The whole world came down on your head. (I'm telling you, brain surgery was the ticket, not cookie baking.)

Was it during the Republican National Convention when you were the Feminist from Hell? Or during the "Billary" humorfest? Or when you were snidely dubbed Saint Hillary for talking about a politics of meaning?

It must have been when you went to Capitol Hill last fall and the senators fell into a state of shock that you "were effortlessly answering complex questions in great detail." Why, one even suggested you were smart enough to go on "Jeopardy."

There's even more black humor in words of the feminists-come-lately. Not a few opponents and commentators insist that they are merely treating you as an equal — showing respect for your power, intelligence and status as one of America's 100 Best Lawyers and a certifiable New Woman. Why, by accusing you of sleazy, greedy behavior and cover-ups, they are actually taking you seriously!

And if this were not enough, too many women have put too much stock in your one basket. There is a chorus of friends and enemies who seem to agree that the advancement of women — nay, the entire women's movement — is riding on your success.

Well, let me offer a few unsolicited words of advice.

Take a good long look at what's on your plate. In the past year, your father died, your mother-in-law died and one of your best friends committed suicide. You've got a widowed mother, a teen-age daughter, a job and a role and a husband with the weight of the world on his shoulders.

On top of that you have an overdeveloped sense of responsibility and a gritty, sometimes grim, determination to prove that you can handle it all. Even when the "all" goes off the charts.

What should you do? First of all, stand up like a big girl and answer the questions about Whitewater all by yourself. When that's done — and it will be — cut loose from the day-to-day internecine warfare of the White House. Step back from the wrangles over appointments and the strategy sessions and the power struggles. Don't get trapped in his or her loyalty tests.

Treat health care reform as what it is — a tough job, but your job. Go to it in the morning. Get an office out of the White House if you have to. Work hard. Do your best. Go home at night.

When you get there, kick back, put on the slippers and the sweats. If you don't have to go downstairs to some state dinner, get something out of the refrigerator, check Chelsea's homework, invite a friend over, put a video on. Let go.

Remember that there are two things you don't have to be. (1) You don't have to be a copresident. (2) You don't have to be everything to everyone. Even to every woman.

At the moment, you're heading somewhere between burnout and flameout. And no, you don't have to be a brain surgeon to see that.

— ***Ellen Goodman*** is Pulitzer Prize-winning journalist for *The Boston Globe*. Her books include *Making Sense* and *Value Judgments*. (March 13, 1994.)

Hillary Clinton Gets Tough as Her Health Plan Falters

Leonard Larsen

AT THIS LATE STAGE of the national debate over health care reform President Clinton's side seems to be running on empty, vague as usual behind "universal coverage" and unnecessarily caustic with both friends and foes.

Congressional Democrats have taken over to rewrite legislation in a last ditch attempt to enact something, anything, before elections next fall.

And, in this late state of affairs, the president's chief health care spokesperson, his wife, Hillary Rodham Clinton, remains disruptive, a target as much as an advocate, turning up partisan heat against critics and still using unfortunate Americans as stage props in her public appearances.

Helping in the Pacific Northwest to send off the "Health Security Express" and busloads of volunteers to speak across the country on behalf of health reform, Mrs. Clinton appeared to be spoiling for a political fight, with anybody.

It's understandable that the highly visible first lady, who's thrust herself into an unprecedented role as her husband's health reform architect and avid defender, would answer the shrill and angry personal criticism she's received with shrillness and anger of her own.

But — again, at this late date when practical politics would seek to narrow dispute and seal alliances — Mrs. Clinton came out with her dukes up, seeming more intent on fighting her critics than for her cause.

And she castigated not only opponents but all of Congress, Democratic majorities as well as Republican minorities she portrayed as too greedy to share with Americans the health coverage they enjoy.

To bolster her arguments, Mrs. Clinton paraded — even carried in her arms — stricken and needy people as she angrily denounced opponents of the Clinton health plan, a plan that survives mostly in name and with the indulgence of Democratic congressional leaders.

The problem for Mrs. Clinton and her husband remains what it's been from the early stages of the health debate: After submitting the broad outlines of the Clinton health package, they didn't fill in the blanks.

And as partisan criticisms piled on from Republicans and paid lobbyists in one of the most expensive public relations and advertising campaigns ever assembled, the Clinton White House responded as it did when Mrs. Clinton participated in the sendoff of the cross-country bus campaign.

Targeted by harsh political rhetoric, the administration keeps answering criticism with the same broad outlines, themes of "fairness" and coverage for every American but without specifics as to what will change and how it will affect — and improve — health care for every American.

Swatting angrily at all criticism — even from Democrats — the White House with Mrs. Clinton in the lead repeats what's now the meaningless mantra of health care that "can never be taken away" but never fully explains the nuts and bolts.

Obviously, as the polls reflect, many Americans have been reached by paid lobbyists and partisans who oppose the Clinton health care plan and fan fears that personal and family health care would be threatened by reform and that "socialized medicine" is lurking.

Instead of laying out the Clinton plan in greater detail — how reform will work for every American, what it'll cover, what it'll cost, everything Americans need to find themselves and their families in the plan — the White House and Mrs. Clinton have answered with their own propaganda.

Whatever the outcome of the health care debate, one judgment that may endure is that Mrs. Clinton — if she had to get involved — should not have got so deeply involved she became as big a part of the argument as the reform plan itself.

Unseemly as it is for partisan opponents to target the nation's first lady for personal criticism, that was the obvious risk and result when Mrs. Clinton took over health care reform as her own project in the Clinton administration.

And, however unfair the observation might be, it's also unseemly when the nation's first lady answers back with angry rhetoric of her own, leaving a traditional White House sanctuary of civility to muck around in raw politics.

— ***Leonard Larsen*** was a reporter and Washington correspondent for the *Denver Post* for almost 40 years. Upon leaving the *Post,* he wrote a national column for Scripps Howard. He retired in 1998. *Denver Rocky Mountain News* (August 2, 1994).

Over the Hill

Martin Walker

THE CO-PRESIDENCY IS OVER. The most distinctive feature of the Clinton campaign and the first 18 months in office, and the boldest experiment in U.S. sexual politics, has been quietly but firmly dropped.

That unique power of the First Lady as czarina of health reform, custodian of the capstone of the entire edifice of Bill Clinton's legislative agenda, is over. And it will not be repeated. There will be no such starring role for her in the next big program to reform the welfare system, even though she had begun working on it.

The reason is simple. Having spent a year on drafting the Clinton health plan, stumping the country to publicize and to sell it, Hillary Clinton has failed. If some pale and watery health reform is passed in this presidency, which is no foregone conclusion, it will not be hers. Nor will it be that his'n'her vision of universal health care for all U.S. citizens that helped elect Bill Clinton to the White House.

If she had been just another hired hand, a top-ranking political adviser, she would probably have been fired by now, like so many of the other Arkansas loyalists who came to Washington with such high hopes. Two of them were her partners in the Rose Law Firm. And Mack McLarty, the president's boyhood friend, has been ditched as White House chief of staff.

The Clinton presidency has been a long battle between the cozy customs and the old loyalties of Arkansas, and the ruthless politicking of Washington where they have a saying, "If you want a friend in this town, get a dog."

Clinton has ditched friend after friend to shore up his crumbling administration with skilled Washington insiders. But the president cannot fire a wife. The First Lady may be off the welfare team but she will remain in the White House, pinned in the spotlight's glare. And one of the urgent issues for a White House team struggling to relaunch itself is the Hillary problem.

What is to be done with a First Lady whose "unfavorable" ratings in the opinion polls are lower than her husband's?

The polls reflect the warring images of the magazine covers. In the month that the venomously right-wing *American Spectator* portrayed her as a sour-faced witch on her broomstick, *Working Woman* had her as confident yuppie. "Hillary hangs tough" ran the headline, over a photo of a smiling First Lady with arms crossed, in a brisk business suit softened at the neckline with a discreet silk scarf.

She has become trapped by images of her own, unwise endorsement. The two most familiar photographs, each personally approved, betray the contradictions. For *Vogue* magazine, she vamped in black, dreamily cool and remote in one shot, breathlessly parted lips and bedroom eyes in another. For the *New York Times* magazine she preened in pious white, for a profile that portrayed her as St. Joan, hoping to convert cynics to her concept of "a politics of meaning." Which is it?

Between Hillary the missionary in white, and Hillary the sophisticate in black, is a vast gap that was last year filled in by a perception of extraordinary competence.

But with the failure of her great venture into health reform, that gap is being filled increasingly by some far less savory perceptions.

There is Hillary the sharp — perhaps too sharp — investor, turning $1,000 in cattle futures into nearly $100,000 in profits, claiming tax relief on everything from her desk to her husband's used underpants, even as they campaigned against "the decade of greed."

There is Hillary the sharp — perhaps too sharp — lawyer. The Clintons claimed that they lost $69,000 in the Whitewater property venture that went wrong. But in her role as a lawyer Hillary Clinton represented and defended Madison — a bank in which the Clintons had an indirect interest through Whitewater — before state banking regulators appointed by her husband.

There is Hillary the sharp — perhaps too sharp — watchdog over the Arkansas skeletons rattling in Washington cupboards. The night that White House counsel Vince Foster died, it was Hillary's own loyalists who searched his office before the police were allowed in.

Small wonder that the deputy Treasury secretary Roger Altman wrote in his diary on Jan. 4 this year, as the Whitewater affair dominated the headlines, "Hillary Rodham Clinton was 'paralysed' by it; if we don't solve this within the next two days, you don't have to worry about her schedule on health care . . . doesn't want poking into 20 years of public life in Arkansas." (Altman's diary said he was quoting Margaret Williams, Hillary's chief of staff. Williams has since told Congress that she has no recollection of saying that to Altman. This week Altman resigned.)

Whitewater will not go away. And running just beneath the surface of respectable journalism, but blaring from the raucous airwaves of right-wing talk-show hosts such as Rush Limbaugh, are suggestions from Arkansas state troopers of a romantic entanglement with Vince Foster.

In this sense, her predicament is exactly that of her husband. Were the Clinton presidency succeeding in its core ambition of delivering fundamental social reforms, Whitewater and sexual harassment suits and questions of character would be blown away in the gale of legislative success. It is in the context of failure that the personal problems of this co-presidency assume such damning weight.

"What I do not like is the amount of hatred that is being conveyed and really injected into a political system," she confided recently to a small group of health care reporters. "This personal, vicious hatred that for the time being is aimed at the president, and to a lesser extent myself, is very dangerous for our political process. Those encouraging it should think long and hard about the consequences of such encouragement. We have to draw the line of violence and protests that incite violence."

It was a revealing choice of words. Last month in Seattle, at a health care rally, she received the worst reception of her life. The secret service was on special alert after an intelligence tip that trouble was in store. Police confiscated two guns from one man and a knife from another, as angry demonstrators carried banners that read "Heil Hillary" and howled

"Stop the Bitch." Even with the microphones and speakers turned up so high that they howled, she barely managed to be heard above the chants and jeers.

After months of assuring her friends that the Whitewater assaults were all part of the foetid atmosphere in inside-the-Beltway Washington, she was jolted by the hostility in one of the most liberal cities in the country. And it was aimed at her, personally, in a way that brought home to her the beleaguered plight of this presidency.

It is a personal as well as a political assault, and the challenge now is to do what the presidential campaign scrambled to achieve in 1992, to reinvent Hillary — again.

Dubbed "the yuppie wife from hell" by Republican commentators after she spoke proudly of her legal career when "I could have sat home and given teas and baked cookies," she acquiesced in a repackaging. New clothes, new hairstyles, photo-ops with children, and she even baked cookies for the Democratic Party convention.

But one tantalizing expectation, of Hillary as the first credible woman presidential candidate, can be discounted. As Bill Clinton said in a little-noticed interview on French TV during his D-Day anniversary trip, "She told me she never wants to run for elected office." Then the president paused, grimaced, and added: "The more I do it, the more I understand why."

— ***Martin Walker*** is former US Bureau Chief for *The Guardian*; he has written for *The New Yorker, The New Republic* and *The New York Times.* His books include *The President We Deserve: Bill Clinton.* This article originally appeared in *The Guardian* (Manchester) (August 16, 1994). Copyright Scripps Howard News Service, 1994. Reprinted with permission.

Religion & Spirituality

IT IS NOT UNCOMMON for American conservatives to root their political agendas in the Bible. Liberals and moderates, however, are far less likely to speak forcefully about their religious faith. Hillary Rodham Clinton is unusual in this regard. The First Lady is unquestionably a very religious woman; her Methodism and moral convictions are central to her efforts to improve people's lives through public policy.

In the midst of the health care reform debate and debacle, several prominent articles presented the spiritual side of Hillary Rodham Clinton to the public. In this chapter, KENNETH WOODWARD and MICHAEL KELLY present profiles that explore the First Lady's religious beliefs and her "old fashioned" Methodism. In a speech from April 1993, MRS. CLINTON discusses her thoughts on the subject — describing the nation as suffering from a "crisis of meaning" and advocating a more responsive, respectful public discussion about how we live and work together. Her comments are all the more poignant given the eventual vitriol after the health care reform debate.

Her critics charged that Mrs. Clinton's public discussion of her religious practices and beliefs were cynical attempts to reposition herself in the midst of the bruising political battle over health care and to preempt the "values" debate by stealing spirituality from conservative Republicans' campaign chest. In the wake of negative publicity over her call for a "politics of meaning" and stories about her "séances" with Eleanor Roosevelt (see chapter 7), Mrs. Clinton went back, at least in the press, to being a policy wonk. In an April, 1995, letter to *Esquire*, she objected to characterizations that she was meeting with "gurus" and complained that "no matter what I do — or do not do — I will be criticized and exploited by some."

The 1993
Liz Carpenter Lecture Series

Hillary Rodham Clinton

THANK YOU SO MUCH. I am reminded, in following Ann Richards, of that old story of the fellow who died in one of the early Arkansas floods and makes his way to heaven and is met at the gates. And St. Peter says, "Well, you're just in time for our monthly seminar. What do you want to talk about?" The man said, "I want to talk about the most important experience that I have ever encountered. I want to talk about what it is like to be in a flood. I feel like I can make a real contribution to that dialogue." St. Peter says, "Fine. You'll go on after Noah." So, here we are after Noah.

You know, when Liz Carpenter asked me to come speak at her little seminar it was one of those conversations that you have with Liz — those of us who are lucky enough to know her and call her a friend — where her enthusiasm just kind of takes over. She said, "I'm going to have some of my friends in, and we're going to do this lecture. It will be fun. I'll get Ann to come over and Mrs. Johnson will come over, and we'll just have a good old time."

And I had this sort of mental image of being over in one of the small rooms at the LBJ School and sitting with a bunch of my friends, maybe with some students around a table. And then I just put it out of my mind. And over the last two weeks, as Liz knows, it's been kind of touch-and-go for me whether I thought I could be here, and I told Liz that I would certainly try. And when it became clearer that I could, I renewed contact with the people who were helping her put this on and was told that there were going to be thousands, maybe 14,000 people at this event.

And my first response was, "No, no, no. You must have heard it wrong; there's an extra zero in there somewhere." But my second was, "Why would I doubt Liz Carpenter on anything? If she's going to put on a lectureship that's like Anne says, it's going to be a big one. And besides, it's in Texas. So what do we expect?" And I'm just pleased to be part of it.

I also want to say a special word of appreciation to Mrs. Johnson. You know, there is that wonderful old saying about how you never quite know what it's like until you've walked in another person's moccasins. Well, I don't know if you've ever worn moccasins, Mrs. Johnson, but I'm getting a sense of what it is like to try to walk in the footsteps of you and the other women who have been in the position that I now find myself in. And every day that goes by, I am more impressed by the kind of qualities that you and other women in this position have brought to taking care of your personal business on behalf of your family and your husband, and also trying to make your contribution to the country. And all of us in this arena are grateful for the grace and beauty by which you carried out both of those functions and as a wonderful example, not just for me, but for all of us. And I very much wanted to say that to you publicly.

You know, after you hear what I have to say, you'll think that Governor Richards and I not only coordinated outfits but coordinated comments. And I suppose the only thing left for me is to get a hair-do like that. You know, I'm actually due for a new one, and I figure that if we ever want to get Bosnia off the front page, all I have to do is either put on a headband or change my hair and we'll be occupied with something else.

But what Ann Richards talked about is what I want to expand on in my remarks leading into the panel discussion with all of these distinguished panelists and with questions from many of you that I understand were submitted. Because the problems that she alluded to are not just American problems; they are not just governmental problems. We are at a stage in history, I would suggest, in which remolding society certainly in the West is one of the great challenges facing all of us as individuals and as citizens.

And we have to begin realistically to take stock of where we are, stripping perhaps away the romanticism that Governor Richards referred to, to be able to understand where we are in history at this point and what our real challenges happen to be.

And I say that it is not just an American problem. Because if one looks around the Western world; if one looks at Europe; if one looks at the merging democracies, at Asia; if one looks certainly here in North America, you can see the rumblings of discontent, almost regardless of political systems, as we come face to face with the problems that the modern age has dealt us.

And if we take a step back and ask ourselves, "Why is it in a country as economically wealthy as we are despite our economic problems, in a country that is the longest-surviving democracy, there is this undercurrent of discontent — this sense that somehow economic growth and prosperity, political democracy and freedom are not enough? That we lack, at some core level, meaning in our individual lives and meaning collectively — that sense that our lives are part of some greater effort, that we are connected to one another, that community means that we have a place where we belong no matter who we are?" And it isn't very far below the surface because we can see popping through the surface the signs of alienation and despair and hopelessness that are all too common and cannot be ignored. They're in our living rooms at night on the news. They're on the front pages; they are in all of our neighborhoods.

On the plane coming down, I read a phrase in an article in the newspaper this morning talking about how desperate conditions are in so many of our cities that are filled with hopeless girls with babies and angry boys with guns. And yet, it is not just the most violent and the most alienated that we can look to. The discontent of which I speak is broader than that, deeper than that. We are, I think, in a crisis of meaning. What do our governmental institutions mean? What does it mean to be educated? What does it mean to be a journalist? What does it mean in today's world to pursue not only vocations, to be part of institutions, but to be human?

And, certainly, coming off the last year when the ethos of selfishness and greed were given places of honor never before accorded, it is certainly timely to ask ourselves these questions.

One of the clearest and most poignant posings of this question that I have run across was the one provided by Lee Atwater as he lay dying. For those of you who may not know, Lee Atwater was credited with being the architect of the Republican victories of the '70s and the '80s; the vaunted campaign manager of Reagan and Bush; the man who knew how to fight bare-knuckled in the political arena, who was willing to engage in any tactics so long as it worked and he wasn't caught at it.

And yet, when Lee Atwater was struck down with cancer, he said something which we reprinted in *Life Magazine*, which I cut out and carry with me in a little book I have of sayings and Scriptures that I find important and that replenish me from time to time, that I want to share with you. He said the following:

> Long before I was struck with cancer, I felt something stirring in American society. It was a sense among the people of the country, Republicans and Democrats alike, that something was missing from their lives — something crucial. I was trying to position the Republican Party to take advantage of it. But I wasn't exactly sure what it was. My illness helped me to see that what was missing in society is what was missing in me. A little heart, a lot of brotherhood.
>
> The '80s were about acquiring — acquiring wealth, power, prestige. I know. I acquired more wealth, power and prestige than most. But you can acquire all you want and still feel empty. What power wouldn't I trade for a little more time with my family? What price wouldn't I pay for an evening with friends? It took a deadly illness to put me eye-to-eye with that truth, but it is a truth that the country, caught up in its ruthless ambitions and moral decay, can learn on my dime.
>
> I don't know who will lead us through the '90s, but they must be made to speak to this spiritual vacuum at the heart of American society — this tumor of the soul.

That to me will be Lee Atwater's real lasting legacy, not the elections that he helped to win.

But I think the answer to his question — "Who will lead us out of this spiritual vacuum?" — the answer is "all of us." Because remolding society does not depend on just changing government, on just reinventing our institutions to be more in tune with present realities. It requires each of us to play our part in redefining what our lives are and what they should be.

We are caught between two great political forces. On the one hand we have our economy — the market economy — which knows the price of everything but the value of nothing. That is not its job. And then the state or government which attempts to use its means of acquiring tax money, of making decisions to assist us in becoming a better, more equitable society as it defines it. That is what all societies are currently caught between — forces that are more complex and bigger than any of us can understand. And missing in that equation, as we have political and ideological struggles between those who think market economics are the answer to everything, those who think government programs are the answer to everything, is the recognition among all of us that neither of those is an adequate explanation for the challenges confronting us.

And what we each must do is break through the old thinking that has for too long captured us politically and institutionally, so that we can begin to devise new ways of thinking about not only what it means to have economies that don't discard people like they were excess baggage that we no longer need, but to define our institutional and personal responsibilities in ways that answer this lack of meaning.

We need a new politics of meaning. We need a new ethos of individual responsibility and caring. We need a new definition of civil society which answers the unanswerable questions posed by both the market forces and the governmental ones, as to how we can have a society that fills us up again and makes us feel that we are part of something bigger than ourselves.

Now, will it be easy to do that? Of course not. Because we are breaking new ground. This is a trend that has been developing over hundreds of years. It is not something that just happened to us in the last decade or two. And so it is not going to be easy to redefine who we are as human beings in this post-modern age. Nor will it be easy to figure out how to make our institutions more responsive to the kind of human beings we wish to be.

But part of the great challenge of living is defining yourself in your moment, of seizing the opportunities that you are given, and of making the very best choices you can. That is what this administration, this president, and those of us who are hoping for these changes are attempting to do.

I used to wonder during the election when my husband would attempt to explain how so many of the problems that we were confronting were not easy Democratic/Republican, liberal/conservative problems. They were problems that shared different characteristics, that we had to not only define clearly, but search for new ways of confronting.

Then someone would say, "Well, you know, he can't make up his mind," or "He doesn't know what he wants to say about that." When instead what I was hearing and what we had been struggling with for years is how does one define the new issues? How do we begin to inject some new meaning? How do we take old values and apply them to these new — for many of us — undreamed of problems that we now confront? And that is what all of us must be engaged in in our own lives, at every level, in every institution with which we interact.

Let me just give you some examples. If we believe that the reconstruction of civil society with its institutions of family, friendship networks, communities, voluntary organizations are really the glue of what holds us together; if we go back and read de Toqueville and notice how he talked over and over again about the unique characteristics that he found among Americans and rooted so many of those in that kind of intermediary institution of civil society that I just mentioned, then we know we have to better understand what we can do to strengthen those institutions, to understand how they have changed over time, and to try to find meaning in them as they currently are.

That's why the debate over family values over the last year, which was devised for political purposes, seemed so off point. There is no — or should be no — debates that our family structure is in trouble. There should be no debate that children need the stability, the predictability of a family. But there should be debate over how we best make sure that children and families flourish. And once that debate is carried out on honest terms, then we have to recognize that either the old idea that only parental influence and parental values matters, or the nearly as old idea that only state programmatic intervention matters, are both equally fallacious.

Instead we ought to recognize what should be a common-sense truth — that children are the result of both the values of their parents and the values of the society in which they live. And that you can have an important debate over how best to make sure parental values are the ones that will help children grow and be strengthened, and how social values equally must be recognized for the role they play in how children feel about themselves and act in the world. And then we can begin to have what should be a sensible conversation about how to strengthen both. That's the kind of approach that has to get beyond the dogma of right or left, conservative or liberal. Those views are inadequate to the problems we see.

Any of you who have ever been in an inner city, working with young people as I have over the years, will know as I do the heroic stories of parents and grandparents who, against overwhelming odds, fight to keep their children safe — just physically safe; and who hold high expectations for those children; whose values I would put up against any other person in the country, but who have no control over the day-to-day violence and influence that comes flooding in the doors of that housing project apartment; and who need a society that is more supportive of their value than the one they currently have.

Equally, all of us know the contrary story of families with enough economic means, affluent enough to live in neighborhoods that are as safe as they can be in our country today, so they have the social value structure of what we would hope that each child in America could have in terms of just basic kinds of fundamental safety and physical well-being, but whose parental values are not ones to promote a childhood that is a positive one, giving children the chance to grow up to achieve their own God-given potential. So that the presence of values of society are not enough, either.

There are so many examples of how we have to think differently and how we have to go beyond not only the traditions of the past, but unfortunately for many of us, well-held and cherished views of the past; and how we have to break out of the kind of gridlock mentality which exists not just in the Congress from time to time, but exists as well in all of us as we struggle to see the world differently and cope with the challenges it has given us.

Yet I am very hopeful about where we stand in this last decade of the 20th century, because for all of the problems that we see around us, both abroad and at home, there is a growing body of people who want to deal with them, who want to be part of this conversation about how we break through old views and deal with new problems. And we will need millions more of those conversations.

Those conversations need to take place in every family, every workplace, every political institution in our country. They need to take place in our schools, where we have to be honest about what we are and are not able to convey to our children; where we have to be honest about the conditions which are confronting so many of our teachers and our students day in and day out; where we have to be honest that we do have to set high expectations for all children and we should not discard any because of who they are or where they come from.

And where we need to hold accountable every member of the educational enterprise — parents, teachers and students. Each should be held accountable for the opportunity they have been given to participate in one of the greatest efforts of humankind, passing on knowledge to children. And we have to expect more than we are currently getting.

We also need to take a hard look at other institutions. As Governor Richards said, we are in the midst of an intensive effort of trying to determine how we can provide decent, affordable health care to every American. And in that process we have to ask hard questions about every aspect of our health care system. Why do doctors do what they do? Why are nurses not permitted to do more than they do? Why are patients put in the position they're in?

But to give you just one example about how this ties in with what I have said before about how these problems we are confronting now in many ways are the result of our progress as we have moved toward being modern men and women: Our ancestors did not have to think about the many of the issues we are now confronted with. When does life start; when does life end? Who makes those decisions? How do we dare impinge upon these areas of such delicate, difficult questions? And, yet, every day in hospitals and homes and hospices all over this country, people are struggling with those very profound issues.

These are not issues that we have guidebooks about. They are issues that we have to summon up what we believe is morally and ethically and spiritually correct and do the best we can with God's guidance. How do we create a system that gets rid of the micro-management, the regulation and the bureaucracy, and substitutes instead human caring, concern and love? And that is our real challenge in redesigning a health care system.

I want to say a word about another institution, and that is the media, because it is the filter through which we see ourselves and one another. And in many ways the challenge confronting it is just as difficult as those confronting any other institution we can imagine. How does one keep up with the extraordinary pace of information now available? How do we make sense of that information now available? How do we make sense of that information? How do we make values about it even if we think we have made sense? How do we rid ourselves of the lowest common denominator that is the easiest way of conveying information? How do we have a media that understands how difficult these issues are and looks at itself honestly, because the role it must play is so critical to our success in making decisions about how we will proceed as a society?

I remember in the beginning of the campaign being asked a question at an editorial meeting in South Carolina that my husband was at to meet a lot of the editors and reporters from a lot of the small-town papers. These were not the folks who you'll see on a TV station anywhere, these are the people who got up every day and did the best they could to put out the paper that covered their community or their region. And one of the men, after hearing my husband speak, said, "Now you've talked about how we have to change — how we have to change government, how we have to change society. But as a journalist, how do I change to be able to understand and report on those changes?" My husband said, "You know, I can't answer that. That's something you have to answer. But I'm really glad you asked the question, because every institution in our life has to ask those hard questions about who we are, what contribution we make to dealing with our problems and to injecting meaning again in the lives of us all."

So every one of our institutions is under the same kind of mandate. Change will come whether we want it or not, and what we have to do is to try and make change our friend, not our enemy. But probably most profoundly and importantly, the changes that will count the most are the millions and millions of changes that take place on the individual level as people reject cynicism; as they are willing to take risks to meet the challenges they see around them; as they truly begin to try to see other people as they wish to be seen and to treat them as they wish to be treated; to overcome all of the obstacles we have erected around ourselves that keep us apart from one another, fearful and afraid, not willing to build the bridges necessary; to fill that spiritual vacuum that Lee Atwater talked about.

You know, one of my favorite quotes is from Albert Schweitzer. And he talks about how the disease in Central Africa is called the sleeping sickness; there exists a sleeping sickness of the soul. The most dangerous aspect is that one is unaware of its coming. That is why we have to be careful. As soon as you notice the slightest sign of indifference, the moment you become aware of a loss of character or a serious longing of enthusiasm, it is best [to] take it as a warning. You should realize that your soul suffers if you can't live superficially. Not just your soul, but your society. Being here on this great campus, with so many thousands of people who care about learning and are committed to making a difference. Let us be willing to remold society by refining what it means to be a human being in the 20th century, moving into a new millennium. Let us be willing to help our institutions to change, to deal with the new challenges that confront them. Let us try to restore the importance of civil society by committing ourselves to our children, our families, our friends; and to reaching out beyond the circle of those of whom we know, to the many others on whom we are dependent in this complex society; and understanding a little more about what their lives are like and doing what we can to help ease their burdens.

Our greatest opportunities lie ahead, because so many of the struggles of the Depression and the World War and the other challenges posed by the Cold War and communism are behind us. The new ones are equally threatening. But we should have learned a lot in the last few years that will prepare us to play our part in remolding a society that we are proud to be a part of.

Thank you all very much.

— ***Hillary Rodham Clinton*** is a lawyer and children's rights advocate. She is the first First Lady to run for the Senate. She is the author of *It Takes a Village, and Other Lessons Children Teach Us,* as well as "Talking It Over," a syndicated weekly column drawing on her experience as First Lady. Mrs. Clinton delivered these remarks at the University of Texas (Austin) on April 7, 1993. Lee Atwater's quotation is from "Lee Atwater's Last Campaign," *Life Magazine*, February 1991.

Saint Hillary

Michael Kelly

SINCE SHE DISCOVERED, at the age of 14, that for people less fortunate than herself the world could be very cruel, Hillary Rodham Clinton has harbored an ambition so large that it can scarcely be grasped.

She would like to make things right.

She is 45 now and she knows that the earnest idealisms of a child of the 1960's may strike some people as naive or trite or grandiose. But she holds to them without any apparent sense of irony or inadequacy. She would like people to live in a way that more closely follows the Golden Rule. She would like to do good, on a grand scale, and she would like others to do good as well. She would like to make the world a better place — as she defines better.

While an encompassing compassion is the routine mode of public existence for every First Lady, there are two great differences in the case of Mrs. Clinton: She is serious and she has power.

Her sense of purpose stems from a world view rooted in the activist religion of her youth and watered by the conviction of her generation that it was destined (and equipped) to teach the world the errors of its ways. Together, both faiths form the true politics of her heart, the politics of virtue.

She is spurred now by a personal matter — the death of her father — and two considerations of practical politics: She recognizes that issues of public values and personal behavior are coming to dominate the politics of this millennial age — but that so far those issues have been mostly defined and championed by conservative Republicans; she is moved by the impatient conviction that moderates and liberals have wanly surrendered the adjective "religious" to the right. She recognizes, too, the need to provide some sort of overarching theme around which the many and varied proposals the Clinton Administration spins out to an increasingly askance public may be made to seem neatly fitting parts of a coherent whole.

The First Lady's vision is singular, formed by the intellectual passions and experiences of a life. But it is also the most purely voiced expression of the collective spirit of the Clinton Administration, a spirit that is notable both for the long reach of its reformist ambitions and the cocky assurance of its faith in the ideas of its own design. It is very much a work in progress, but its emerging shape is, even by the standards of visions, large.

Driven by the increasingly common view that something is terribly awry with modern life, Mrs. Clinton is searching for not merely programmatic answers but for The Answer. Something in the Meaning of It All line, something that would inform everything from her imminent and all-encompassing health care proposal to ways in which the state might encourage parents not to let their children wander all hours of the night in shopping malls.

When it is suggested that she sounds as though she's trying to come up with a sort of unified-field theory of life, she says, excitedly, "That's right, that's exactly right!"

She is, it develops in the course of two long conversations, looking for a way of looking at looking at the world that would marry conservatism and liberalism, and capitalism and statism, that would tie together practically everything: the way we are, the way we were, the faults of man and the word of God, the end of Communism and the beginning of the third millennium, crime in the streets and on Wall Street, teenage mothers and foul-mouthed children and frightening drunks in the parks, the cynicism of the press and the corrupting role of television, the breakdown of civility and the loss of community.

The point of all this is not abstract or small. What Mrs. Clinton seems

— in all apparent sincerity — to have in mind is leading the way to something on the order of a Reformation: the remaking of the American way of politics, government, indeed life. A lot of people, contemplating such a task, might fall prey to self doubts. Mrs. Clinton does not blink.

"It's not going to be easy," she says. "But we can't get scared away from it because it is an overwhelming task."

The difficulty is bound to be increased by the awkward fact that a good deal of what Mrs. Clinton sees as wrong right now with the American way of life can be traced, at least in part, to the last great attempt to find The Answer: the liberal experiments in the reshaping of society that were the work of the intellectual elite of . . . Mrs. Clinton's generation.

THE CRUSADE OF HILLARY RODHAM CLINTON began on April 6 in Austin, Tex. There, speaking from notes she had scribbled on the plane, she moved swiftly past the usual thanks and jokes to wade into an extraordinary speech: a passionate, at times slightly incoherent, call for national spiritual renewal.

The Western world, she said, needed to be made anew. America suffered from a "sleeping sickness of the soul," a "sense that somehow economic growth and prosperity, political democracy and freedom are not enough — that we lack at some core level meaning in our individual lives and meaning collectively, that sense that our lives are part of some greater effort, that we are connected to one another, that community means that we have a place where we belong no matter who we are."

She spoke of "cities that are filled with hopeless girls with babies and angry boys with guns" as only the most visible signs of a nation crippled by "alienation and despair and hopelessness," a nation that was in the throes of a "crisis of meaning."

"What do our governmental institutions mean? What do our lives in today's world mean?" she asked. "What does it mean in today's world to pursue not only vocations, to be part of institutions, but to be human?"

These questions, she said, led to the larger question: "Who will lead us out of this spiritual vacuum?" The answer to that was "all of us," all are required "to play our part in redefining what our lives are and what they should be."

"Let us be willing," she urged in conclusion, "to remold society by redefining what it means to be a human being in the 20th century, moving into a new millennium."

It is easy to mock this sort of thing, and some people immediately did. What, asked *The New Republic* in a question the First Lady finds to be a perfect small example of the cynicism she deplores, was all that supposed to mean?

Mrs. Clinton has been groping toward an answer to that question for much of her life. She has read her way from the Methodist founder John Wesley to Paul Tillich, Reinhold Niebuhr and Dietrich Bonhoeffer, three left-of-center theologians who sought to link their religious beliefs to a critical involvement in politics and government, to, most recently, Michael Lerner, a liberal Jewish thinker who coined the phrase "politics of meaning," which Mrs. Clinton adopted in her Austin speech.

She gropes still. "I don't know; I don't know," she begins, when asked to define her philosophy. "I don't have any coherent explanation. I hope one day to be able to stop long enough actually to try to write down what I do mean, because it's important to me that I try to do that, because I have floated around the edges of this and talked about it for many, many years with a lot of people, but I've never regularly kept a journal or really tried to get myself organized enough to do it."

But she is well along in her musings. Working her way through a thicket of theologies and ideologies, she offers in language that is a mix of Bible and Bill Moyers, of New Testament and New Age, a tentative definition of what she believes.

"The very core of what I believe is this concept of individual worth, which I think flows from all of us being creatures of God and being imbued with a spirit," she says. She speaks carefully, sitting upright and leaning slightly forward at a small table in a neat and modest White House garden.

"Some years ago, I gave a series of talks about the underlying principles of Methodism," she goes on. "I talked a lot about how timeless a lot of scriptural lessons were because they tied in with what we now know about human beings. If you break down the Golden Rule or if you take Christ's commandment — Love thy neighbor as thyself — there is an underlying assumption that you will value yourself, that you will be a responsible being who will live by certain behaviors that enable you to have self-respect, because, then, out of that self-respect comes the capacity for you to respect and care for other people.

"And how do we just break this whole enterprise down in small enough pieces? Well, somebody says to themselves: 'You know, I'm not going to tell that racist, sexist joke. I don't want to objectify another human being. Why do I want to do that? What do I get out of that kind of action? Maybe I should try to restrain myself.'

"Or somebody else says: 'You know, I'm going to start thanking the woman who cleans the restroom in the building that I work in. You know, maybe that sounds kind of stupid, but on the other hand I want to start seeing her as a human being.'

"And then maybe the next step is I say to myself: 'How much are we paying this woman who works the 3 to 11 shift. And who's taking care of her kids while she's here working? And how do we make it possible for her to be able to both be a good parent and perform a necessary function?'

"And these are little pieces, and a lot of those little pieces can be done on a very small scale that then aggregates. So I think what we're basically, what we're really looking at is, you know, millions and millions of changes in individual behavior that are motivated by the same impulses, even if we're not doing a very good job of describing them."

This rambling passage seems to validate *The New Republic*'s impertinence. What does it all mean? This is, as it turns out, a fair question. The meaning of the politics of meaning is hard to discern under the gauzy and gushy wrappings of New Age jargon that blanket it. Michael Lerner, who has been expounding on the subject for several years in the pages of *Tikkun*, a magazine of liberal Jewish thinking, has described the new politics as all about "how to build a society based on love and connection, a society in which the bottom line would not be profit and power but ethical and spiritual sensitivity and a sense of community, mutual caring and responsibility."

Mrs. Clinton says the right language remains to be invented. "As Michael Lerner and I discussed, we have to first create a language that would better communicate what we are trying to say, and the policies would flow from that language."

The problem with the language goes right to the core of the question of what it all means. Is there one unifying idea that is at the heart of the politics of meaning? "I don't think there is one core thing," Mrs. Clinton says. "I think this has to be thought through on a variety of planes. I don't think there is one unifying theory."

Meanwhile, words somewhat fail her. "It is like when you tell someone for the first time that you love them," she says. "You're not fully aware of what that means, but it's the best effort you can make to kind of convey the full range of emotions and feelings and intentions and expectations that you can articulate at the time."

BUT THERE ACTUALLY IS, as the mists of New Age mysticism slip away, a clear line to Mrs. Clinton's message. It is, fundamentally, an old and very American message, one that goes purposely beyond the normal boundaries of politics into the territory of religion. It is concerned not just with how government should behave but with how people should. It is the message of values, not programs. It is the message of the preacher, a role Hillary Rodham Clinton has filled many times delivering guest sermons from the pulpits of United Methodist churches.

It seems odd at first to contemplate Mrs. Clinton in such terms. The public debate over her that swirled throughout the 1992 Presidential race centered on two lesser questions — how left-wing was she and how hungry for power — but failed to consider the larger point of her life.

She appeared before the public in a series of roles, some of the news media's design, some of the Republicans' and some of her own. She was, by bewildering turns, a calculating and radical feminist lawyer and a cookie-baking mom, Lady Macbeth and the little lady.

In an election that Republicans failed to win on the strength of much the same sort of "values" issues that Mrs. Clinton now talks about, one thing the Democratic candidate's wife was not was a moralist.

"American women don't need lectures from Washington about values," she said then. "We don't need to hear about an idealized world that was never as righteous or carefree as some would like to think."

Now, questions of values and matters of morals are the heart of what Mrs. Clinton sees as the way toward national salvation. In truth, they always have been at the core of what she is about, but the many faces of the Hillary of 1992 obscured the larger point of her life.

The politics of Hillary Rodham Clinton are indeed largely liberal (although, the post-election evidence indicates, no more so than those of her husband), but they are of a liberalism derived from religiosity. They combine a generally "progressive" social agenda with a strong dose of moralism, the admixture of the two driven by an abundant faith in the capacity of the human intellect and the redeeming power of love.

They are, rather than primarily the politics of left or right, the politics of do-goodism, flowing directly from a powerful and continual stream that runs through American history from Harriet Beecher Stowe to Jane Addams to Carry Nation to Dorothy Day; from the social gospel of the late 19th century to the temperance-minded Methodism of the early 20th century to the liberation theology of the 1960's and 1970's to the pacifistic and multiculturally correct religious left of today.

The true nature of her politics makes the ambition of Hillary Rodham Clinton much larger than merely personal. She clearly wants power, and has already amassed more of it than any First Lady since Eleanor Roosevelt. But that ambition is merely a subcategory of the infinitely larger scope of her desires.

Hillary Rodham was born in 1947, into the world she wishes to restore, a place of security and community and clear moral values, to Hugh and Dorothy Rodham and raised in the solidly upper-class, solidly conservative Chicago suburb of Park Ridge, Ill. Her childhood was, by all accounts including her own, grounded in the old-fashioned, uncomplicated absolutes of her parents' ethical code.

"My father was no great talker and not very articulate, and wouldn't have known Niebuhr from Bonhoeffer from Havel from Jefferson, and would have thought a conversation like this was just goofy," Mrs. Clinton said in an interview several weeks after Rodham's death on April 7. "But he gave me the basic tools, and it wasn't fancy philosophical stuff.

"He used to say all the time, 'I will always love you but I won't always like what you do.' And, you know, as a child I would come up with 900 hypotheses. It would always end with something like, 'Well, you mean, if I murdered somebody and was in jail and you came to see me, you would still love me?'

"And he would say: 'Absolutely! I will always love you, but I would be deeply disappointed and I would not like what you did because it would have been wrong.'"

The lesson Mrs. Clinton drew from this is one she says is at the core of her philosophy: "It was so simplistic, but it was so helpful to me, because, I mean, it gave me the basis of unconditional love that I think every child deserves to have — and one of our problems is that too many of our children don't have that — but it also gave me from the very beginning a set of values based on what I did."

Mrs. Clinton says the 16 days she spent in Little Rock as her father lay dying led her to give the Austin speech. Her reflections went back to 1961, when she was 14 and began attending Sunday-evening youth sessions conducted by the Rev. Donald G. Jones, the youth minister at the First Methodist Church in Park Ridge. It was Jones who taught her the lessons that would most profoundly shape her idea of the way things ought to be.

Jones, who now teaches social ethics at Drew University in Madison, N.J., was 30 years old, "just out of the seminary, full of vim and vigor," and a believer in the theology of Paul Tillich, whom he considers a theological mentor. Tillich had propounded a theory that sought to redefine the Christian role in the modern world.

"He said that the two major problems of contemporary society were the crisis of meaning and alienation," Jones said in a recent interview. "He contrasted this with the 16th century, where the two major problems were death and guilt.

"The point he was making was that because death and guilt were the two major problems back then, Protestantism had defined grace in terms of answers to those problems: eternal life and the forgiveness of sins. But now, with the two major problems being the crisis of meaning and alienation, he said, our religious language should speak in terms of unity, of connectedness, of overcoming alienation, of giving meaning."

When Jones read the texts of Mrs. Clinton's Austin speech, he was struck by the obvious parallels between the oratory of the First Lady and the teachings of Tillich on alienation and meaninglessness: "These were precisely the terms Hillary struck in that speech in Austin. She talked of the discontent lurking beneath the surface and the politics of meaning."

Indeed, this theme runs deep in Mrs. Clinton's sense of things.

"If you go back and read the correspondence that existed in the 19th century between people of all different walks of life," she says, "you know, it may not be some kind of heavy theological inquiry, but there will be all kinds of flashes about what happened in a way, that, you know, that the whole cycle of life and its meaning is tied into their daily life.

"And you know, by the nature of how we spend our time today, we have walled ourselves off from that. I mean, we get up in the morning and we go to work and our children don't know what our work is, because they don't see us plowing a field or making a quilt. We go off and push papers and then come home and try to explain it. Our relatives age and die often in places far away from our homes. We've compartmentalized so much of our lives that trying to find even the time to think about how all of it fits together has become harder and harder."

Jones was a dedicated proponent of the idea, then and now the driving force of the United Methodist Church, that Christian duty lay in taking a direct, helpful interest in the lives of the less fortunate. He organized the white, suburban children of Park Ridge to help provide baby sitting for the children of migrant workers in the Chicago area. Hillary was among the students he took on an eye-opening visit to talk with young black and Hispanic gang members at a community center on Chicago's South Side and also among those taken to meet the Rev. Dr. Martin Luther King Jr., who was speaking in the city.

Now, asked if she has always been impelled by what she called, in a recent interview with *The Washington Post*, "a burning desire" to "make the world . . . better for everybody," Mrs. Clinton says, with a slight, self-conscious laugh: "Yeah, I always have. I have not always known what it meant, but I have always had it."

Then, on a moment's reflection, she amends her answer in a way that shows clearly the effect Jones's field trips had on the sensibilities of a child of well-off suburbia: "Especially since I was in junior high and high school and got a sense of what people were up against, and how lucky I had been, a sense, you know, that I was a very lucky person in what I had been given."

But there was more to Hillary's education than the inculcation of a guilt-induced sense of obligation. Jones also exposed her to the writings of Niebuhr, who argued that the tragedy of history proved that the hope for a better world could not depend on any sentimental view of human behavior but must encompass the legitimate use of power.

"My sense of Hillary is that she realizes absolutely the truth of the human condition, which is that you cannot depend on the basic nature of man to be good and you cannot depend entirely on moral suasion to make it good," Jones says. "You have to use power. And there is nothing wrong with wielding power in the pursuit of policies that will add to the human good. I think Hillary knows this. She is very much the sort of Christian who understands that the use of power to achieve social good is legitimate."

There is a Niebuhrian hardness under the fuzzy edges of Mrs. Clinton's discourses on the politics of virtue — an acknowledgment that some sorts of behavior are acceptable and other sorts are not, that every right is married to a responsibility, that a civilized society must be willing to condemn those who act in ways destructive of that society.

"We do this in our own lives," she says. "I mean, we pass judgments all the time. I can remember sitting in a law school class years and years ago in which a hypothetical was being discussed about terrorists. . . .

"And I remember sitting there listening to the conversation as so many people tried to explain away or rationalize their behavior. And I remember saying, 'You know, there is another alternative. And the other alternative is that they are evil.' I mean, you know? There are evil people in the world. And they may be able to come up with elaborate rationalizations to attempt to explain their evil, and they may even have some reasonable basis for saying their conduct needs to be understood in the light of pre-existing conditions, but their behavior is still evil."

Mrs. Clinton argues passionately for a "reaffirmation of responsible behavior rooted in what I view as a value system in which people respect one another and in which they care for one another."

She offers an example of what she sees in society as the opposite sort of value system.

"We have two friends who just moved out of a big city to a smaller town, because they found that their high-school daughter was basically being shunned because she had a curfew, she was not permitted to run wild with other kids, she was not permitted to go out to dance clubs till 2 or 3 o'clock in the morning. She was basically being made fun of for being a good kid.

"Now, it is not government's fault that the parents of those other kids are letting their kids engage in behavior and court dangers that they are not emotionally or psychologically prepared to do," she says. Rather, it is the fault of individuals: "affluent parents in this society who drop their 10- and 11-year-olds off at the mall, that let their 13- and 14- and 15-year-olds go off to places that they've never met the parents of the kids, they've never met the kids or anything like that — that is a failure on the part of the adult community to care for our children."

A critical aspect of Mrs. Clinton's analysis suggests the rejection of rights-based liberalism as it now exists. She favors, as does the President, welfare reform, and she argues that society has extended too freely rights without responsibilities, which has led to a great decline in the standard of behavior.

She cites a recent article by Daniel Patrick Moynihan on what the New York Senator called "defining deviancy down."

"Senator Moynihan argues very convincingly that what we have in effect done is get used to more and more deviant behavior around us, because we haven't wanted to deal with it," she says. "But — by gosh! — it is deviant! It is deviant if you have any standards by which you expect to be judged."

This line of argument, central to Mrs. Clinton's view, is, of course, precisely what social conservatives have been saying for years. Social liberals, who dominate the national Democratic Party, have held that it is not the place of either government or society to lay down a set of behavioral standards based on moral absolutes, and that individual freedom necessitates moral relativism.

"I think that is a theoretical and to a great extent an elitist argument," says Mrs. Clinton, with some heat. "I think a person would have a hard time making that argument to the kind of people who I know who are working hard and living in fear and are really taking the brunt of a lot of the social and political decisions that we've either made or failed to make in the last 20 years. There are standards. We live by them. We reward them. And it is a real fallacy to jump from what we do in our individual and work lives to expect us not to have standards in our social community lives."

Those standards are, it is suggested, the standards of the Ten Commandments.

"That's right," she says. "And in nearly every religion I am aware of, there is a variation of the Golden Rule. And even for the nonreligious, it is a tenet of people who believe in humanistic principles."

We could do a lot worse, she says, than live according to the Golden Rule. "That means: Should we let whole sections of our city be like Beirut? Would we want that to be the place where we live with our children? Of course not. Well then, what would be reasonable policies to pursue in order to avoid that? Would we want young children to be exposed to a lot of the dangers that might lead to drug addiction or abuse or violence or all of the problems we face, if there were ways we could band together as adults to help them avoid that? Of course, we much would prefer that."

IT IS AT THIS POINT that some awkward questions arise:

If it is necessary to remake society, why should Hillary Rodham Clinton get the job?

Can someone who helped lead the very generation that threw out the old ways of moral absolutes and societal standards now lead the charge back to the future?

At Wellesley College, from 1965 to 1969, Hillary Rodham gradually moved away from the conservatism of her parents and embraced the predominant attitudes of a campus that was steeped in the tradition of liberal, social service-oriented Protestantism and heady with the conviction that the young people of the moment were fated to remake the world.

The times encouraged dreaming of great, sweeping change. Alan Schechter, who taught Rodham political science and remembers her transformation from a Goldwater Girl to "secular liberalism," recalls: "The aura of the martyred Kennedy was strong on the campuses then, and everyone was full of talk about doing something about the race crisis, about the Peace Corps. The mood was one of youthful idealism, commitment, that cliched line of Kennedy's — ask not what your country can do for you."

By the time she graduated from Wellesley to head on to Yale Law School, Hillary Rodham had become a radical, in the true sense of the word: dedicated to the imperative of profound societal change, and confident in her own ability to direct that change.

She began thinking then about the ideas she is giving voice to now. The student commencement speech delivered by Hillary Rodham for the class of 1969 is the direct ancestor of the Austin speech delivered by the Hillary Rodham Clinton of today. They share all the same traits: vaulting ambition, didactic moralizing, intellectual incoherence and the adolescent assumption that the past does not exist and the present needs only your guiding hand to create the glorious future.

Then, she spoke of "attempting to come to grasp with some of the inarticulate, maybe even inarticulable, things that we're feeling." Today, she speaks of the struggle to "put into words what is often for most of us inarticulate or inarticulable."

Then, she spoke of the attempt "to forge an identity in this particular age." Today, she speaks of "redefining who we are as human beings in this post-modern age."

Then, she spoke of "our questions, our questions about our institutions, about our colleges, about our churches, about our government." Today, she asks "what do our governmental institutions mean? What do our lives in today's world mean?"

At the heart of the Wellesley speech, she argued for what she then called the "experiment in human living" and would come to call "excessive individualism" and "rights without responsibility."

The "prevailing, acquisitive and competitive corporate life," she said, "is not for us. We're searching for more immediate, ecstatic and penetrating mode of living."

When asked if the social experiments of the 1960's and 1970's led to the systemic problems she now sees in the 1990's, Mrs. Clinton replies, "I don't know if it's unfair to say that, but it's probably incomplete."

The roots of the problems go back farther and spread wider than that, she says. But still, she carefully acknowledges that the questioning and searching of her generation did produce some "excesses" and "wrong decisions."

It is suggested that for Hillary Rodham Clinton, a career liberal activist and former seeker of ecstatic living, to sound the call for a return to traditional ethics will strike some people as a bit much. As easy, moralistic preaching. After all, the last person who tried this sort of thing, Dan Quayle, was mocked for his pains. And he, at least, had been elected.

The First Lady jumps hard on the point.

"That's irrelevant to me," she snaps back. "I know that no matter what I did — if I did nothing, if I spent my entire day totally disengaged from what was going on around me — I'd be criticized for that. I mean, it's a no-win deal, no matter what I do, or try to do.

"But from my perspective, there are millions of people who are worried about the same things I'm worried about. I don't care who gets the credit. I don't care who has to be criticized in order to move this conversation forward. I want to live in a place again where I can walk down any street without being afraid. I want to be able to take my daughter to a park at any time of day or night in the summertime and remember what I used to be able to do when I was a little kid."

At that moment, irritation still edging her voice, she doesn't sound at all like the Hillary Rodham of 1969. She doesn't sound like a politician or a preacher. She sounds like just another angry, sincere, middle-aged citizen, wondering how everything went so wrong.

Which brings up the second difficult question.

What exactly can Mrs. Clinton and the new politics do about it all?

It is clear that there will be immense practical problems in making the transition from theory to practical politics.

The reason harks back to the question of language. Several weeks ago, when Michael Lerner accepted Mrs. Clinton's invitation to come to the White House and talk about the politics of meaning, they agreed that, he says, "the question was how to take, in a practical, hard-nosed way, the sum of the ethical ideas of the Bible and apply them to this moment in time."

They fell into disagreement, however, as soon as they began talking about how that might be done. "I proposed that the Clinton Administration establish a policy where, for any proposed legislation or new program, there would have to be written first an Ethical and Community Environmental Impact Report, which would require each agency to report how the proposed legislation or new program would impact on shaping the ethics and the caring and sharing of the community covered by that agency."

Mrs. Clinton, Lerner says, "liked the idea, but was worried about using words like 'caring' and 'sharing' and 'love' in talking about government policies. And this concern became the central question of our discussion: Would the press kill us on this?"

Unintentionally hilarious Big Brotherism is, in fact, a hallmark of Lerner's ideas for implementing the politics of meaning. In the May-June issue of his magazine, *Tikkun*, Lerner offers a series of specific proposals by which the Clinton Administration could turn the theory of the politics of meaning into reality in the workplace.

These include: that the Department of Labor order "every workplace" in America "to create a mission statement explaining its function and what conception of the common good it is serving and how it is doing so"; "sponsor 'Honor Labor' campaigns designed to highlight the honor due to people for their contributions to the common good," and "train a corps of union personnel, worker representatives and psychotherapists in the relevant skills to assist developing a new spirit of cooperation, mutual caring and dedication to work."

The reason Lerner's proposals for the application of the politics of meaning focus so heavily on bureacratic irrelevancies is the same reason Mrs. Clinton is struggling still with words.

Any clearly expressed, serious proposal to do anything to improve public values runs immediately against the fundamentals of social liberalism that are the guiding ethos of Democratic policies.

Mrs. Clinton argues that the concepts of liberalism and conservatism don't really mean anything anymore and that the politics of the New Age is moving beyond ideology. But that is not at all true in the area of values where she seeks to venture. It is easy for social conservatives, who have been writing and debating for years about the moral values Mrs. Clinton is now addressing, to speak bluntly about what is morally right and what is not. Conservatism is purposely, explicitly judgmental. But liberalism, as defined by Mrs. Clinton's generation and those who came after, has increasingly moved away from the entire concept of judgment and embraced instead the expansion of rights and the tolerance of diversity.

Returning to moral judgment as a basis for governmental policy must inevitably mean curtailing what have come to be regarded as sacrosanct rights and admitting a limit to tolerance. And that will bring the politics of meaning hard against the meaning of politics.

— ***Michael Kelly*** covered Clinton's 1992 presidential campaign for *The New York Times*. He has written for *The New Yorker*, *National Journal* and *The Washington Post*. He is the editor-in-chief of *National Journal*, editor of *The Atlantic Monthly* and author of *Martyrs' Day: Chronicle of a Small War*. (May 23, 1993.)

Soulful Matters

Kenneth L. Woodward

HILLARY RODHAM CLINTON HAS been called many things since she became the nation's first lady.

To her fiercest critics she is a radical feminist; to her most ardent admirers she is a disciplined political operative, an eloquent advocate who needs no notes when speaking.

In softer profile, Mrs. Clinton comes across as a well-organized working mother and her husband's closest confidante. But long before she was a Democrat, a lawyer or a Clinton, Hillary Rodham was a Methodist.

And that, say those who know her now as well as those who knew her when, is the way the first lady is best understood.

She thinks like a Methodist, talks like a Methodist and wants to reform society just as a well-Sunday-schooled Methodist churchwoman should.

"I am," she tells *Newsweek* in an exclusive interview at the White House, "an old-fashioned Methodist."

In any other place, from almost any other woman, such an admission would be insignificant.

Americans want their first family to be religious but not strongly so. As Ronald Reagan understood — and Jimmy Carter painfully learned — vague belief firmly held is the most appropriate White House religion.

Politicians may not care and the media may scoff, but the Clintons are perhaps the most openly religious first couple this century has seen.

The president is a hymn-humming, sermon-loving, liberal Southern Baptist who studied under the Jesuits at Georgetown and feels at home in any kind of pew.

But Mrs. Clinton is cut from old, less expressive Methodist stock; and these days she feels like a battered woman. Her public role has diminished, and she's being blamed for the failure of health care reform in a bitter political season.

Meanwhile, evangels of the religious right scorn her as a Mary Magdalene, while pundits in the secular press ridicule her spirituality as flaky New Age blather.

All this has taught her a "great deal of sympathy" for Christian fundamentalists. Like them, she believes she has to prove that she isn't a figment of other people's prejudices. Indeed, at one point in the conversation, the first lady even submitted to a brief examination of her faith:

Do you believe in the Father, Son and Holy Spirit?

"Yes."

The atoning death of Jesus?

"Yes."

The resurrection of Christ?'

"Yes."

The interview was conducted in the Map Room around a makeshift folding table that looked as if it had just been cleared of dishes.

The first lady, dressed in black, glances down often at her hands.

For three months *Newsweek* had sought an interview about her religious faith and her aides were fearful that no matter what she said, Mrs. Clinton would be accused of trying to manipulate her public image. She even hesitated to name her favorite Bible passages, convinced she'd be misunderstood:

"If I quote a Bible Scripture, people are always looking for the hidden meaning in it."

Or, worse, that her words might be turned against her in the latest rush to judgment. Can this Hillary Clinton be real?

Though conservatives may doubt her religious convictions, and liberals wish them away, Hillary Rodham Clinton is as pious as she is political. Methodism, for her, is not just a church but an extended family of faith that defines her horizons.

Through her father's family, she can trace her roots back via her grandparents' stories to early-19th-century England and Wales — close to the beginnings of the original Methodist movement.

PARENTS' EXAMPLE

HER MOTHER TAUGHT Sunday school. Though her father was seldom seen at First United Methodist Church in Park Ridge, Ill., where young Hillary grew up, she vividly recalls that "he said his prayers kneeling by his bed every night of his life, until he had his stroke."

The first lady is a Methodist by choice as well as by chance. Of the three Rodham children, only Hillary continued to attend Sunday services as an adolescent. "She's really a self-churched woman," says the Rev. Donald Jones, her former youth minister, who developed his privileged suburban students' social consciences by taking them to visit migrant workers' children.

More than other Protestants, Methodists are still imbued with the turn-of-the-century social gospel, which holds that Christians have been commissioned to build the Kingdom of God on earth.

As a bright, well-educated woman growing up in the turbulent '60s, Hillary Rodham defied that generation's rebellious stereotype. At Wellesley, she continued to attend church, joined the interdenominational chapel society and took a year of required Bible study — an experience, she says, "I'm very grateful for."

She also read *Motive*, a now defunct magazine for college-age Methodists. "I still have every issue they sent me," Mrs. Clinton says.

But the issue she remembers best contained an article by a Methodist theologian, Carl Oglesby, called "Change or Containment."

"It was the first thing I had ever read that challenged the Vietnam War," Mrs. Clinton recalls. Partly because of that war, she switched from being a Goldwater Republican to a McGovern Democrat.

But she remained a devout Methodist. Although the United Methodist Church had by then dropped most of its traditional taboos against alcohol and dancing, Hillary was conservative in her social habits. In a letter to Pastor Jones from college, she wrote that she was having "as much fun as any good Methodist can."

Even today, says Mr. Jones, "when Hillary talks it sounds like it comes out of a Methodist Sunday school lesson."

That should be no surprise. In Arkansas, Mrs. Clinton taught Methodist Sunday school. She also attended church regularly and, in the Methodist tradition of favoring lay preachers, she spoke often at church gatherings on "why I am a United Methodist."

Even her campaign to reform Arkansas' public schools, says the Rev. Clint Burleson, her former pastor in Little Rock, was "grounded in Methodist social concerns. "That's who Hillary is. She's not a woman who would be in harmony with (Methodism's conservative) evangelical movement."

Perhaps, but after two years in the White House, Mrs. Clinton is showing another side of her Methodist self. The religious books she reads are mostly by popular evangelical and spiritual-guidance authors, like Tony Campolo, Father Henri Nouwen and the Rev. Gordon MacDonald, and the only religious magazine she sees these busy days is *Christianity Today*, an evangelical weekly.

She says she also keeps a copy of *The Book of Resolutions* of the United Methodist Church in her private quarters, along with the Bible. The two volumes reflect her search for religious balance.

"I think that the Methodist Church, for a period of time, became too socially concerned," she says, "too involved in the social gospel and did not pay enough attention to questions of personal salvation and individual faith. It is, for me, both a question of grace and of personal commitment."

In the White House family quarters, the ethos is more Methodist than Baptist.

LIQUOR QUESTION

A TELLTALE EXAMPLE: liquor is served — something a staunch Southern Baptist would hesitate to do. But you have to ask for it, which is the moderate Methodist way.

On Sundays, it's a Methodist, not a Baptist, church the first family most often attends. And like her mother, 14-year-old Chelsea Clinton is being raised a Methodist.

The Methodist ethos extends to politics as well. The first lady's speech in April 1993 calling for "remodeling society by redefining what it means to be a human in the 20th century" may have startled some listeners, but its ambitious optimism was fully consonant with the Methodists' liberal social creed.

Indeed, Mrs. Clinton's many speeches defending the universal health care coverage resonated with the moral rhetoric of resolutions adopted by the church's governing General Conference. Her favorite adjective is a Methodist byword: "inclusive."

"Hillary views the world through a Methodist lens," says Mr. Jones, who is still a welcome guest at the White House. "And we Methodists," he adds wryly, "know what's good for you."

If the Kennedy era was Camelot and the Reagan White House a ranchero on the Potomac, the Clinton presidency — in the figure of its formidable first lady — is Washington's Methodist Moment.

Despite what some critics believe, the nation's first lady is not markedly feminist in her religion. She thinks abortion is "wrong," but, like her husband, she says, "I don't think it should be criminalized."

She does not follow feminist theology and seems unaware of the upheaval its most radical exponents have created among Methodists in the name of greater inclusiveness.

As long as they are in the White House, the first family has elected to worship at Foundry United Methodist Church, less than a mile away. There they find spiritual support from Pastor J. Philip Wogaman, a liberal social-ethics professor who tries, he says, to be "prophetic" in his sermons "without embarrassing the president."

Generally the first family slips into the same pew, three rows down from the front off the right center aisle. It's a mixed congregation in a mixed urban neighborhood.

As Mr. Wogaman proudly points out, young singles and married couples usually sit up front on the far left, gays prefer the far right, African-Americans congregate in the center and older white congregants — including Senate Republican leader Robert Dole and his wife, Elizabeth — favor the sections near the door.

Very inclusive. Very Methodist. Very Hillary Rodham Clinton.

— ***Kenneth Woodward*** has been *Newsweek*'s Religion Editor since 1964. He is the author of several books, including *Making Saints*, and has written for *Commonweal*, *McCall's*, *The New York Times* and *The Washington Post*.

1994 Elections

THE 1994 ELECTIONS WERE A SLAP in the face to Democrats and the Clinton Administration. While the opposition often gains seats during a midterm election, few analysts expected the Republicans to capture both the House and Senate for the first time since 1946. Republicans gained eight seats in the Senate and 52 in the House, including that of Speaker Tom Foley. In the Governor's races, Republicans kept all of their incumbents and won 11 new seats, including key states like Texas, New York, California, Illinois and Michigan.

The incoming Republican powerbase was conservative and activist, guided by a sense of revolution and their *Contract with America*. The results of the 1994 elections set the stage for later developments including welfare reform, 1995's budget showdown, Congressional Whitewater hearings, the Lewinsky scandal and the President's impeachment trial.

The failure of health care reform, for which the public and press laid significant blame on Hillary Rodham Clinton, was one key element of the Republican landslide. Throughout the election cycle, the First Lady was the target of bruising political commentary and attacks. In just one example, Mrs. Gingrich, mother of the Speaker of the House of Representatives, reported to the press that her son thought Hillary Rodham Clinton was "a bitch."

After the election, Hillary Rodham Clinton apologized for her (and the Administration's) failure to communicate the health care plan, calling herself politically "dumb" and regretting that the proposal was misunderstood as big government interference. She began to concentrate on more traditionally "female" issues (education, children's development, foster care) and adopted a less official role. In this chapter, the BBC's BRIDGET KENDALL looks at the wake of the 1994 elections, and what they bode for Mrs. Clinton.

The First Lady's Not for Turning?

Bridget Kendall

THIS HAS BEEN A SHOCKING WEEK for Bill and Hillary Clinton. Whatever the degree of Democrat fears before the mid-term elections, nothing can have prepared them for the landslide that left both the Senate and the House of the Representatives in Republican control, and some of the country's leading Democrat governors ousted from office.

Clinton's own problems are obvious: how to govern and how to get himself re-elected in two years' time; but the First Lady is not immune to the aftershocks. Tuesday's elections will have been devastating proof that, despite her reputed perspicacity, both she and her husband have sorely misjudged the mood of the nation.

I met Mrs. Clinton on the eve of the elections, and if she had been hoping for a miracle she was certainly preparing herself for disappointment. It is rare for journalists now to be granted an interview with the First Lady, but in the past few months, after criticism of her plans for health care reform, she has had to reassess her public persona. Her relationship with the press has been showing signs of a new openness. I talked to her while compiling a profile for BBC 2's "Assignment."

With the Democrats on the defensive, Mrs. Clinton's attempt to reshape her role and image is even more of a priority. As she remarked recently, with a wry smile, "I've been re-zoned." She cannot afford to be seen as a Lady Macbeth figure, haunting the Oval office, neither does she want to be pushed into becoming a spiritual successor to Barbara Bush, hosting White House tea parties.

Mrs. Clinton's keenness to stress that she is not the president's handmaiden has, in the past, landed her in trouble. During the presidential campaign in 1992 she twice annoyed traditional women voters. Once when she scornfully denied she was like Tammy Wynette, standing by her man. And again when she upset homemakers by saying in a disparaging voice that although she could have stayed at home and baked cookies, she decided to work as a lawyer.

These days Hillary Clinton rarely puts a foot wrong. She almost never makes unguarded comments.

On the contrary, into her well-ordered phrases and rounded paragraphs are woven deliberate and subtle hints to suggest she is the model of tradition, the perfect wife, mother, hostess and God-fearing American citizen. Yet Mrs. Clinton is not simply giving herself a new image. By doing so she is attempting to reposition herself politically. If there was any doubt before this week's elections that the Clinton presidency needs to reach out to the traditional, conservative, middle ground of American politics, there can be none now.

She is keen to stress the theme of her instinctive conservatism. "I had a wonderful upbringing by my parents, schooling and church," she said. "Although my father had very strong beliefs, they were of a Republican party that unfortunately seems to be vanishing in many parts of our country. He was conservative in the sense that he believed in conserving and investing to conserve. He moved his family when he got out of the navy to a suburb that had high school taxes because he believed in the best education for his children. He didn't begrudge his responsibilities to the larger community.

"So although he was a Republican and a conservative, those are values I still feel I hold. I believe strongly in the responsibility of individuals. I happen to think that government can either impede or assist in individuals becoming more self-sufficient, and I don't see any contradiction in that."

No longer does Mrs. Clinton want to be seen as champion of liberal causes, it seems. She is now a conservative Democrat, proud to be the daughter of a Republican, deliberately resisting being categorised, trying to broaden her appeal across the nation.

When we met, the Clintons were already rehearsing their response to this week's predicted heavy losses, with a call to the Republicans to put aside political differences and work together. Later, she put it even more succinctly: "A lot of problems today do not give themselves easily to answers labelled Republican or Democrat or conservative or liberal. That's often an excuse for not thinking through and coming up with pragmatic problem-solving approaches."

That new bipartisan message fits well with the conciliatory style on which President Clinton is now pinning his political future. On the lips of his wife Hillary it is less expected. It highlights the contradictions in her character that make her such an enigma.

On the one hand there is practical Hillary, willing to change her hairstyle if it will win more votes, willing to paint herself as half Republican if that is the way the political wind is blowing. But how does that square with the uncompromisingly principled Hillary, who was seen as the White House's moral backbone? The one who explained to me that the lesson she learnt from her favourite former First Lady, Eleanor Roosevelt, was not to listen to other people: "No matter what you do you will be criticised," she said. "So better to have done what you believed in and accept whatever criticism comes from that, than to have tried to twist yourself into some other image."

This attitude has shielded Hillary Clinton from painful criticism, whether on health care matters, Whitewater, or alleged sex scandals involving her husband. But has it also isolated her, insulated her from her critics?

"It is, on occasion, hurtful," she admitted. "It always is, when someone says something that's not true or accuses myself or my husband of something. I just try to remember that they often do it for their own personal reasons, usually for political or financial advantage."

Her middle-class, moral, conservative upbringing may help to explain a lot about her disavowal of personal political ambition. Equally though, it is in her interests at the moment to play down her own political influence and depict herself as a modest helper. Since her ambitious health care reform plan ran into trouble, she has been careful to avoid the limelight.

"I don't think you have to be in elective office to serve," she said, when I asked her why, as a young woman, she had abandoned the promise of a career in Washington to follow Bill Clinton to his home state of Arkansas. "We are a nation — and always have been — of citizen activists, and that has been my tradition.

"And besides," she added with a smile, "I am married to the greatest political person of our generation, I think. He has such enormous capacity for understanding the problems facing America and I've often said he has that wonderful marriage of head and heart not often found in political leaders. So any way I can assist him in his elective office is very satisfying to me."

When asked directly, though, she was quite open about her role as chief presidential adviser. She remains in close partnership with her husband, she said. They had always confided in each other. She saw nothing wrong with having taken a job in his government to head the Health Care Task Force. It was risky, she admitted. But no one in the government except the Vice President was directly elected, so why shouldn't she accept a post?

The reason, in Hillary Clinton's eyes, that health care reform failed was only partly to do with the way she handled the issue. She and her team should have countered hostile advertising and direct mail earlier, she conceded. But the main culprit was the power of special-interest groups intent on resisting changes.

So what happens next? She had clearly already prepared her answer, and launched a political manifesto. Neither she nor the President intended to abandon the fight for health care reform, she said — whatever, apparently, the political mood in the next Congress. "We'll be back," she said, "because our problems will not go away, and we know we're going to have to continue to try to provide quality health care at affordable cost to every American."

She went on: "But I also want to talk, maybe more often than I have in the last 20 months, about how we all bear dual responsibility for our children and families ... because in our country we have this false debate. There are those on the right who say the family is totally responsible, society has no obligations; and there are those on the left who say everything's the fault of society or the government and absolve neglectful parenting. They are both inadequate explanations for what's going on, and I think we ought to be more sensible."

There was no hint in what she said that she believed her involvement in these areas could raise the same controversies that she did with health care. So, I asked, were those who said she was going to retreat into a more traditional role wrong?

She laughed, shaking her head from side to side: "They've never been right. It gives me a good laugh every time I read it, especially given my schedule, which is as busy as ever . . . Taking the message of change the President has out to the country."

— ***Bridget Kendall*** is the BBC's Diplomatic correspondent. She was previously the BBC's Moscow correspondent, reporting on the collapse of Communism and Boris Yeltsin's Presidency, and the Washington correspondent, covering the Clinton Presidency. Her article was based on an exclusive television interview with Hillary Clinton for the BBC's "Correspondent" series. This article appeared in *The Independent* (London) (November 11, 1994,).

Eleanor Roosevelt

DURING THE 1992 CAMPAIGN, when asked which First Lady she would model herself upon, Mrs. Clinton cited Eleanor Roosevelt, the reformer and activist who worked tirelessly to improve conditions for Americans throughout the 20th century. The two women shared commitment, intelligence, ambition and the drive to create public service careers alongside their husbands'.

In 1992, candidate Bill Clinton remarked: "If I get elected President, it will be an unprecedented partnership, far more than Franklin Roosevelt and Eleanor. They were two great people, but on different tracks. If I get elected, we'll do things together, like we always have." Writing at the start of the Clinton Administration, Presidential scholar DORIS KEARNS GOODWIN offers advice to the First Lady on mobilizing "a real power base on behalf of children's rights," but warns of the possibility of a backlash. In a less flattering comparison, A. M. ROSENTHAL looks at how Mrs. Clinton and Mrs. Roosevelt used their position as First Lady, and criticizes the policy-making role the former adopted during the first term.

In 1996, *Washington Post* reporter Bob Woodward published a story intimating that Mrs. Clinton had been working with a "psychic" to spiritually contact the ghost of Eleanor Roosevelt. In the resulting furor, Hillary Rodham Clinton was accused of communing with gurus and other New Age fringe figures. In fact, Mrs. Clinton had been conducting exercises with a respected psychologist in order to help develop her agenda and learn from Mrs. Roosevelt's experience. DEBORAH TANNEN looks at the controversy in the context of business development practices, noting that "men have 'leadership sessions.' Women have 'séances.'" She places this controversy in the context of corporations and individuals seeking innovative ways to maximize their potential (economic or personal) through similar strategic planning and skills-building exercises.

Hillary & Eleanor

Doris Kearns Goodwin

Dear Hillary,

Throughout your husband's campaign, you pointed to Eleanor Roosevelt as evidence that an independent first lady can influence policy and still remain popular. I see many similarities between you and Eleanor; and I think you can learn from her approach to the job, not only from her successes but from her mistakes as well. With only a few days left before you and Bill move into the White House, I'd like to pass along some advice I've gleaned from studying the past.

Take this time before the inauguration to decide exactly what you want to make of the office. Otherwise you'll have your days taken up by the requests that will flood you. Eleanor had a terribly difficult time turning anybody down. Late in life, she said that she wished she had been more selective. She answered every letter that came to her, and she spoke to every group that asked. Consequently she wasn't focused enough on the issues that she could really do something about. You will have one of the best platforms in the country from which to advance your concerns, but you must have a plan beforehand — days go quickly, and time will slip away from you.

I assume you will remain an advocate for children's rights. That's a powerful cause because it acts as an umbrella for a whole rubric of concerns: minorities, women, child care, health care, refugee situations, even famine in Somalia. The more broadly you can define it, the more influence you can have. But make sure to stay within the realm you stake out and the issues close to your heart. Lady Bird Johnson was so successful with conservation and beautification because they genuinely interested her. To be honest, it's hard to remember what Pat Nixon or even Barbara Bush did as first ladies. Sure, Barbara Bush made symbolic appearances for literacy every now and then, but she wasn't a warrior on a contested battleground. That's what I'm suggesting for you, Hillary. You will be in a position to mobilize a real power base on behalf of children's rights.

As I write this, there's been speculation — fear; on the part of some— that Bill might appoint you Attorney General. While I think you would be entirely qualified (certainly more qualified than Bobby Kennedy was), serving as both First Lady and Attorney General would probably weaken both positions. I understand why you might want to be a cabinet officer. While Eleanor was First Lady, she also had an abiding desire for a job of her own. Because her role as First Lady was so loosely defined, she felt she couldn't know at the end of the day whether she had really made a difference. Finally, in 1941, President Roosevelt appointed her assistant director of the Office of Civil Defense under Mayor La Guardia — and it turned out to be a disaster. The fact that she was now a government employee bollixed everything up: Everyone knew there were people working under her and people working above her, but, after all, she was married to the president. The whole chain of command was out of whack. Ultimately she had to resign the office.

As it turned out, Eleanor did much more as first lady than she ever could have done in any other one job. The first-ladyship doesn't put you in conflict with the president in the same way a cabinet post would you have more leeway to build a constituency. You can move the president be yond where he otherwise might go on some issues. It's a rich power base if used correctly. On the other hand, there's an immediate backlash waiting for anyone who uses it badly. As you know, you have to stay on your own turf and steer clear of the president's, at least in public. Even though Eleanor often discussed a variety of issues with FDR, she never once said that she influenced him in making decisions. Nor did she ever sit in on a cabinet meeting, as Rosalynn Carter did. The advice Eleanor would give you: Don't talk openly about the influence you have on Bill Clinton.

I know it's nuts, Hillary. You would think people would realize the great advantage in allowing a strong, popular, smart woman to advise the president. But there's this craziness out there that fears that somehow she's "running the show" or "wearing the pants." We're at a strange moment in our history now. There is still an unease about women assuming positions of power, even as women are more powerful and accomplished than ever before. The mere fact that you are so smart and outspoken is going to produce a backlash from certain elements of society.

Don't try to become something different than you are to avoid this backlash. Instead, organize a "frontlash" by making sure that the groups behind you are strong and supportive. Go on the offensive. There's such a power base among women now that, if you mobilize them, you will be even stronger than Eleanor ever was. You're already partway there, thanks, ironically, to the Republicans. Millions of women sided with you when the GOP attacked you for being a working mother. The support you got after the convention was a demonstration of this "frontlash" approach I'm talking about. But you won't be able to depend on the Republicans anymore.

It will be like a political campaign on behalf of your issues. You have to mobilize the constituency and the pressure to make something happen. That means going to Congress, fighting the cabinet members where it's relevant, and utilizing the media. Although you've done all this in Arkansas, it's going to be much more difficult on the national level. You might consider writing something like "My Day," Eleanor's daily column and diary. It gave ordinary people insight into what her day was like.

Get away from Washington as often as you can. To become a successful advocate for any issue, you'll have to absorb what's really happening in the country. It will help you, and Bill as well. Eleanor's remarkable ramblings around the country brought FDR vivid, human, anecdotal details. Although Bill does not suffer from the physical paralysis that made FDR dependent on Eleanor's eyes and ears, these days all presidents are paralyzed by Washington. I suspect that Bill's campaign bus trips were a metaphor for his determination not to be imprisoned by the White House. But no matter how hard presidents try to escape, they get stuck. When you bring back those human details freshly and vividly to him, you'll be playing a valuable role.

As you stake out your positions, some people will be angry with you. Thirty percent of the country probably thought Eleanor was the worst person ever to exist, a subversive agitator. Many southerners, for example, thought she was too far out on civil rights. They wrote letters to FDR, saying that she should be muzzled and kept on a chain. There were rumors (none of them true, of course) that Eleanor had created "Eleanor Clubs" for black maids who promised to get out of white people's houses and go somewhere else to work. "Whenever you see a Negro wearing a wide-brimmed hat with a feather in it," they said, "you know it's a sign of the Eleanor Club." There were warnings of "Eleanor Tuesdays," when black women were supposed to bump into white women on the street in honor of Eleanor.

Although Eleanor engendered controversial feelings in some, at the same time she was an inspiration for others, particularly blacks but also young women, who saw her doing things women had never done before. The advice Eleanor would give you is: Don't worry about your public-opinion polls. Know that you're doing a good job when your friends respect you and your enemies are angry. One of the reasons Barbara Bush has had a 90 percent popularity rating is that she hasn't done anything. She may be warm and affectionate, but she won't leave any accomplishments behind. Don't feel constrained by polls, and don't worry about hurting your husband's political standing. Whenever southerners got mad at Eleanor for taking down "Colored Only" signs, FDR could always say, "Well, it's my missus and I can't control her." In the same way Bill Clinton can simply say with a smile that you are your own person.

Finally, behind the incredibly powerful national platform of the first-ladyship lies an equally important family role. Eleanor traveled away from home too many days. She admitted this at the end of her life. As much as her ramblings around the country helped build her political base and allowed her to serve as FDR's eyes and ears, she wasn't there when he needed her. A wife and mother can allow a president to relax, to feel affectionate, and to have an oasis from the pressures of the White House. Eleanor would have been the first to admit that she wasn't very good at that. At the end of the day, FDR would have his cocktail hour, where he had a rule that you could only talk about movies and gossip. He had to unwind and he had an amazing capacity to do so, even without Eleanor. In the middle of the worst battles of the war, for example, he would sit there playing with his stamp collection. Much later, Eleanor said she wished she had learned to enjoy that with him, that she thought he needed somebody just so he could relax and play with stamps.

Whatever it is that the two of you do together for leisure — movies, sports, games — those are as important as sharing the partnership of presidency and first-ladyship. You seem to have found the right balance between activism, legal practice, and family in Arkansas, but it's going to be much more difficult in the White House.

I'm not suggesting that you be a dependent wife in the traditional mold. One of the strengths of the Roosevelts' relationship was that it was one of partnership, not dependence. You and Bill appear to have this strength as well. At least in part, this similarity may result from the rough patches both you and Eleanor worked through in your marriages. In Eleanor's case, the partnership was born with the discovery of her husband's affair with a young woman named Lucy Mercer. The affair rocked the marriage, but ultimately gave Eleanor the freedom to go outside her home to find fulfillment and even establish political power. In the years that followed, while Eleanor and Franklin each drew sustenance from other "friendships," there's no question there was great affection and a renewed respect between them. As a law-school graduate and a career woman, you brought independence to your marriage long before you hit the rough spots that you have acknowledged. I imagine that working out your difficulties has helped you and your husband to stand as equal partners. Like Eleanor and Franklin's, this partnership you and Bill bring to the White House may be great for the country.

The critical thing is that you not feel a need to do anything that's not authentic. If those advisers try to tell you to start off slow, don't listen. If you feel confident and comfortable about what you're doing, public acceptance will be far deeper than what you would gain by simply avoiding offensive acts. In the end, you have to find your own balance between how much time you want to give to your issues, to your daughter, and to your husband. You must shape the role for yourself, and, if you do it well, the people will ultimately support you.

Good luck.

— ***Doris Kearns Goodwin*** is a noted historian and biographer. Her works include *Lyndon Johnson and the American Dream* and *No Ordinary Time: Franklin and Eleanor Roosevelt: The Home Front During World War II*, for which she won a Pulitzer Prize. This article appeared in the January/February 1993 issue of *Mother Jones*. Ms. Goodwin's comments were given through an interview with Josh Clark.

On My Mind
Hillary and Eleanor

A. M. Rosenthal

THREE YEARS AGO THIS WEEK they were dancing and singing and telling happy jokes at all the balls and parties given for them in Washington.

Now he is campaigning for another term in office as president. She is campaigning too — desperately, to save what is left of her reputation.

The President stands by her, of course. But he seems to cast himself as an observer — warm and interested, but somehow aside from and beyond what is going on that is eating her up. He may win again, but compared with how she saw herself and her role in government, she cannot.

We do not know exactly what they did in Whitewater. But it is impossible to believe he did not know that she would so tortuously try to talk her way around it — or that she had pressured for firing the White House travel staff without telling him.

We do know this: The most important decision they took after Bill Clinton became President, the worst and most dangerous, they made together. That was to transform the chivalrously intended position of First Lady into The First Ladyship and make it the second most important political post in the land.

That decision skewed the Government, skirted its law, twisted its Constitution. It was outrageous in concept and practice — the anointing of an unelected person to dominate a large part of the Government because she wore his wedding ring.

The law provides that a president should not appoint a member of his family to run a Federal agency. He dodged that by appointing his wife to rule over the most important work of a whole batch of agency heads — writing a new health care program.

She became not only an equivalent of a cabinet member but the most powerful one. Her influence touched their fears. High officials who are part of her domain lost their ultimate right — to appeal over the head of a team leader to the president.

The first time you complain about the work of a president's wife he may nod and say thank you. The second time he will ask: Will nobody rid me of this fool?

Somebody will.

They transferred power — part of the power he held by vote of the people, he not she. And incidentally they besmirched feminism. Feminism does not rely on the wedding ring to achieve political power. The Clintons just didn't get it.

When I wrote this two years ago, from her supporters I got a furious argument that we hear more and more now that the hole she is in gets deeper. "Eleanor did it."

No, Eleanor Roosevelt did not do it. The contrary — she used her influence as a President's wife not to exert executive power inside the Government, but to bring in unheard voices from outside.

Doris Kearns Goodwin details this magnificently in her book about the Roosevelts, *No Ordinary Time*. Eleanor traveled the country to talk with people her husband showed no wild desire to meet — blacks, the unemployed, working women. Then she kept telling him that war or no war, he was the leader of all the people and many were suffering.

She kept nagging him about black rights, day care for working mothers, job training for women. She drove him almost crazy with her notes and memos, but she never stopped. She had influence, as every spouse does — but she was not Hillary, and Hillary is not Eleanor.

After FDR had been president nine years he appointed her assistant director of civilian defense under Fiorello La Guardia, former Mayor of New York. The two spent their time not getting along. Finally FDR said he didn't want to hear from either of them. She quit and said publicly that it had been a mistake to take an official job.

She went back to her real life's work — not First Lady but First Gadfly — after he died. I met her in 1947 in a cafeteria line at the U.N. She was the U.S. human rights delegate and kept biting the Soviet ankle.

Presumably Mrs. Clinton will not try again to be The First Ladyship if her husband is re-elected. Presumably is not enough. Long ago the Clintons should have said it was a mistake to give her executive power that evaded law and democratic practice.

The longer they wait the less will be the inclination to believe them when they get around to it. Tomorrow would be an excellent time to start.

— ***A. M. Rosenthal*** is a Pulitzer Prize-winning columnist and former executive editor of *The New York Times*. He retired in 1988 after almost 50 years at the paper, but continued as an op ed columnist until 1999. Rosenthal now writes for the *Daily News.* He has written two books and some 100 magazine articles. (January 19, 1996.)

The Guru Gap

Deborah Tannen

LAST WEEK, IN THE SAME ISSUE that excerpted Bob Woodward's account of Hillary Rodham Clinton's conversation with psychologist Jean Houston, *Newsweek* reported that Dan O'Brien, an Olympic decathlete, had "found redemption" after he failed to make the Barcelona team. The magazine described how he had consulted a sports psychologist who trained him to "free up his mind" in order to focus better.

Successful men in sports and business regularly hire consultants and psychologists to guide them and even to help them tap into their own inner wisdom. They keep a straight face when they tell stories about using visualization and other mind exercises. And the press takes them seriously.

The corporate world is replete with such gurus. The mostly male executives who hire them win respect — even if it means (according to a recent account in the business press) being led blindfolded through the foothills of the Colorado Rockies as part of a $7,400, five-day "Leadership at the Peak" course.

What about those brisk-selling business books that draw management insights from the minds of professional sports coaches? Books like

Everyone's a Coach by Don Shula, *Sacred Hoops* by Phil Jackson and *The Winner Within* by Pat Riley have all found their way onto the corporate bookshelves.

Indeed, such business favorites as Anthony Robbins (*Awaken the Giant Within*) and Stephen Covey (*The Seven Habits of Highly Effective People*) are among the authors the Clintons have met with at the White House, according to Mr. Woodward's book, *The Choice*.

These meetings didn't come in for much ridicule. So how did a short conversation in which Hillary Clinton imagined herself talking to Eleanor Roosevelt get so blown out of proportion last week?

Why was this interchange between the First Lady and a respected psychologist compared to Nancy Reagan's consultations with an astrologer about her husband's schedule?

Perhaps because the stereotypical image of a woman consulting a guru is too delicious to pass up, whether the facts add up or not.

Ridicule is often based on such images, and those that come to mind for women and for men are different. Business-book writers don't fit into the risible stereotype of women seeking help through earnest self-reflection. Indeed, when it turned out that Ms. Houston, who holds a doctorate in humanistic psychology, had been a consultant to such companies as Xerox, the corporate imprimatur lent her credibility — and nobody laughed at Xerox.

But by then Dr. Houston had already been tarred as a "spiritual advisor," a "guru" and a "psychic." That's how her short talk with the First Lady (according to Dr. Houston, it lasted "four minutes — maybe") became a séance in the news accounts based on excerpts from Mr. Woodward's book.

As one chagrined journalist, who asked for anonymity, told me: "I had to write a story under deadline, so I didn't have time to check it out, and I took Woodward's word for who she was. Now she turns out she isn't a psychic at all, but is a much more serious person."

To me, Hillary Clinton's conversation with Jean Houston sounds less like consulting a guru than like something much more mundane: talking to a friend about a problem. This activity may seem odd to many men, since it isn't the way they tend to deal with troublesome issues.

Besides, for them problems dealing with feelings are just less serious than the really grave questions — how to win at sports or get ahead in business.

The "séance" characterization has turned out to be baseless, and therein lies a lesson for reporters and commentators: ridicule, which often draws on stereotypes, is always likely to distort the facts.

It's time to leave the stereotypes behind. That's what will help us get closer to the truth.

— ***Deborah Tannen*** is a University Professor and Professor of Linguistics in the Department of Linguistics at Georgetown University in Washington, D.C. Her books include: *You Just Don't Understand: Women and Men in Conversation* and *Talking from 9 to 5: Women and Men in the Workplace: Language, Sex, and Power.* *The New York Times,* June 29, 1996.

1996 Elections

IN THE 1996 PRESIDENTIAL ELECTIONS, Clinton faced Republican Bob Dole and became the first Democratic President to win reelection in 60 years. One factor in Clinton's success was the overwhelming support of female voters, solidified by Republican attacks on the First Lady and by Mrs. Clinton's tireless campaigning. Republicans retained control of Congress, albeit with a smaller majority, setting up later showdowns over the budget and social spending.

Prior to the elections, Hillary Rodham Clinton redeemed herself with the American public by softening her approach. She wrote a best-selling book on child development, promoted home decorating and fashion, adopted a muted political presence and consciously wooed the press. And she worked hard on the campaign; Mrs. Clinton's popularity was so great that she received a four-minute standing ovation before her remarks at the Democratic National Convention.

In contrast to the 1992 elections, Hillary Rodham Clinton backed away from any assertion that she would hold a major policy role, recognizing, perhaps, that she could exert influence and get results without benefit of an official position. Chastened by the defeat of her health care reform plan and the devastating 1994 elections, Mrs. Clinton entered her husband's second term with a far better understanding of how Washington works, and how to make it do so to her advantage. In this chapter, MARIANNE MEANS looks at the election, and Mrs. Clinton's role in promoting her husband's candidacy.

Hillary Clinton
The Latest Model as a Role Model

Marianne Means

FOR FIRST LADY HILLARY CLINTON, this campaign is not about what "we" will do in a second term, but strictly about the leadership of "my husband".

She's not quite as gooey as Elizabeth Dole in those mushy odes to spouse, Bob, nor anywhere as stupefyingly adoring as the silent Nancy Reagan gazing up at Ron.

But there's an unmistakable feminine resemblance here.

Hillary's on the run, and she's fighting back against her critics the same way her husband has against his. Her language has changed to give him preeminence, and her topics have changed to emphasize traditional womanly concerns, such as children.

In public at least, she has become pretty much what they want her to be, which is nonthreatening.

Since her smooth, upbeat speech at the Democratic convention in defense of her husband and his achievements, Hillary Clinton — the independent public figure — has virtually vanished as a campaign force.

She either travels modestly at the president's side or speaks before friendly audiences about safe topics such as administration efforts to help children and families.

She said she got a great charge out of greeting a fan club in the White House. The Vice President's wife, Tipper Gore, was more visible on the team's joint bus trip.

And the first lady never, ever talks about the equal political partnership they said they had in the 1992 campaign.

It was the president himself who almost blew her cover last week. In a joint ABC *20/20* interview with his wife, he suggested that he might appoint her to head legislative efforts to reform further the welfare-reform bill that he signed but purports to disapprove partially.

"The real advocates of children, including the first lady, have to weigh in here," Clinton said. "I think the business people will listen to her. I think people at the state level will."

The First Lady quickly demurred. She said she hadn't heard that notion before and had absolutely no assignment for a second term.

Clinton backed off, insisting, "It's not a formal role. It's not a formal role."

Hillary Clinton has shouldered the lion's share of the fallout from failure of the administration's sweeping health care reforms, for which she led the legislative battle.

Voters uncomfortable with powerful women were quick to blame her for a defeat at the hands of influential lobbyists that was caused more by the president's miscalculations than hers.

This left her with an exaggerated image of being too pushy, too liberal and too darn independent for a middle-aged female whose influence depended upon her husband's position.

It has been compounded by nasty legal accusations that she covered up shady financial dealings, lied about odd happenings in the White House travel office and with Federal Bureau of Investigation files and is generally a bad egg. She is the only First Lady to be compelled to testify before a grand jury and be a focus of a long-running corruption probe by a federal independent counsel.

So far, the charges are unproven. But her popularity is lower than the president's.

Dole naturally seized the opportunity handed him by the president to raise the spector of Hillary Clinton, liberal feminist on the prowl again. Just Dole's prediction that she would be in charge of welfare reform as she had been in charge of health reform drew boos from a partisan audience.

But Dole used the first lady as proof of Clinton liberalism (a supposed philosophical commitment that escapes much of the Democratic Party) in order to contend that Clinton in a second term would not be the moderate he seems today. Dole did not attack her moral standards or judgment, as other Republicans freely do.

Dole's message is that putting Hillary in charge of welfare re-reform means that the president secretly plans to expand the federal government with more big programs such as the failed health care plan. There's no evidence of this, but, hey, symbols count in campaigns, and Dole is behind.

But Dole cannot weave attacks on the first lady into his campaign in any larger context without a potential backlash.

He already suffers from an astonishing gender gap. This is caused mostly by perceptions that his policies of ending affirmative action and unpaid worker family leave, denying illegal Hispanic children the right to an education, opposing Medicare and Medicaid, cutting student-loan funds and blocking a woman's right to abortion are not family-friendly.

Yet Hillary Clinton is a role model to many working women, who think women should influence policy and speak for themselves.

In any case, Hillary's defiance of traditional gender roles may be off the table in this campaign, not because of who she now pretends to be, but because of who the opponent's wife is. Elizabeth Dole is a former two-time Cabinet officer not known as a shrinking violet averse to exerting authority. Her own financial investments have been questioned.

The real political scandal is that both women feel that they can most help their husbands' candidacy by sublimating their own talents.

— ***Marianne Means***, the Washington columnist for Hearst Newspapers, is syndicated by the New York Times News Service. Means has covered Washington for almost 40 years and has reported on every presidential convention and campaign since 1960. She is the author of *The Woman in the White House*. This article appeared in the Orlando Sentinel (September 26, 1996).

Whitewater

THE "WHITEWATER" INVESTIGATION centered on financial dealings connected to the eponymous Arkansas land development project, but encompassed other activities that ranged from the firing of White House Travel office staff to Clinton's affair with Monica Lewinsky (see chapter 14 also). The complexity of the issue is reflected in the *New York Times* reference to the scandal as "the convoluted issue known broadly as Whitewater."

By late 1993, enough reports were circulating about questionable Whitewater-related practices that Congress called for hearings to investigate the charges. In 1994, the Attorney General appointed a Special Counsel to investigate charges of corruption and graft. Later that year, Congress renewed the Independent Counsel law and appointed Kenneth Starr to look into charges connected to Whitewater.

The investigation addressed many issues, including: Mrs. Clinton's talent in turning an investment in cattle futures into almost $100,000 in profits; her role in the mismanaged Whitewater land development scheme; her legal representation of the failed Madison Guaranty Savings & Loan institution; her role in removing several White House travel office employees; and the possible disappearance of Whitewater-related documents from Vincent Foster's office after his suicide.

Both the House and Senate conducted inquiries into the matter. Mrs. Clinton was investigated by Independent Counsel Starr, questioned at least six times and, in 1996, became the first First Lady ever subpoenaed to testify before a grand jury. The White House's inability to provide documents related to the case — and the Clintons' reluctance to discuss their roles in the various matters — fueled the controversy. The later discovery of subpoenaed Rose Law Firm billing records inside the White House also presented serious problems for the First Lady's credibility.

The Whitewater investigation resulted in several convictions, including Webster Hubble, a partner at Mrs. Clinton's Little Rock

law firm; Jim McDougal, owner of Madison Guaranty; and Jim Guy Tucker, then Governor of Arkansas. Mrs. Clinton was never indicted for any Whitewater-related matter. Nonetheless, the scandal hung over both Clinton terms, and particularly tainted the First Lady's efforts to promote health care reform.

In this chapter, JOHN BRODER and JAMES RISEN provide an overview of her role in the spiraling investigation and controversy. WALTER SHAPIRO offers a spirited defense of the First Lady, while WILLIAM SAFIRE and MAUREEN DOWD describe her role in the scandal and possible cover-up activities. In one of the stranger Whitewater moments, President Clinton responded to Safire's article by saying he wanted to punch the noted *New York Times* columnist in the nose.

First Lady in Spotlight for Her Role in Whitewater Inquiry

John M. Broder and James Risen

As THE WHITE HOUSE STRUGGLES to contain the controversy surrounding the First Family's involvement in the tangled Whitewater real estate and banking affair, First Lady Hillary Rodham Clinton's role has begun to raise as many questions as her husband's.

Indeed, the Whitewater matter now seems to be a controversy befitting the Clintons' modern, two-career political marriage: Just as the First Lady has played a critical role in major policy decisions on health care and other issues, she now finds herself a central figure with her husband in this politically threatening affair.

It is Hillary Clinton's independent career as a top attorney in Little Rock, Ark., while her husband served as governor — and her reputation for being the financial brains of the household — that have prompted questions about her role in the Whitewater matter.

Even friends in Arkansas are wondering why she has not come forward with a fuller account of what she did and what she knew at the time the events in Arkansas were unfolding.

"I don't know why she hasn't been more open about explaining" her work as a lawyer for the defunct savings and loan at the center of the affair, said Beverly Bassett Schaffer, a former Arkansas state regulator and longtime acquaintance. "I don't understand why they (the Clintons) were in business with someone like McDougal," the thrift's owner.

James B. McDougal, a friend of Clinton's, owned Madison Guaranty Savings & Loan and was half-owner with the Clintons in an Ozark Mountain real estate venture called Whitewater Development Corp.

The President and Hillary Clinton have said they were innocent bystanders as McDougal drove his lending institution into the ground with a binge of bad loans and frittered away nearly $70,000 of their assets on the bankrupt Whitewater project.

Unresolved, though, is the mystery of how to reconcile this image of naivete in the world of high finance with Hillary Clinton's reputation as a top corporate lawyer and board member of some of the nation's biggest corporations.

The question being asked more openly in Washington and Arkansas is: How could Hillary Clinton — whom one legal journal called one of the 100 most influential lawyers in the United States — be unaware of gross mismanagement at a savings institution she represented as an attorney and neglect her family's only substantial financial asset?

Those questions intertwine with a web of others as federal investigators continue their inquiry.

Specifically, they are trying to determine whether, amid the careening disorder in the runaway S&L and Whitewater, money from a federally guaranteed thrift was diverted into Clinton's 1984 campaign coffers. Also, there is the matter of whether the institution got favorable treatment from Arkansas authorities that helped keep it in business before federal regulators finally shut it down in 1989.

It is Hillary Clinton's role as a former attorney for the savings and loan that has raised concerns about her actions.

McDougal, who worked with Clinton in Sen. J. William Fulbright's office in the 1960s, bought Madison Guaranty in 1982 and soon began using it to make loans to important figures and to finance an assortment of speculations including his four-year-old Whitewater venture with the Clintons, according to records filed with state regulators.

Before long, the S&L was on dangerous ground, and in 1984 federal regulators warned that they considered its lending practices questionable. The Federal Home Loan Bank Board directed the S&L — along with others in Arkansas — to raise more capital and put its house in order.

McDougal hit upon a quick way to raise money: selling stock. But that was not normal practice for savings and loans in Arkansas, and the proposal needed approval from the Arkansas Securities Commission. So McDougal had Little Rock's Rose Law Firm — and specifically partner Hillary Clinton — make his case for the stock sale to state regulators.

The White House has acknowledged that Hillary Clinton, then on a $2,000-a-month retainer with Madison Guaranty, worked on the proposal in 1985. But senior presidential adviser Bruce Lindsey said her involvement was minimal and that most of the legal work was done by a junior associate, Richard N. Massey, then a 28-year-old, first-year lawyer at the firm.

Joe Madden, the current commissioner of the Arkansas Securities Department, said there are at least three Rose Law Firm documents to the commission that refer questions back to either Hillary Clinton or Massey. But he said the case was fairly routine and that a "competent first-year attorney (as Massey was at the time) could have been primarily responsible for doing the research and doing the drafting."

Schaffer, who had just been appointed securities commissioner by then-Gov. Clinton when the case arose, said Massey handled meetings with her staff and that Hillary Clinton was the only senior attorney at the Rose firm with whom she or her staff communicated.

Ultimately, Schaffer and her staff decided that the unusual capital-formation plan did not violate Arkansas law and approved it. Because of its growing financial problems, though, the plan was never carried out by the thrift.

Schaffer, now an attorney in private practice in Fayetteville, Ark., said she did not feel pressured to rule favorably because the governor's wife was involved in the case. But she expressed frustration at her old friend's seeming hesitation to publicly explain her role as a senior attorney in the case and thereby allow suspicions to grow.

Repeatedly, Hillary Clinton has insisted that questions arising from private matters a decade or more ago are not a fit subject for public scrutiny. She has refused to respond to any detailed inquiries, including the central one: whether it was proper to represent a business partner before a state regulatory board run by a personal friend and appointee of her husband's.

She has expressed bewilderment that the press and investigators are interested in the aftermath of a money-losing private real estate investment. Jack Pitney, a political scientist at Claremont McKenna College in Claremont, said the First Lady's response created a credibility problem. It is difficult, he said, to believe she would ignore a major family investment and overlook a potential conflict of interest. "She can't just throw her hands in the air and say she doesn't understand all this legal stuff. She can't claim ignorance of legal details," he said. "It is not a credible defense. Her involvement is a fix of her own making."

Friends and associates said the two images of Hillary Clinton — meticulous lawyer and absentminded investor — are not mutually exclusive. While she was a keen professional at work, she had little interest in acquiring wealth or closely monitoring her family's finances, according to her defenders.

Lindsey, a longtime Arkansas friend of the First Family, said the Clintons got into the Whitewater deal on the assumption that McDougal would manage the property and the Clintons would simply make payments periodically on loans taken out to purchase the undeveloped land.

"They went into a real estate development with a developer with the clear understanding that he would manage the investment and with the clear understanding they would be passive investors," Lindsey said.

"When they were asked to write a check to Citizens Bank of Flippin (Ark.) or even to the McDougals when McDougal said there weren't sufficient funds from property sales to cover that month's mortgage payments, that didn't seem unusual."

He said the Clintons were aware that the property appeared to be losing value, but rather than questioning McDougal or seeking detailed financial statements on the deal, they just wrote it off as "bad business judgment," Lindsey said.

Another family friend's assessment is that neither of the Clintons was interested in getting rich; they concentrated through the 1980s on Clinton's political career and his wife's policy crusades. "They don't know beans about business," said this Arkansas friend, who asked to remain nameless.

According to McDougal, the Clintons early in 1985 expressed interest in Madison Guaranty's affairs — as well as their personal enrichment — and sought the thrift's legal work for the Rose Law Firm. McDougal said he put Hillary Clinton and the Rose firm on the $2,000-a-month retainer at then-Gov. Clinton's request — a claim the White House has denied.

In 1988, when Madison Guaranty clearly was on the verge of failure and McDougal was suffering personal problems, records show that Hillary Clinton wrote to McDougal to seek power of attorney over all Whitewater-related business.

She received that power but apparently did not use it until 1992, when she authorized Rose firm law partner Vincent Foster to work on Whitewater's delinquent tax returns.

In an unrelated case, she took a distinctly active role in a family investment involving much less money. In 1983, she, Foster and Webster L. Hubbell, another law firm partner, formed an investment partnership called Mid-life Investors, with each contributing an initial $15,000.

Roy P. Drew, a stockbroker who helped them set up the venture, said neither Foster nor Hubbell later expressed much interest in the performance of the partnership but that Hillary Clinton called frequently to ask about her investment, at times phoning him daily with questions and instructions.

The partnership eventually foundered, paying annual dividends of between $2 and $20 from 1986 to 1992, according to the Clintons' income tax returns. Lindsey, who follows the Clintons' personal business closely, said he knew virtually nothing about Mid-life Investors except that it was an insignificant part of the family's portfolio.

Some of the White House defensiveness about Whitewater questions over the last three weeks can be attributed to concern for Hillary Clinton's potential exposure to political damage. The chief item on the White House agenda for 1994 is the health care reform initiative, which the First Lady has headed. White House aides — and ultimately the Clintons — concluded this week that until questions are resolved about the First Family's business matters, little progress can be made on affairs of state, officials said.

"There ain't going to be no health care campaign if they don't get Whitewater out of the way," said Betsey Wright, Clinton's former gubernatorial chief of staff and an informal adviser.

—***James Risen and John Broder*** are staff writers at the *Los Angeles Times*. Mr. Broder is a White House correspondent and Mr. Risen is an investigative reporter covering national security issues. (January 16, 1994.)

Blizzard of Lies

William Safire

AMERICANS OF ALL POLITICAL PERSUASIONS are coming to the sad realization that our First Lady — a woman of undoubted talents who was a role model for many in her generation — is a congenital liar.

Drip by drip, like Whitewater-torture, the case is being made that she is compelled to mislead, and to ensnare her subordinates and friends in a web of deceit.

1. Remember the story she told about studying *The Wall Street Journal* to explain her 10,000 percent profit in 1979 commodity trading? We now know that was a lie told to turn aside accusations that as the Governor's wife she profited corruptly, her account being run by a lawyer for state poultry interests through a disreputable broker. She lied for good reason: To admit otherwise would be to confess taking, and paying taxes on, what some think amounted to a $100,000 bribe.

2. The abuse of Presidential power known as Travelgate elicited another series of lies. She induced a White House lawyer to assert flatly to investigators that Mrs. Clinton did not order the firing of White House travel aides, who were then harassed by the F.B.I. and Justice Department to justify patronage replacement by Mrs. Clinton's cronies.

Now we know, from a memo long concealed from investigators, that there would be "hell to pay" if the furious First Lady's desires were scorned. The career of the lawyer who transmitted Hillary's lie to the authorities is now in jeopardy. Again, she lied with good reason: to avoid being identified as a vindictive political power player who used the F.B.I. to ruin the lives of people standing in the way of juicy patronage.

3. In the aftermath of the apparent suicide of her former partner and closest confidant, White House Deputy Counsel Vincent Foster, she ordered the overturn of an agreement to allow the Justice Department to examine the files in the dead man's office. Her closest friends and aides, under oath, have been blatantly disremembering this likely obstruction of justice, and may have to pay for supporting Hillary's lie with jail terms.

Again, the lying was not irrational. Investigators believe that damning records from the Rose Law Firm, wrongfully kept in Vincent Foster's White House office, were spirited out in the dead of night and hidden from the law for two years — in Hillary's closet, in Web Hubbell's basement before his felony conviction, in the President's secretary's personal files — before some were forced out last week.

Why the White House concealment? For good reason: The records show Hillary Clinton was lying when she denied actively representing a criminal enterprise known as the Madison S&L, and indicate she may have conspired with Web Hubbell's father-in-law to make a sham land deal that cost taxpayers $3 million.

Why the belated release of some of the incriminating evidence? Not because it mysteriously turned up in offices previously searched. Certainly not because Hillary Clinton and her new hang-tough White House counsel want to respond fully to lawful subpoenas.

One reason for the Friday-night dribble of evidence from the White House is the discovery by the F.B.I. of copies of some of those records elsewhere. When Clinton witnesses are asked about specific items in "lost" records — which investigators have — the White House "finds" its copy and releases it. By concealing the Madison billing records two days beyond the statute of limitations, Hillary evaded a civil suit by bamboozled bank regulators.

Another reason for recent revelations is the imminent turning of former aides and partners of Hillary against her; they were willing to cover her lying when it advanced their careers, but are inclined to listen to their own lawyers when faced with perjury indictments.

Therefore, ask not "Why didn't she just come clean at the beginning?" She had good reasons to lie; she is in the longtime habit of lying; and she has never been called to account for lying herself or in suborning lying in her aides and friends.

No wonder the President is fearful of holding a prime-time press conference. Having been separately deposed by the independent counsel at least twice, the President and First Lady would be well advised to retain separate defense counsels.

— ***William Safire*** is a Pulitzer Prize-winning author and journalist; his columns appear twice-weekly in *The New York Times*. He is the author of several books, including *Spread the Word* and *Scandalmonger*. (January 8, 1996.)

All About Hillary

Maureen Dowd

THIS WAS SUPPOSED to be Earth Mother Week.

The First Lady is going on tour with her book, *It Takes a Village: and Other Lessons Children Teach Us*. "For more than twenty-five years, First Lady Hillary Rodham Clinton has made children her passion and her cause," says a Simon & Schuster press release.

Mrs. Clinton is accustomed to stepping behind an apple-pie and motherhood scrim. During the '92 campaign, Clinton strategists wrote a secret memo, including advice about how to make Mrs. Clinton seem more affectionate and maternal. It suggested staging an event where "Bill and Chelsea surprise Hillary on Mother's Day" and advised her to talk more about her family.

Since the health care debacle, she has taken to the hearth with a vengeance. She appeared on Martha Stewart's Christmas special, chatting about wreaths. She wrote her newspaper column about New Year's resolutions ("I will try to keep the same hairdo for at least 30 days . . . . I will try to show more enthusiasm for my husband's golf game.")

On the President's recent trip to London, the First Lady's anodyne demeanor caused one journalist to mourn that she had become "the first Stepford Wife."

Mrs. Clinton uses rituals of domesticity to make her desire for "systematic" change seem less threatening.

Her latest fluffer-nutter make-over was to be capped by the book tour. But the timing turns out to be extremely awkward, as revelations about the travel office fiasco and the mysteriously disappearing and appearing Whitewater files have once more cast doubt on Mrs. Clinton's probity and put her at the center of what she dismisses to *Newsweek* as "all the spider webs that are spun."

The confidential memo written by David Watkins about the travel office gives the maternal image a Joan Crawford twist, portraying the First Lady as a scary "Mommy Dearest."

Mr. Watkins said he realized there was a more humane way to handle the situation than firing seven people, sticking the F.B.I. on them, leaking it to the press and pretty much ruining their lives.

He starkly contradicts the story of Mrs. Clinton, who had Administration lawyer Neil Eggleston tell the General Accounting Office last year that "Mrs. Clinton did not know the origin of the decision to remove the White House Travel Office employees."

Now comes the Watkins "soul cleansing," as he calls his memo. "Once this made it into the First Lady's agenda, Vince Foster became involved, and he and Harry Thomason regularly informed me of her attention to the Travel Office situation — as well as her insistence that the situation be resolved immediately by replacing the Travel Office staff . . . We both knew there would be hell to pay if . . . we failed to take swift and decisive action in conformity with the First Lady's wishes."

An associate of the First Lady through all this confirms Mr. Watkins' portrait: "She's a good screamer. She can cut someone to ribbons and make them feel like an idiot. It was a lot easier to do what she wanted."

And there's more: 116 pages of copies of documents from the Rose Law Firm — which have been searched for and subpoenaed for two years — have suddenly turned up in the White House residence, showing that Mrs. Clinton had billed for a wide range of legal services on behalf of Madison Guaranty.

At her Whitewater press conference in 1994, Mrs. Clinton wore pink and professed ignorance about the Madison account: "It was not an area that I practiced in, it was not an area that I really know anything to speak of about."

Mr. Watkins said that he had been trying to be as "vague and protective as possible" with investigators. But apparently he wrote his scalding memo after he grew tired of taking the fall for the First Lady.

Mrs. Clinton is at the center of a web of fall-takers. People say what they are expected to say, and are rewarded with monstrous legal bills. And the more candid associates keep contradicting her. In the coming weeks, she will need Houdini-like skills to dodge the collision of her images. She will be spreading sunshine in bookstores while in hearing rooms her former colleagues speak under oath about her legal activities.

Earth Mother meet Mommie Dearest.

— ***Maureen Dowd,*** a columinist for the *The New York Times'* op ed page, received a Pulitzer Prize for her coverage of the Clinton White House. (January 7, 1996.)

She is Not a Crook

Walter Shapiro

FEW DAYS BEFORE Hillary Clinton's January interview with Barbara Walters, the First Lady was presiding over a prep session with her team of advisers, including her poised and polished attorney, David Kendall. "Before I moved to Little Rock, I had spent a lifetime dealing with David Kendall-type people," she said, gesturing toward her lawyer. "I thought it would be nice to deal with the colorful people in Arkansas for a change. Well, all those colorful people keep coming back to haunt me."

Every day has become Halloween for Hillary — the ghosts and goblins of the long-buried Arkansas past keep converging on the East Wing. Any hope that the First Lady had of striking a noncontroversial pose for the election year exploded with the arrival of the phrase that Washington obfuscators fear most: newly discovered documents. As someone who had enjoyed interviewing Hillary during the campaign and the early days of the administration, I thought I had a good handle on who she was. And for nearly four years, I have regarded Whitewater as a fat-free muffin of a scandal — it looks like the real thing until you bite into it and discover that it's all puffed up with hot air and artificial ingredients. But how could the First Lady sink into such a morass of missteps, misstatements, and presumed mendacity?

So, with perjury indictments swirling around Hillary's cohort, it is time for a revisionist history of the First Lady. Could I have been that much of a sucker in my positive portrayals of her in *Esquire*? Could she really be the Queen of the Cover-ups, the Whitewater Witch depicted by columnist Bill Safire as a "congenital liar"?

In the end, I found her culpable not of impeachable offenses (eat your heart out, Al D'Amato) but of self-righteous blunders. If Hillary is to be pilloried, it should be for venal sins like these:

THE ARKANSAS MARTYR. In 1974, Yale-educated female lawyers did not squander their careers to run off to Dogpatch to be with the man they loved. Hillary never lost sight of what she had sacrificed, and this sense of moral entitlement blinded her to some ethical considerations.

Against this backdrop, consider what to my nonlawyer's mind remains the most troubling aspect of the Hillary saga: her uncanny ability to turn $1,000 in pocket change into a $100,000 profit in the cattle-futures market. She plunged into commodities in 1978, when Clinton was first running for governor. (The job paid just $35,000 a year.) With no family money on either side, Hillary knew that she had to be the good provider.

My guess is that her commodities guru, Jim Blair, was acting as a close friend eager to share a good thing — and not as a bagman for his legal client, Tyson Foods. Blair was such a good friend that he guaranteed Hillary's profits, either by insider trading or by making sure that winning trades were assigned to her account after the fact. Commodities regulation in those day was so loose that it's likely that no laws were broken, although Hillary did exceed the margin limits on her early trades and in 1994 paid $6,000 in back taxes on some of her swag. Alarm bells should have gone off in Hillary's mind as her winning streak rose to Charles Van Doren levels. But she was bathed in the light of her own righteousness — she and Bill could do so much for the poor benighted people of Arkansas.

For all her Watergate-honed government ethics, Hillary as not as meticulous as she should have been in walling herself off from possible conflicts of interest at the Rose Law Firm once her husband was governor. She carefully skirted any legal work for the state and later even refused to take any partnership profits from the firm's lucrative state-bond practice. Having gone that far, Hillary believed that she did not have to be excessively prissy on the little stuff. Little stuff like her 1985 phone call on behalf of Madison Guaranty to Beverly Bassett Schaffer, the state banking commissioner appointed by her husband. She was Hillary the Good, the call was innocuous, so why sweat the details?

THE WHITE HOUSE MESS. Travelgate had its roots in the two biggest mistakes that the Clintons made during the prepresidential transition: keeping the campaign pledge to cut the White House staff by 10 percent and then deferring all the personnel decisions until they laboriously selected a Cabinet. More time was spent choosing a secretary of transportation (for $100,000 in commodities pro, name him) than in devising a White House organizational chart. The Clintons simply shunted most of their Arkansas retainers to safe administrative jobs in which they would oversee minor matters like keeping track of files.

David Watkins, author of the famous ass-covering Travelgate memo that was so damaging to Hillary, had the exalted title of special assistant for administration and management. His rise was sufficiently accidental that, in mid-1993, Clinton asked a friend, "How did David Watkins get his job?" Hillary haters hail Watkins as a lonely truth teller in a den of intrigue. But they conveniently forget that Mr. Credibility was fired in 1994 for commandeering the presidential helicopter for a golfing expedition and then insisting it was for a training flight.

But what about the heinous Hillary factor? The First Lady's role in Travelgate had already been partly revealed in the 1993 report on the scandal. The Clintons deserve scorn for allowing their Hollywood chums Harry Thomason and Linda Bloodworth-Thomason to get anywhere near the White House and scheme to get charter business for one of Thomason's companies. Why did otherwise sensible people like Mack McLarty approve the Travelgate purge? Not to cater cravenly to Hillary's whims but to free up seven coveted staff slots in the radically downsized White House.

THE WAY LAWYERS LIE. Al D'Amato's Whitewater hearings, which are moving as fast as Freudian analysis, keep foundering on one question: So what? Hillary's only apparent sin is that she dissembled at her famed 1994 pink press conference — and might have repeated her answers in her two interviews with Special Prosecutor Kenneth Starr. TV has endlessly repeated the aw-shucks press-conference footage showing Hillary responding to a question about her representation of Madison by claiming that a "young attorney [Richard Massey]. . . did all the work. But because I was what you call the billing attorney . . . my name was at the bottom of the letter."

For Hillary, the jig was up when the missing billing records miraculously materialized. They showed that she had done a total of sixty hours of work on various Madison projects. To critics like Safire, the whole point of the White House cover-up was to conceal that Hillary "was lying when she denied representing a criminal conspiracy known as the Madison S&L."

There's just one problem: Hillary was asked only about her "regulatory" work for Madison. Her sin was to exploit this narrow loophole in the question to convey the false impression that her overall work for Madison had been nominal. Lawyers make their careers out of twisting the precise wording of questions to their own tactical advantage. This approach may work in a deposition, but it is precisely the wrong way to contain a political scandal. As for Safire's "congenital liar" crack, neither of us is qualified to speak of the First Lady in such terms. I don't know where she gets it, but she can dodge with the best of them. By not coming clean, and by not realizing that some of her actions were suspect, Hillary has put Bob Dole's valet, D'Amato, on to the scent of a cover-up and allowed him to shanghai the more important business of the country. For that, she deserves the ire of reasonable people everywhere.

FEEDING THE BLAST. If the First Lady could take back three words, they might well be "milk and cookies." In March 1992, after Jerry Brown attacked her integrity in a campaign debate, Hillary angrily snapped, "I suppose I could have stayed home, baked cookies, and had teas, but what I decided to do was to fulfill my profession." Afterward, in an uncharacteristic admission of error, she said privately, "I made a big mistake."

From that moment on, Hillary put herself in the hands of the image police. Before the convention, there was a conscious decision to play up her role as wife and mother and to try to make her legal career seem as if it were volunteer work. The more she struggled to become Barbara Bush, the more her image seemed draped in inauthenticity. The emphasis on the ever-changing hairstyles became a metaphor in the eyes of the public for not knowing exactly who she was.

The same pattern repeated itself after she was tarred and feathered over the failure of health-care reform. Every political half-wit in the country knew her plan was going down, but Hillary remained cloistered — hunched over arcane studies of the German system — when she should have been wading among common reporters, as her enemies were. Equal parts superior, stubborn, and paranoid, she was incapable of doing this and never developed the reservoir of goodwill that might have buttressed her in future crises.

The First Lady has pretended to be Superwoman for so long that it is hard to get used to her as Hillary the Blunderer.

She has made her mistakes and shares with the president a reluctance to own up to them. None of this means that she is the ethical inferior of that noted philosopher-king Al D'Amato. But that obvious judgment will not prevent the all-too-colorful ghosts of Whitewater from haunting Hillary right through the election.

— ***Walter Shapiro*** covers politics for *USA Today*. He has reported on the last six presidential elections, and his books include *Ten Lessons from Election '96*. This article originally appeared in *Esquire Magazine* (vol. 125, no 3, March 1996) and is reprinted with the generous permission of the author.

Feminism, Critique & Analysis

HILLARY RODHAM CLINTON often appears to be beloved or despised solely on the basis of her feminism. Many people love her because they believe she is a feminist. Others hate her because they suspect exactly the same thing. The fear and hope engendered by Mrs. Clinton's commitment to women's equality serves as a lightening rod for both popular support and criticism. Other authors touch on this subject as well (see Katha Pollitt and Pat Schroeder), but this chapter specifically addresses the issue of Mrs. Clinton's role in American feminism.

Despite Hillary Rodham Clinton's feminism, her friends describe her as conservative — less a radical than a transitional figure in women's rights. Some commentators have, in fact, questioned the strength and effectiveness of her feminist beliefs. In defense, SUSAN FALUDI explores the connection between sexual and political pleasure and suggests that Hillary's sin lies in "visibly, tangibly having fun." HENRY LOUIS GATES, JR. looks at the national pasttime of "Hillary Hating" and why the First Lady "does seem an especially inviting target." MRS. CLINTON'S remarks on the 150th anniversary of the Seneca Falls Convention speak directly to her commitment to "a society based on equality and mutual respect."

Clinton Administration critics have effectively used satire and cartoons to promote images of Hillary Rodham Clinton as a radical feminist whose views endanger the American way of life. Jokes about her (as power-monger, lesbian, shadow president, etc.) started during the 1992 campaign. CHARLOTTE TEMPLIN examines political cartoons about the First Lady and describes "the backlash against professional women, as evidenced by the obsession with Hillary among cartoonists."

The Power Laugh

Susan Faludi

I HAVE READ AND HEARD — and repeated — the now standard feminist explanation for the hysteria over Hillary Clinton.

It goes like this: The guardians of the rusting social order — the pundits, the political hacks, the religious right — have their shorts in a knot over Mrs. Clinton because she's an independent woman.

They feel threatened by this emblem of the modern women's movement — by her professionalism, her role in her husband's career, her feminist views, her failure to produce a brood of young 'uns and, last but not at all least, her financial independence.

But is that the whole answer? After all, Mrs. Clinton is hardly the first first lady to have an egalitarian relationship with her husband. From Abigail Adams to Sarah Polk to Rosalynn Carter, numerous first ladies have refused to play the I-don't-know-nothin'-about-makin'-policy role.

They have been involved in their husbands' political decisions, attending Cabinet meetings (Helen Taft), writing speeches (Bess Truman) and monitoring political correspondence (Edith Wilson). Nor is Mrs. Clinton the first feminist in the East Wing.

Eleanor Roosevelt fought to revoke laws that locked married women out of the Depression-era job market. Betty Ford lobbied for the Equal Rights Amendment; she even installed a separate phone line in her office just for this purpose.

Hillary Clinton's failure to demonstrate mega-maternity is no departure either: Neither the Washingtons nor the Polks had children.

And her final indignity — drawing an income that makes her the family's breadwinner — is also no aberration. As Betty Boyd Caroli observes in *First Ladies*, most presidential wives have been richer than their husbands. But none of these women has taken half the licking in the press that Mrs. Clinton has. Why not?

Mrs. Clinton's autonomy is only half the story. What galls her detractors isn't so much that she is independent — but that she enjoys it. She is doing something her predecessors didn't dare. She's abandoned the earnest, dutiful demeanor. She doesn't bear the grim visage of the stereotypical female policy wonk; she's no Jeanne Kirkpatrick.

Nor does she make any pretense that power and visibility were forced on her. And therein lies her sin: Hillary Clinton is visibly, tangibly having fun.

Eleanor Roosevelt loved the public life, but she rarely revealed her exuberance. Before the media, Mrs. Clinton throws back her head and laughs, kicks up her heels and breaks into a dance.

Wipe that smile off your face, the media instructed. In the *National Review*'s many anti-Hillary broadsides, the magazine's contributors were in highest dudgeon over the pleasure the first lady-elect takes in politics, calling her "that smiling barracuda."

Time magazine too was put out by Mrs. Clinton's displays of enthusiasm and political passion: "At first, she seemed insufficiently aware that she was not the candidate herself. Instead of standing by like a potted palm, she enjoyed talking at length about problems and policies."

Other columnists wagged their fingers at her for "beaming" and "throwing her arms open wide" as she "seized the stage." *The American Spectator* was particularly disgusted by Mrs. Clinton's embrace, in her 1969 Wellesley commencement speech, of an "ecstatic . . . mode of living."

By combining equality with ecstasy, liberty with laughter, Mrs. Clinton violated the cardinal trade-off rule of American womanhood. Women are told: OK, gals, go ahead and do your liberated thing, but you must pay the price with personal happiness.

Women have taken this lesson to heart. To prove our femininity and avoid the slings and arrows of anti-feminism, we have learned to assure the world that while we may have more mastery of our lives, we've balanced it with more misery. We are careful to stress that we are working only because we have to, not because we might also take pleasure from our jobs.

Sexuality for women comes with the same warning: If you have sex and enjoy it, prepare to face the consequences. That may be why many who favor a ban on abortion are willing to look the other way when the woman in question has been raped or is the victim of incest; she doesn't need to be punished because she hasn't gotten any pleasure out of the encounter.

Enthusiastic activism is cast in the same dim light as sexual activity. Indeed, the phrase "public woman" has traditionally meant a prostitute; the lady of the evening and the lady of social advocacy often seem interchangeable in society's eyes.

Victorian male pundits raged against the "whorish" behavior of the decidedly unwhorish women of the era who were reformers and suffragists. In his 1844 address to the Young Ladies' Institute of Pittsfield, Mass., William Buell Sprague intoned that he would rather his daughter join a nunnery than go "up and down the world haranguing promiscuous assemblies."

The connection between sexual and political pleasure explains one of the more bizarre slips of the tongue by a media man contemplating the Hillary Threat.

In a "Nightline" report this fall about the first lady's proper "role," Ted Koppel asked R. Emmett Tyrell, editor of *The American Spectator*, "What would you do with (Hillary), put her in a convent for the next four years?"

Eleanor Roosevelt noted that women could be either biblical "Marthas" or "Marys." Take the part of the giggly party girl or assume the role of the dowdy activist. Mrs. Roosevelt cast her lot with the Marys.

Historically, first lady Marys have presented themselves as dour and self-denigrating. They have insisted their political activities were really a terrible burden — a "splendid misery," as Abigail Adams put it.

The list of first ladies who moaned about their ineptitude at public speaking is endless — and the most adept moaned the loudest.

Mrs. Roosevelt "never missed an opportunity to discount her influence," biographer Blanche Wiesen Cook writes, and she "was rarely direct or confrontational."

Mrs. Clinton, however, is a Martha-Mary, an independent woman who has happily and openly ventured into the stream of public life. It's her refusal to play the penitent Mary that most enrages the anti-feminist commentators. "There is no reason she ought to be forgiven, when she hasn't repented," fumed Daniel Wattenberg in *The American Spectator.*

For a moment, when the Gennifer Flowers story broke, it looked as if Hillary Clinton might play the long-suffering Mary after all. But no, she rolled her eyes and asserted she was no Tammy Wynette. Later in the campaign, misogynist hopes rose again as she softened her looks and toned down her impassioned speechmaking. But these efforts were pure cosmetology, and both Hillary and her enemies knew it.

The joy of female independence is what Hillary Rodham Clinton will bring to the White House. By showing us that an independent woman doesn't have to don a hair shirt and hang her head in shame, Mrs. Clinton has already advanced women's rights.

Her presence will remind us that the Founding Fathers guaranteed Americans more than life and liberty.

They promised us the pursuit of happiness, too.

— ***Susan Faludi*** is author of *Backlash: The Undeclared War Against American Women.* She won a Pulitzer Prize for reporting for the *Wall Street Journal.* (December 20, 1992.)

Hating Hillary

Henry Louis Gates, Jr.

WE'RE SITTING TOGETHER at one end of a long mahogany table in the Map Room, on the ground level of the White House. A little awkwardly, the table is set up for twelve, with a White House notepad by each chair; it seems that nobody has been around to pick up since the President had a meeting here just before Christmas. Half a century ago, the American conduct of the Second World War was largely overseen from this room; here President Roosevelt could send messages to commanders around the world and receive up-to-the-minute reports from the battlefields. More recently, the once top-secret room has fallen into disuse; Hillary Rodham Clinton tells me that its restoration was one of her pet projects when she first arrived. A red damask sofa stands off to one side, and there are half a dozen pleasant, undemanding oils and engravings on the wall. But what draws your eye is a map of Europe, hand-labeled "Estimated German Situation," which was prepared and posted on April 3, 1945. Areas under Nazi occupation were outlined in red, with blue arrows to indicate invading enemy troops. It was the last situation map seen by President Roosevelt, who died nine days later.

All these years after, the map still lends an aura of the war room — of tactical maneuvers against desperate odds, of moves and countermoves. In the light of the First Lady's embattled position, it may also lend the comfort of control, the assurance that V-E Day is around the corner. You're almost tempted to stick different-colored pins in the thing, the way generals in old war movies mark enemy battalions; over here, a Senate panel and an independent counsel clustered together; over there, a *Times* columnist; and, in scattershot formation, a Fifth Column of disaffected ex-supporters. Maybe it isn't war but it is hell. "I wouldn't wish this on anybody," she says. This morning's William Safire column happens to be the one that pronounced her a "congenital liar." She has been out taking a long walk by herself — which, given the recent blizzard, shows real determination, or maybe need.

Actually, the strain isn't visible. With nearly flawless skin, she defies all logic by looking younger than she does in photographs. She's in what you might call her civvies; she's wearing a purple turtleneck and a blue St. John's knit suit ("It's great to travel in, you can crumple it, and it doesn't show wrinkles," she offers in a hints-from-Heloïse spirit), and her hair is pulled back in a black velvet headband. I'm impressed by her equipoise. She explains that she's been trying to practice something called "the discipline of gratitude," and refers me to a book by a Jesuit priest, Henri Nouwen. "The discipline of gratitude," Father Nouwen wrote, "is the explicit effort to acknowledge that all I am and have is given to me as a gift of love, a gift to be celebrated with joy." She points to a bowl of fresh roses on the table and says, "I mean, you look at those flowers and you think, 'My gosh, if my life were to end tomorrow, how lucky I've been that nearly all my life, I've been surrounded by flowers.'" If you are Hillary Clinton, the discipline of gratitude means reminding yourself that you are not a Bangladeshi peasant foraging for grains of rice — you are the First Lady and there are fresh-cut flowers in every room in your house. As with any mental discipline, concentration sometimes wavers, and the press of daily life intrudes. These days, what with one thing and another, Bangladesh may not be entirely without its attractions.

Earlier, I had asked Maggie Williams, who has spent the past three years as the First Lady's chief of staff, whether she would do it all again, knowing what she knows now. It wasn't something she had to stop and think about. "Absolutely *not*," she replies, lolling her head. "Are you *kidding*?" I put the same question to Hillary Clinton, whose daily schedule now has to accommodate things like depositions with Kenneth Starr, the Independent Counsel for the Whitewater investigation. "Absolutely," she says, and she speaks of the sense of adventure. "I wake up every day just wondering about what's going to happen next." She's not the only one.

Like horse racing, Hillary-hating has become one of those national pastimes which unite the elite and the lumpen. Serious accusations have, of course, been leveled against the President's wife, but it's usually what people think of her that determines the credence and the weight they give to the accusations, rather than the reverse. At times, she herself sounds at a loss to explain the level of animosity toward her. "I apparently remind some people of their mother-in-law or their boss, or something," she says. She laughs, but she isn't joking, exactly.

The remark chimes with something I've been told by the redoubtable Sally Quinn, who — in part because she's a frequent contributor to *The Washington Post*, in part because she's the wife of the *Post*'s legendary editor Ben Bradlee — must herself count as a figure in the so-called Washington establishment. "There's this old joke about the farmer whose crops fail," she says. "One year, he's wiped out by a blizzard, and the next year there's a rainstorm, and the next year there's a drought, and so on every year. Finally, he's completely bankrupt — he's lost everything. He says, "Why, Lord? Why, why me?" And the Lord says, "I don't know. There's just something about you that pisses me off." She pauses, then says, "That's the problem — there's just something about her that pisses people off. This is the reaction that she elicits from people."

Well, from many people, anyway. "A lot of Americans are uncomfortable with her self-righteousness," Arianna Huffington says. "I think gratitude is great if you can communicate it, but if you have to keep telling people how grateful you are. . . ." William Kristol, a Republican strategist and, since September, the editor and publisher of *The Weekly Standard*, puts it this way: "She strikes me as a sort of moralistic liberal who has a blind spot for actions that are in her own interest. These are exempt from that cold gaze that she casts over everyone else's less than perfect actions." On the whole, though, he's one of the more dispassionate voices you're likely to hear on the subject. Peggy Noonan, who came to prominence as a speechwriter for Presidents Ronald Reagan and George Bush, speaks of "an air of apple-cheeked certitude" that is "political in its nature and grating in its effects," of "an implicit insistence throughout her career that hers were the politics of moral decency and therefore those who opposed her politics were obviously of a lower moral order." She adds, "Now with Whitewater going on, nonliberals are taking a certain satisfaction in thinking, Uh-huh, you're not my moral superior, Madam."

Some of this glee relates to a discomfort with Hillary's political identity. In the 1992 campaign, her husband presented himself as a different kind of Democrat. Many people who wanted a different kind of Democrat to be president fear that the president's wife is not a different kind of Democrat. (In Ben J. Wattenberg's *Values Matter Most* — the book that prompted Bill Clinton's infamous midnight-of-the-soul telephone call to the author — Hillary is identified as "a lady of the left" and compared with Mikhail Suslov, who was for years the Kremlin's chief ideologist.) Of course, if you ask why they fear she is not a different kind of Democrat, the answers are less than entirely satisfying. It's true that she served on the board of a liberal advocacy group, the Children's Defense Fund, but then many CDF members regard the First Lady with heartfelt disappointment. It's also true that the Clinton health plan, which she spearheaded, involved significant governmental oversight, but then congressional conservatives routinely pass complicated bills in which the government has a complicated role. (Consider, even, the tort reform movement, which Vice President Dan Quayle spearheaded, and which sought to vest the federal government with new powers to regulate product liability and other civil legislation.) But if you want to understand how conservatives perceive Mrs. Clinton these matters are ultimately a distraction. For they recognize her, almost on a gut level; in a phrase I've heard countless times, they "know the type." In a word, they look at Hillary Clinton and they see Mrs. Jellyby.

Mrs. Jellyby, you may recall, is the Dickens character in *Bleak House* who is as intent on improving humanity as she is cavalier towards actual human beings; thus she heartlessly neglects her own family while high-mindedly pursuing charity abroad — "telescopic philanthropy," in Dickens' classic phrase. Mrs. Jellyby is a pretty, diminutive woman in her forties with handsome eyes, Dickens writes, "although they had a curious habit of seeming to look a long way off." ("As if," he adds, "they could see nothing nearer than Africa!") And, in Mrs. Jellyby, Dickens' achievement was to have captured everything that people would come to detest about a certain strain of do-gooding liberal; the zealous reformer with a heart as big as all Antarctica. However much you may protest that you are not Mrs. Jellyby — however un-Jellybylike you in fact may be — once she has been attached to you by the adhesive of archetype, there is not much you can do to banish her.

In the '60s and '70s, neoconservatives liked to talk about the ascent of "the New Class," consisting of highly educated professionals who were, in Norman Podhoretz's words, "making a serious bid to dislodge and replace the business and commercial class which had on the whole dominated the country for nearly a century." Podhoretz ascribes to Irving Kristol (father of William) the insight that the New Class "represented itself as concerned only with the general good, the good of others (especially the poor and the blacks), but what it really wanted was to aggrandize its own power." As the only First Lady thus far to have come from its ranks, Hillary Clinton has suffered the fluctuating fortunes of the New Class itself. Among her peers, you'll hear, variously expressed, a very basic sentiment: finally, a First Lady who's one of us. "It was just as if we'd known each other all our lives," says Carly Simon, who has spent time at Martha's Vineyard with the First Lady; when Hillary admired a naïve Haitian painting in Simon's house, Simon made a present of it. "It was an easy, Ivy League kind of camaraderie. Like, 'You went to Wellesley? Oh, I went to Sarah Lawrence.' And, 'Oh, you like that kind of art? I like that kind of art.'" But if you do not feel part of that "us" — if, indeed the very idea of Haitian folk art on the Vineyard makes you shift uneasily — you may feel the tug of an answering sentiment: that this First Lady is *one of them*. The writer and social activist Letty C. Pogrebin (who must herself count as New Class, if you see the world in such terms) was at a White House lunch on a day when the papers carried a story about testimony given by a messenger at the Rose Law Firm. "And Hillary said, 'How could they believe a messenger and not me?'" Pogrebin recalls. "For me, that was such a real, human reaction. It's like, 'I have a history here, I'm a hardworking, caring person, I've worked on good causes, I'm a trained lawyer. How could your first assumption be that he's telling the truth and I'm lying?' Her reaction was such pure, authentic surprise. It says a lot about her." Well, yes, but if you ask *what* it says, you find yourself in the realm of the Rorschach.

Hillary Clinton's supporters have their own theories about the slings and arrows, many of which have to do with her role as a prominent working woman, and hence a symbol of feminism at a time when feminism is under siege. Gloria Steinem offers the canonical feminist explanation: "She and the President are presenting, at a very high, visible level, a new paradigm of the male-female relationship. And that is very much resented." Mandy Grunwald — a consultant who worked closely with the Clintons in 1992, as media director of the campaign — notes that women in politics often make other women uncomfortable: "They feel threatened — they're looking at a woman who is close to their age and has made totally different choices." Hillary, she says, "forces them to ask questions about themselves and the choices they've made that they don't necessarily want to ask."

Hillary herself identifies a cultural component of her difficulties. "I don't want to get grandiose," she says, "but I believe that we're going through a significant transition — economically, politically, culturally, socially, in gender relations, all kinds of ways — and so someone as visible as I am is going to get a lot more attention. I think if the spotlight were turned on many of my friends in their own private lives somebody could make out of it what they would: 'My goodness, she didn't take her husband's name,' or 'She's the one who travels while her husband stays home and takes care of the children,' or 'She has a very traditional role — does that mean she's sold out her education?' There could be questions like that raised about nearly every American woman I know. It's just that I'm the one in the public eye right now, and so a lot of the issues that are being talked about around kitchen tables or office water coolers or college classrooms get focussed on me."

Nothing goads her detractors more than the claim that her travails have anything to do with gender relations — "the 'strong woman' bogey," as one of them refers to it. "That's nonsense, that's old, it's not true, and it no longer applies," Peggy Noonan says, with her usual diffidence. "And for her to suggest that her problems stem from the fact that there are many Americans that just can't stand a strong woman is *infuriating* to people, because she's hiding behind charges of 'You are a sexist,' and they think she is trying to divert attention from the real problem, which is who she is and what she's doing." Sally Quinn, too, is impatient with such explanations: "I do not think that was an issue with the press, because half of the people who are covering her are working women, and the other half are men whose wives work."

It's clear enough that many of Hillary's most severe critics, especially in the mainstream media, are women; it's less clear what to make of that fact. When I broach the subject with her, she says vaguely, "Maybe it's something to do with the insecurity that people feel about their own lives and the roles that they find themselves in and how that is changing." Ann Lewis, who was recently named deputy campaign manager and director of communications for Clinton/Gore '96, is more plainspoken. She sees it, basically, as a way for a woman reporter to prove she's one of the boys. "There are women in the business of communications who are striving very hard by what they think of as impartial standards, and they prove that by being as hard on women who run for political office as the guys. In your head, you think that the way to succeed is to win acceptance by that crowd, and those are the standards. But I have got to tell you, I have worked for a lot of women candidates and — guess what? — there's nothing impartial about those standards."

Speaking more generally, a close friend of the Clinton's brings up yet another theory: "The President thinks that they are treated so harshly because he is 'white trash' as they put it. The way somebody put it is, Imagine Washington as a country club, and Clinton as the golf pro. They think he's perfectly competent at what he does, they think he's a nice guy. You want him to have a drink at your table with you and your friends and maybe even come to dinner. But the golf pro is never 'one of us,' never a real member."

None of this lets the golf pro's wife off the hook, of course. For the historical role of the First Lady has always involved the more delicate reaches of social diplomacy. And it's in the practice of these exquisite arts that Mrs. Clinton is widely perceived to have faltered. Mandy Grunwald, who during the two years following the election was an advisor to the White House, tells me of a sense of exhaustion after a bruising campaign requiring constant interaction with the media: on some level, she thinks, it was as if the Clintons "thought they could close the door." They're still living with that mistake. "There were people who covered the campaign who were ideologically sympathetic to the President, who were essentially the New Democrats of the press corps," Grunwald says. "And they were not cultivated by the Clintons, and that was silly. Certainly there were people who could have been friends, who didn't go to dinner, who could have and should have and wanted to, and who drew conclusions about having been cultivated and then essentially dropped after the campaign — drew conclusions about the Clintons' sincerity which were unnecessary."

"She hates the press, and that's not smart," a senior official in the Bush Administration tells me. "You can see the tightness around her mouth. That's where you really see it. And in the eyes. Even when she's smiling, you can see that tightness." One consequence is that people who have met her socially always talk about how different she was from what they'd expected in a way that people who met Barbara Bush, say, did not. Arthur Schlesinger, Jr., had lunch with his friend Jacqueline Onassis on a day when he had been invited to have dinner at the White House. He mentioned to her that he'd never met Hillary and that he assumed she was very bright but also stern and humorless. "Jackie said, 'Not at all — she's great fun, she's got an excellent sense of humor, and you'll like her very much,'" Schlesinger recounts. "At the dinner, I found myself placed next to her and, indeed, Jackie was absolutely right. She's a charmer." What's remarkable isn't that she can be funny, spontaneous, and mischievous, and has a loud, throaty laugh; what's remarkable is the extent to which she has sequestered her personality from the media.

Indeed, when it comes to handling the press Hillary Clinton sometimes seems to have a positive talent to annoy. Her troubled relationship with Sally Quinn, some argue, is itself a revealing example of diplomatic failure: the wages of well-meant counsel spurned. "I have watched First Ladies for thirty years, and it just seemed to me that Hillary could be potentially very damaging to him if she went about things the wrong way," Quinn tells me. "And so I literally said, 'Here is what I have learned over the years from observing First Ladies and here are some mistakes not to make.'" Today, Quinn's coolness toward Mrs. Clinton is a popular topic of Beltway conversation. A longtime friend of both women puts it this way: "It's like the blond girl in the class — you don't even know why you hate her." Whatever the roots of Quinn's disaffection, her assessments of both the Clintons do tend to be unsparing. "I just think that, time after time, they have responded to things with no class," she offers tartly. "It would appear that there is sometimes a certain lack of loyalty."

The list of Clinton friends and supporters who now feel abandoned is a long one. Lani Guinier wrote mordantly in the *Times Magazine* about encountering Hillary in the West Wing at a time when her nomination to head the civil-rights division of the Justice Department was beginning to look doomed: Hillary, whom she'd known since law school, had breezed by with a casual, "Hi, kiddo," announcing that she was late for lunch. Then, there is the tale of Michael Lerner, who is the editor of the magazine *Tikkun*, and the inventor of the phrase "the politics of meaning," which seeks to meld progressive politics with spiritual values. That was a phrase, and an idea, that the First Lady started to introduce into her speeches shortly after she arrived in Washington. Lerner met her at the White House in April of 1993, at a ceremony for the opening of the Holocaust Memorial Museum. "And when she was introduced to me," he recounts, "her first words were 'Am I your mouthpiece, or what?' I said, 'Well, we seem to be talking a similar language,' and she said 'We're completely on the same wavelength.' And 'When can we get together and talk?'" As he goes on, he sounds like a wounded soldier reliving a combat experience. When the two did get together at the White House, Lerner says, Hillary made a point of explaining that the so-called politics of meaning wasn't anything he had introduced her to, that it was really a way of talking about the things she had learned as a Methodist when she was growing up. "And I said to her, 'Absolutely right — this is an attempt to speak Biblical values in a nonreligious language,'" he recalls. "And she said, 'Yeah, that's why I love it.' So I have no sense of exaggerated importance or anything like this. I was giving her permission in a way — the politics of meaning gave her a vehicle through which to say things that she already believed."

Their intellectual comity did not last. Some people point to letters that Lerner sent to a small group to *Tikkun* supporters, sprinkled with turns of phrase like "Hillary and I believe. . . ." It was a presumption that the White House couldn't be expected to warm to, and especially not in the light of several caustic articles that portrayed him as her guru — alternatively Svengali and Rasputin. Lerner thinks the attack was led by people whose allegiance was really to Vice President Al Gore and who were unhappy that Hillary was playing the role in shaping domestic policy that they'd sought for Gore. "They wanted Hillary's influence to decrease and Gore's to increase, and thus theirs to increase, because they were coming into the White House through Gore," he says. What really incensed Lerner, though, was her response to the bad press. "The second she was attacked, she backed completely away." The final straw came when Hillary, in a later effort to disassociate herself from him, referred in print to his cherished White House meeting as a mere "courtesy call." "So here is Safire saying this woman is a 'congenital liar,'" Lerner adds, sounding not at all displeased by it. "I am sure glad he didn't know about all these things, because he might have been able to use them to bolster his case."

The truth is that the bristly Michael Lerner was not cut out to be a Camelot companion. And plenty of others now departed from the charmed circle had themselves to blame. But the traditional standard of politesse involves never giving offense *intentionally*, and Hillary hasn't always met it. Indeed, it's become a Washington commonplace that when Mrs. Clinton arrived in the White House, she failed to understand that being the First

Lady was itself a job. Marilyn Quayle says, "It was a basic misunderstanding of the power and importance you can have in what some might call a traditional role of First Lady — a lack of understanding that this wasn't just cutting ribbons. My presumption is that she was given advice or pushed by feminists to the point where the traditional role of First Lady was denigrated." But, even to the most apt pupil, the culture of Washington — and, indeed, the White House — can be daunting. Susan Porter Rose, who was the director of scheduling for Mrs. Nixon and Mrs. Ford and the chief of staff for Mrs. Bush, is a savant on the subject, and she addresses the question with Jeeves-like discretion. "The place has its own sociology, and it's filled with banana peels and land mines," Porter Rose says. Another member of the Bush Administration talks about the shortage of "seeing eye dogs" on the Clintons' staff and goes on, "You have to remember that, in Washington, real estate and titles are everything. They are how you draw distinctions — one of the few ways, really. They *serve notice*. Mrs. Bush came in with one commissioned officer. Mrs. Clinton, on the other hand, came in with three — Maggie and two others. What this means is this: Going in, she told the world, 'This is a new day.' Not everyone was pleased." And Jan Piercy, an old friend of Hillary's from Wellesley who now sits on the board of the World Bank, hints, "There was also a kind of resistance in parts of the White House itself, a kind of ambivalence about Hillary's role."

When it comes to the subject of social diplomacy — to her performance in the "charm offensive," the tablecloth front — Hillary offers only a partial defense of her record. "Part of the urgency that my husband felt about the agenda he brought with him to Washington made all of us rush in and try to do things before we really understood how Washington worked," she says. "It's one thing to stand outside, as we did, and to look at it and to criticize it, but there really is a culture here, and it is something that I certainly did not understand, and would have spent more time trying to understand and would have tried to figure out better how to do what I wanted to do." Now, she says, "I would have gone at it differently. I would not have made some of the mistakes that I think we made, that got us on the wrong side of some of the perceptions from the very beginning." Still, Hillary clearly thinks that this culture has a lot to answer for, too. "I suddenly came to a place where perception is more important than it had ever been in my life — where I thought I was being painted in ways based almost on tea-leaf reading," she says. "But I finally realized this is serious business for the people who cover politics in this town and think about it, and so I had to pay at least some attention."

Certainly I've met Washingtonians who wonder whether Hillary the New Woman hasn't shortchanged Hillary the hostess. She's slightly nettled by the idea, and invokes the priorities of a mother. "I regret, for example, that I haven't had as much time to socialize or spend with friends. I don't get out a lot in Washington, and I didn't get out a lot in Little Rock, because when I have time that is not spent on my work and my public activities, I want to be with my family. I think *that's* one of the reasons why people say, 'Well, who is she? We don't know her.' I don't get out as much as many people do, because the years of childrearing go by so fast — I mean, Chelsea's going to be gone. I can go to dinner parties from now to kingdom come when she's in college and when she's grown up." She sounds philosophical. "You know, you pay a price no matter what decision you make."

As a working mother in the White House, Hillary says, "it has been very hard, because there wasn't any blueprint. I really didn't know what to do or what was expected. I really did feel that I was pretty much having to make it up as I went along. I made lots of mistakes. But by and large I think it was a necessary 'learning experience' — at least for me." She laughs at the euphemism. "I think for the country, too — we still seem to be learning together."

At the same time, she maintains that if she has come up short in the charm offensive it hasn't been for lack of trying. "I've tried to do all those things — we've tried very hard to be as hospitable as we can, we've entertained more people than anybody has ever entertained in the White House before." She shakes her head. "I think if there were something that I would do differently it would be to try earlier than I have to rezone my sense of privacy, so I could give people a broader view of who I am and what I do." Part of the trouble, though, is that who she is and what she does is itself hopelessly ill-defined — not so much divided as multiple.

She often refers to the book *Composing a Life*, by the anthropologist Mary Catherine Bateson, who is the daughter of Gregory Bateson and Margaret Mead. Reading it, I'm struck by a passage that must have had particular resonance for Hillary. "There has been a tendency to look ahead to some sort of utopia in which women will no longer be torn by the conflicting claims and desires that so often turn their pathways into zigzags or, at best, spirals," Bateson writes. "It would be easier to live with a greater clarity of ambition, to follow goals that beckon toward a single upward progression. But perhaps what women have to offer in the world today, in which men and women both must learn to deal with new orders of complexity and rapid change, lies in the very rejection of forced choices: work or home, strength or vulnerability, caring or competition, trust or questioning. Truth may not always be so simple."

Now Hillary Clinton has published a book of her own, *It Takes a Village*, that is all about parenting and politics, but though Chelsea makes an appearance in its pages, Hillary has been resolute about shielding her daughter from the glare of public politics. Mandy Grunwald, the media consultant, tells me of an inspiration she had for the 1992 Democratic National Convention. After the presentation of the short film, "The Man from Hope," Clinton's campaign biography in documentary form, the hall would go completely dark. Then out of the darkness, there would be a single spotlight on Chelsea, who would say, "I want to introduce the next President of the United States — my dad, Bill Clinton."

It had everything: not only drama but also, implicitly, an affirmation of family values. It would remind viewers at home that, whatever else he might be, this man was somebody's *daddy*. The crowd at Madison Square Garden would go wild. Home viewers, already softened up by an inspirational biopic, would get just a little misty. It was a surefire, time tested device, a perfect realization of the lump-in-the-throat magic of political theatre: *And a little child will lead them*. Mandy Grunwald explained her brainstorm to Chelsea's mother, who got it at once, and didn't hesitate to deliver her verdict. "Absolutely not," Hillary said. "I would *never* put my daughter in that position."

"And I felt horrible, crass, manipulative — everything people think of political consultants," Mandy Grunwald tells me. "Bad politics, good parenting," is how she describes the trade-off.

If you're as serious about it as Mrs. Clinton, being a mother, especially in the White House, demands a lot of time and energy. ("I wish Africa was dead!" Mrs. Jellyby's poor daughter is finally moved to exclaim.) But then so does being a wife. Can you really be both policy wonk and helpmeet? Barbara Bush says, "I had to have priorities, and my priorities were things in the private sector." By that, she means providing her husband with the sanctuary of a real home and also serving as her husband's sounding board and confidante: "safe" is the word she uses. "I think every person, man or woman, needs someone who is a safe person to talk to," she says. "In order to get that trust, you have to be safe, and I think I was that for George Bush." If all this sounds, to modern tastes, a bit *Kinder, Kirche, Küche*, you can argue that the role isn't gender-specific. Washington, Noonan reminds me, "is increasingly full of *women* who are in power and important, and married to *men* who are tough critics and advisors. It is wrong to think that this is necessarily a sexist set up."

And, while Hillary may not be "safe," in Mrs. Bush's sense of a neutral, nonpartisan sounding board, few doubt the intimacy of the Clintons' political relationship. "She is the intellectual half — the person he can always bounce ideas off," Ann Lewis says. Actually, I saw something of this dynamic last month, at a dinner where President Clinton was soliciting themes and ideas from a group of academics, mostly political theorists. You could tell when something was said that he took to be valuable, because he'd make eye contact with Hillary and nod, as if to say: make a note, let's discuss it afterward.

Maggie Williams puts it this way: "I used to think that she would be a great President, before I took this job, and she's certainly *smart* enough to run the country. But Hillary's intelligence is specific and concrete — she's task-oriented, she's a great problem solver. The President, on the other hand, is vision-oriented — he's obsessed with the grand design. They depend upon each other."

A onetime friend of theirs from law school says, "She and the President have a private arrangement that is based on power sharing — she is his equal and he acknowledges it. But they realized that the American people weren't ready for that, and so they are trying to do it without telling people. And that is what is creating this sense that they are hiding something." Williams, for her part, emphasizes the simple fact of companionship: "He doesn't have Haldeman. Leon Panetta is doing a brilliant job, but I don't believe they are close like Nixon and Haldeman were close. I think it's difficult for the President to have friends the way we have friends. He has a *best* friend, though, and that best friend is Hillary."

Of course, the nature of the Clintons' personal relationship has itself long been the subject of scrutiny and conjecture, some of it uncharitable. One fixture of the Washington scene says, "She was the one who was always right and always superior — he was the fuckup," and argues that Hillary's troubles have marked a change in the dynamic: "When Bill Clinton came out to make a comment at that press conference about Bill Safire, he looked like a happy man. He didn't look mad. He was really thrilled: 'My wife's screwing up again and I get to be the good guy, I get to be the morally superior one in this relationship.'"

The view is different from inside. People who have spent a lot of time around the two speak of moments both of tension and of tenderness. Maggie Williams admits, "Sometimes I'm embarrassed to be in the same room with them. They are very affectionate with each other. Sometimes the President will call different members of her staff throughout the day and ask, 'How's my girl? How's my girl doing?'"

A former close associate of theirs tells me, "All her friends are going to work in New York and Washington law firms, she's a hot-shot lawyer, she goes to Arkansas? There is one, and only one, reason for it: she's crazy-ass in love with him — and it is still true. And, if you see them together, you know. She gets that goofy look on her face. She lights up around him. It's the thing people don't understand about her at all — they just don't see that side." I've noticed it, too. Hillary reminds me of the girl in high school who was brainy and pretty, friends with the cheerleaders but not one herself, the nerds all admired her, but she was into the jocks. In Bill Clinton, Hillary found a big, lumbering guy who happened to be an intellectual equal. One law-school friend talks of it as "a magic combination."

But if Mrs. Clinton were simply the President's private counselor and public hostess she would not have become the lightening rod she is. The fact remains that the First Lady's greatest reversal of fortune occurred not in the realm of the salad fork and the demitasse but in the rough-and-tumble of the political arena, where the Administration's health care plan met its demise. If Hillary Clinton is a wife and a mother, she is also a working woman, with an office suite in the Old Executive Office Building. To pay a visit there is to be reminded that Mrs. Clinton is a professional — a fact that has proved both her greatest asset and her greatest liability.

In Hillary's offices — Suite 100 on the first floor of the O.E.O.B. — an item evidently clipped from the personal ads has been blown up, mounted, and hung on the wall:

> HILLARY RODHAM CLINTON TYPE SOUGHT by single Jewish attorney, 31, who is bright, witty, sincere, and cute. There's nothing sexier than an intelligent, powerful, an successful female who knows what she wants.

It's a clue to the ethos of the place. Fifteen of the 16 people who work for Hillary are women, and, despite the 16-foot ceilings, there's an almost dorm-room air of camaraderie in Suite 100. Both on and off the record, members or Hillary's staff are quick to acknowledge it; many have their own theories on the merits of what they view as a managerial style.

Earlier, I had breakfast with Maggie Williams, at the Hay-Adams Hotel: she had her hair in a great rope coiled around her head, like a Yoruba headdress, and was wearing a blue turtleneck, sweat-pants, and black snow boots. "She allows you to be a woman in the modern way but also in the traditional way," Williams told me. "Like my mother always says, there is just something basically different between women and men. She's the one who'll lend you jewelry for that special date." Another woman close to Hillary says, "Hillary's the sort of friend who'd undo an extra button on your blouse when you are about to go on a date. She wants to know who you're going out with." Ideally, a single Jewish attorney, 31, who is bright, witty, sincere, and cute.

"She's a real girl," Mandy Grunwald says. "There's a part of her that is constantly commenting on whether you got your hair cut, how it looks, your clothes." And sometimes she plays Emma Woodhouse. Grunwald recounts, "Hillary and I were talking about a man I knew who worked for the Senate, and she said, 'He's really good-looking. Does he go out with anyone?' And I told her that he did. She said she was disappointed, because she was thinking about him for one of the single women on her staff. She was matchmaking."

"Hillary's approach is closer to circle or matrix management than to hierarchical management," Ann Lewis, who has been walking me through the cluttered O.E.O.B. suite, says. "Women have a different management style. You encourage people to sit around the table and contribute — and she will do that. She will sit around the table, too, and listen and take suggestions from people and give suggestions back." And while Hillary's staff is known to be fiercely loyal, Maggie Williams suggests that this, too, may be a sex-linked trait: "I think women tend to be loyal. I just think we work differently; I think we're more task-oriented, more cooperative. And she's a big delegator. I mean, she's got people that she trusts. Not that we're a bunch of lemmings." It's a phrase she has used before. Williams has been threatened by Senator Alfonse D'Amato, who is chairman of the Senate Whitewater Committee, with perjury charges; one witness told the Senate panel that shortly after Vincent Foster's death Williams had removed folders from his office, and she testified that she hadn't. So when she says she isn't a "lemming" she means that, all loyalty aside, she isn't someone who would perjure herself to protect her boss. (Amid her own recent travails, Williams, too, has been trying to practice the discipline of gratitude. She explains, "I try and be grateful for the fact that there is an Al D'Amato. Having him at such a distinct extreme from everything that I am or want to be or that my people are — that brings a certain peace to me when I see him.")

The Hillary Clinton that Williams describes is more den mother than martinet. "We all have our disagreements with Hillary, on policy and on procedure and all kinds of things," she says. "And you *can* disagree with her." Williams previously worked with Marian Wright Edelman at the Children's Defense Fund, and remains devoted to her, despite a certain *froideur* between the Edelmans and the Clintons these days. Still, she finds the contrast in executive styles to be instructive. "Marian tends to know how she wants to solve a problem — she's very fixed on it," Williams says. "Hillary wants the opposition view, always, because she might even adopt some of it. She can be *convinced*. She can be convinced even when it comes to things she thinks she knows everything about."

So Williams' experience does seem to complicate Hillary's bad-cop reputation. "The interesting thing is that people need to box her and have her be one way for all time," Williams says. "But the idea that she is the enforcer is based on, one, her having concerns about things, two, speaking her mind, three, having people call and ask her opinion about things. Now, I think that Harold Ickes — I mean, who would mess around with Harold Ickes? I think that people are more afraid of Harold than they are of Hillary."

Besides, would Harold Ickes, a deputy White House chief of staff, ever help you preen for a date? I'm struck, somehow, by that, detail about the unbuttoned blouse. It's an image of Hillary, I realize, that runs counter to many of the stereotypes people have of her — and, sadly, to many of the stereotypes people have of feminists in general. Understandably, the true nature, of feminism is a subject that both Hillary and most of her associates have strong feelings about. Ann Lewis says to me, with some indignation, "To this day, I read articles by women who say, 'I've always stayed home and taken care of my family, and I don't like to be put down by the women's movement.' And I think, Hey, *I'm* the women's movement. It would never occur to me to put down a woman who takes care of a family. I spent years of my life at home with children. That's hard work." And Maggie Williams says, "This is about choice, isn't it? Let's face it — when white feminists were talking about getting jobs and being in the workplace and coming out of the home, my mother was saying, 'God, I wish I could stay home.' Maybe this is the maturity of both the country and its movements, but they should be about choice." Hillary herself tells me of a phrase she picked up when she was in Belfast, meeting with women who had been working to unite people across the religious divide. "One of the women said she considered herself a 'family feminist.' I loved that phrase, because I believe that, if you are a human being, one of your highest responsibilities is to the next generation. I mean, I have fought all my life for women to have the right, to make the decisions that are best for them, and for me that included getting married, having a child."

Yet Hillary is, demographically speaking, a white upper-middle-class female baby boomer, which is to say that feminism has carved out the very contours of her life. For feminists, moreover, the '60s and '70s were a time of laying tracks, not coasting down the rails. Or so she quickly came to recognize. We're talking about Yale Law School, where she got her law degree, and where I was briefly enrolled not long afterwards. "When I went to take the law-school admissions test, I went with a friend of mine from Wellesley," she recalls. "We had to go in to Harvard to take the test, and we were in a huge room, and there were very few women there, and we sat at these desks waiting for the proctors or whoever to come and all the young men around us started to harass us. They started to say, 'What do you think you're doing? If you get into law school, you're going to take my position. You've got no right to do this. Why don't you go home and get married?'" She sits up very straight. "I got into Harvard and I got into Yale, and actually I went to a cocktail reception at the Harvard Law School with a young man who was, I think, a second-year Harvard Law student. And he introduced me to one of the legendary Harvard Law professors by saying, 'Professor So-and-so, this is Hillary Rodham. She's trying to decide between us and our nearest competitor.' And this man, with his three-piece suit and his bow tie, looked at me and said, 'First of all, we have no nearest competitor, and, secondly, we don't need any more women.' And that's how I decided to go to Yale."

In the early '70s, Yale Law School was itself no enclave of feminist enlightenment. In those days, for instance, the law-school film society was famous all over the campus for its soft-porn evenings, and though I never made it to the screenings myself, I somehow can't imagine the law school playing host to an event like that today. I remind her of that bygone porn festival, since it might be taken as at least one measure of a changing social climate. "*I* never went," the First Lady says, straight-faced. "You and Clarence Thomas must have gone." I'm just about to protest when she starts laughing.

There's a small shelf of books in Suite 100 of the O.E.O.B. where you'll find some titles that are almost comically appropriate: *Public Like a Frog*, by Jean Houston; *The Pursuit of Love & Love in a Cold Climate*, by Nancy Mitford; *The Norton Book of Women's Lives*, edited by Phyllis Rose; *All That She Can Be*, by Carol J. Eagle and Carol Colman; and *First Ladies*, by Margaret B. Klapthor. Just two books — *The Logic of Health-Care Reform*, by Paul Starr, and *Making Managed Healthcare Work*, by Peter Boland — betray what was the all-consuming project of Hillary's first year in Washington. Her plan for health care reform began as triumph and ended as ignominy; and, like investigators at the scene of a high-tech disaster, political analysts are still trying to sort through the wreckage.

These days, when Hillary refers to the health-plan debacle she speaks of the missteps she made. Indeed, for someone often accused of being obnoxiously self-certain ("She has not once said, 'I made a mistake,' there's never a sense of her being a fallible human being," Arianna Huffington maintains), she can sound practically Chinese in her self-criticism. "Certainly here in Washington one of the big mistakes was going along with the recommendation that we shouldn't brief reporters even off the record, because there was a legitimate concern, from both people in Congress and here in the Administration, that trying to put together a health care plan to meet our original date, which was May 1st, was a huge undertaking. Everybody felt that was going to be hard even under the best of circumstances, and they worried that talking about it as we went along would create all kinds of false expectations or misunderstandings. But I think in retrospect that was the wrong call — we should have gone ahead and risked whatever problems might have come from that, in favor of having a much more open relationship with the press from the very beginning. You know, you follow the advice you get, trying to make sense of it, but when you're in a new environment, as we were, you don't really know the players and you don't understand the history and the nuance."

Some fault the complexity of the proposal, which made it hard to represent to voters and easy to misrepresent to them. Ironically, its complexity was a result of its essential conservatism: the constraint of leaving intact, as much as possible, preexisting structures of health care and insurance. Others blame not the plan itself but the way it was created: out of the head of Zeus, so it seemed, rather than the loins of the legislature. Even Brooke Shearer, who was Hillary Clinton's aide during the 1992 campaign and now directs the White House Fellows program, points to a certain neglect of political courtship. "I think that, when you do something as large as that, you would probably want to try and speak to individual constituencies first to get their support." Less sympathetic voices portray Hillary Clinton as having sabotaged it through her own crusading intransigence.

In truth, had the Administration done nothing other than win the fight for universal, or near-universal, health coverage — no matter how it calibrated the mechanisms of employer mandates, business alliances, managed competition, and spending caps — it could have rested on its laurels. That one measure would have gone some distance toward addressing the other high-profile items on the Clinton agenda — reducing the deficit and reforming welfare. (Bringing medical spending under control would have made it easier to arrive at a balanced budget in the foreseeable future. And research had shown that for many welfare recipients a major barrier to employment is the forfeiture of medical coverage, which they would otherwise not be able to afford.) By the same token, Republican strategists swiftly figured out that passage of the Clinton plan, however modified, might have devastating electoral consequences: as William Kristol wrote in an influential memo, the plan would "strike a punishing blow against Republican claims to defend the middle-class by restraining government." A receptive atmosphere quickly soured as Republicans scrambled to enlist the firepower of business interests, some of which had earlier been sympathetic to reform. "In an odd role reversal," the political journalist E. J. Dionne, Jr., observes, "conservative Republican leaders *lobbied* the business *lobbyists*." The rest is an unedifying chapter in the history of negative advertising.

Both Hillary Clinton and her detractors are correct in pointing to mistakes she made — in the planning phase at the O.E.O.B. and in the lobbying phase on the Hill. Yet so nearly perfect an alignment of partisan and industry interests is hard to defeat in the best of circumstances; and to view the outcome as a referendum on Hillary's character is to indulge either vanity or spite. "Every President who has touched it has got burned in one way or the other because the interests involved are so powerful," Hillary points out.

Maggie Williams is blunter. "Any time you start down the road of messing with people's money, they have to kill you," she says. What she's talking about is, among other things; character assassination. In her view, the failure was in no small part related to the politics of perception: "First of all, health care defined her instead of her coming out and defining who she was." What should they have done? "I probably would have done three or four months of people just getting to know her, who she was, people getting a sense of her and her complexities." William Kristol — who has been variously praised and deplored as the man who did more than anyone else to derail the proposal —believes that Hillary "actually helped get their health care plan off to a stronger start than it might have had if it had just been championed by some Cabinet Secretary." In his view, "she has gotten an easier ride than she deserved as the Administration's main spokesman on health care — at least, for the first few months." Ironically, Kristol's remarks dovetail with something Ira Magaziner — who worked closely with Hillary on the health care plan and shared much of the public blame for its failure — tells me about those first few months. "She impressed the heck out of everybody and you could see alarm bells going off all over town, in terms of the opponents of this plan saying that as long as her popularity remains that high and she is that impressive, we're not going to beat it," he says. "All sorts of stories began to get back to us about meetings among the opposition about how to discredit her. And the Whitewater thing and the commodities thing and so on were, in part, the means that were used."

If a year of intensive research, legislative draftsmanship, and political lobbying failed to result in health care reform, it did much to promulgate the so-called Hillary problem. William Kristol says, "There is a problem with asking your wife — who has not been elected, who has not been selected for the staff, can't be fired, hasn't been confirmed — to take charge of a huge policy area. I think that hurt in some way that is hard to put one's finger on." He adds, "It was too monarchial — it was like the Queen gets to do stuff because she's married to the King." And Marilyn Quayle says, "You're not breaking ground by being appointed by your husband to a quasi-Cabinet-level position; that's just getting an office through your husband."

Mrs. Bush, too, takes a dim view of the situation, though she seems to see it departure less from the Constitution than from political etiquette. "If you take on a job you've got to be accountable for it," she says. "And obviously that was a great mistake, because nothing happened and it caused great ill will. And there were other people who were appointed and confirmed by the Senate to do that very job — I would think that you would be already causing friction with the people who were hired for the job. I would never have done that, nor would George have asked me to."

He might well have asked Elizabeth Dole, though. Mrs. Dole is someone who, like Hillary, is an accomplished professional and, like Hillary, has been seen as more of a political animal than a domestic one. She has announced her determination to stay on as president of the American Red Cross if her husband is elected President. But there's no comparison between the role she imagines for herself and the one Hillary has taken on, Mrs. Dole observes: "Hers involved what percentage of our G.N.P.? Quite a large percentage. It was the whole health care system for America, and it was very much a different focus. It was inside the White House." She adds, "You see, I've *served* as a Cabinet member in two Presidents' Cabinets — I don't want to sit in on Cabinet meetings."

And yet the Hillary problem does have the air of something slightly factitious. It's easy to point to previous First Ladies who have wielded significant power (and Hillary notes that "you can go back and find Mrs. Taft consulting with Cabinet members, Eleanor Roosevelt doing everything, Mrs. Carter appointed to chair a commission"). More to the point, perhaps, is the fact that voters do not elect a President's friends, either, yet they often have an incalculable sway over the President's Administration. Nor is the position of White House Chief of staff; arguably the most powerful one in most Administrations, subject to Senate confirmation. Hillary's sex may well prevent us from seeing how familiar the role she plays really is in Presidential history. As Garry Wills has argued, the best parallel is with such Presidential companions as FDR's confidant Louis Howe or Dwight D. Eisenhower's brother Milton. Then, too, it isn't so obvious that, as the familiar claim goes, "you can't fire her," when one could argue that this is, in effect, just what the President did.

To judge from the way many conservatives talk, what they'd really like to do is *impeach* her. Some Republicans who weathered the Senate hearings of the Nixon era may have decided that one good scandal deserves another. Watergate, of course, had all the hallmarks of the modern scandal: it was, in essence, not about the precipitating illegality, but about the act of covering it up. Whitewater, in turn, is the perfect postmodern scandal: the latest and most serious charges allege an act of covering up an act of covering up, while so far nobody has unearthed an original sin.

It was in the 1992 primaries that the Jerry Brown campaign first raised the question about a possible conflict of interest posed by Hillary Clinton's having represented Madison Guaranty Savings & Loan before a state agency. You'll recall that it prompted her most notorious comment of the Campaign: "I suppose I could have stayed home, baked cookies, and had teas, but what I decided was to fulfill my profession." (With some asperity, Marilyn Quayle tells me, "If the press had done its job when Jerry Brown first brought it up, we wouldn't *be* in this position.") And yet you might argue that from the perspective of modern feminism a practicing attorney married to a governor is in something of a double bind. On the one hand, Mickey Kaus, writing in *The New Republic*, has accused Bill Clinton's wife of being a "false feminist" for hitching her star to his. On the other hand, if you are an attorney and you continue your professional career in a poor Southern state where your husband is the chief executive (and where the prospects of patronage are, let us say, loosely bounded), you will have a difficult time avoiding, at the least, the appearance of impropriety. Political candidates and officeholders can be expected to accentuate the positive and minimize the unseemly; but was a line crossed? It would be one thing if Hillary were found guilty of criminal misconduct. The findings, however, are likely to be far more equivocal. We are alas, all fallen creatures, and politicians are more fallen than most. (It would be hard to explain to a Martian why what PACs do, for instance, isn't just a form of legalized bribery.) So at the end of the day you need to decide not only how much of the opposition's case is true but also how much it matters. "Follow the money," the old muckraker's shibboleth has it. But one place the money trail leads is to right-wing millionaires like Richard Scaife, who have lavishly funded "investigative journalism" into the Clintons' finances, Vincent Foster's death, and the like.

Now, for all we know, Hillary Clinton may be guilty of everything she's accused of and more. You might say the point is that we *don't* know. And it's in those dark gaps in our knowledge that the political unconscious makes itself felt: you can't tell a gun from a cigarette by the smoke alone. Which inference you prefer depends on which story you prefer — assuming you've been given one. (What's with those mysteriously rematerialized files, anyway? Some free advice from Aristotle's *Rhetoric*: "A likely impossibility is always preferable to an unconvincing possibility.")

If you're a Republican, of course, you may find poetic justice in the Senate hearing, the subpoena, the federal investigator, the Independent Counsel. A conservative friend of mine sees instructive similarities in the prosecution of Michael Deaver. Starting in 1986, Deaver, as a prominent member of the Reagan Administration who subsequently cashed in as a high-powered lobbyist, found himself the subject of a House investigation into whether he had violated "revolving door" rules meant to discourage profiteering from public service. There's real doubt whether, technically speaking, he had actually violated any such rules, but there's no doubt that he let himself be pictured on the cover of *Time* in a lavish-looking limousine, and holding a cellular phone to his ear. Deaver had become the symbol of a hated political class — of the get-rich-quick culture of Reaganism — and it was for the collective guilt of that class that he to be punished. (The original charges remain unproved, though Deaver, having been flushed into a self-serving fib, was ultimately convicted of lying to Congress and a federal grand jury.) It's true that Deaver, by playing fast and loose with the ethics rules, made himself vulnerable to the inquisition in the first place. But it's also true that Mike Deaver, in the end, went down for being Mike Deaver. Without granting any moral equivalence, you can accept the claim that Hillary Clinton — by, for example, her relationship with people like Jim McDougal — made herself vulnerable to the toxic combination of an instinctively adversarial press and the conservative attack machine, and yet you can also recognize that Hillary Clinton, New Class hero, has been targeted because she is an emblem of an elite that so many wish to humble and bring low. Senator D'Amato's zeal stems from the perfectly transparent, and understandable, desire to proclaim, "See — they're no better than us."

"Modern liberals like Hillary thought Republicans were hounded by special prosecutors for 20 years because Republicans were bad and deserved it," Peggy Noonan tells me. "I truly feel she did not have the wit to understand that the prosecutorial atmosphere that she and her friends unleashed and encouraged would engulf them, too. You know, for 20 years now I've been seeing Democrats torment Republicans. Remember when Ray Donovan, the Labor Secretary, was exonerated of all charges and came out with the great statement of the '80s: 'Where do I go to get my reputation back?'" For a moment, I hear a flicker of compassion in her voice: "I can see her as a woman, and I have a sense of horror for her —

for what she's going through. I just think it's awful." Then she pauses to consider. "I don't mean it's *unfair*."

Hillary's latest bouts of bad press do suggest someone whose sense of public relations is less than finely honed. Take the miscalculation that led to what Katha Pollitt has dubbed "Thankyougate." It started with the decision to hire Barbara Feinman to help out with the research for and writing of *It Takes a Village* (and not since Clark Clifford's memoirs has the publication a book had such exquisitely bad timing). Feinman was a journalism instructor at Georgetown who had previously worked on books by Ben Bradlee and Bob Woodward, among others; but although her involvement in the project was announced publicly last spring, Hillary Clinton decided not to name her — or anyone else — in the book's acknowledgments. Sally Quinn says, "All she expected was 'Many thanks to Barbara Feinman, whose tireless efforts were greatly appreciated.' She would have died and gone to Heaven."

In fact, Thankyougate was only the unhappy outcome of a less than smooth collaboration. The manuscript's original due date was Labor Day. At that point, about eight or nine chapters — which Feinman had helped to organize, draft, and edit — were submitted to the publisher. According to Feinman, she was told that her work was satisfactory, and she subsequently left for a three-week vacation in Italy. A White House aide says that Hillary was appreciative of Feinman's efforts but was not fully satisfied with the direction of the book, and the bulk of the writing, revising, and editing took place after Labor Day — that is, after Feinman's involvement with the project had largely ceased. Then matters got a little stickier. There were discussions between Simon & Schuster and Feinman's agent about whether Feinman would be paid in full. "She was absolutely distraught," Sally Quinn says. "For one thing, she is planning to adopt a baby by herself, because she's 36. So she's saving up all this money to go to China and adopt a baby girl. That was part of this little nest egg that she had." (Other, associates of Feinman reject any suggestion of financial extremity.) In the end, Feinman was paid when the final manuscript was delivered. Even so, it would be understandable if Feinman felt that she hadn't been treated with the dignity that a writer and researcher with her credentials was entitled to; and it would be understandable, too, if the failure to thank her by name might have added insult to injury.

It Takes a Village, we should be clear, really is Hillary's book. Nobody denies that its themes and subjects have preoccupied Hillary for far longer than she's had a publishing contract; whatever its failings, this book isn't something that could simply have been sent out for, like Chinese food. But it's also hard to argue when Sally Quinn says, "Hillary versus Barbara Feinman is a big loser, P.R.wise." She goes on, "Barbara's a single woman, who lives alone in a one-bedroom apartment off Dupont Circle. Not only that, but she has been a researcher at *The Washington Post*, and all her best friends are journalists. Everyone loves her, and she knows every journalist in town. This is what I'm saying about Hillary being book-smart and street-stupid." Indeed, out of all the writers and researchers for hire in the world, why choose one who is closer friends with your critics than with you? Was the choice meant, in fact, to be a conciliatory gesture, a peace offering — giving a plum and profitable assignment to a favorite of the *Post*'s illuminati? If so, the attempt went disastrously wrong.

It would, of course, be absurd to look for the source of the First Lady's plight as if it were the Nile: some of her troubles have been created or else wildly amplified by the formidable machinery of the right-wing media; some of them are, as she admits, of her own making; some of them are, no doubt, the result of well-meant actions by friends; and some reflect the mischief of personal (rather than ideological) antagonists. You might say it takes a village to demonize a First Lady. And demonized she has been, even in the mainstream press: a recent *Newsweek* story suggested that, to Mrs. Clinton, Madison and McDougal must have looked "like Banquo's ghost," which would make her Macbeth. In the Harvard library, you can find at least three books on each of the past four First Ladies, but only Hillary is the subject of a book entitled *Big Sister Is Watching You*. The helpful subtitle: "Hillary Clinton and the White House Feminists Who Now Control America — and Tell the President What to Do.") A recent issue of a New York weekly describes the First Lady as "a scumbag, a hand job and knife-in-the-back Babbitt from the depths of the American horror." Then, there was that Safire column.

All, this has led some to wonder whether there is a qualitative difference at least in the tone of the coverage Hillary Clinton has received. And yet she is plainly not the first wife of a President to suffer such treatment. William Safire on Hillary Clinton is tame stuff compared to the columnist Westbrook Pegler on Eleanor Roosevelt. And Peggy Noonan says, "I thought Nancy Reagan was damned for everything. They said she had fat legs, they said she was a bad mother, they said she had an affair with Frank Sinatra — on the front page of the *Times*. They said she manipulated her husband, they said she had a political agenda, they said she fired Don Regan, they said she was a bully and a cheat." Hillary Clinton herself prefers to speak of broader trends: "I don't think there's anything that has happened to me that is, frankly, very new, but I thank that the environment in which it's happening is significantly different, even different from the 1980s." And she cites a study of Presidential press coverage by the political scientist Thomas Patterson, who found that, in 1960, 75 percent of the evaluative references to Kennedy and Nixon were positive, while in 1992 only 40 percent of the references to Bush and Clinton were positive. Elizabeth Dole tells me, "I think there's a point where there *are* excesses. You don't want to drive talented, capable people away from public service, and I think that probably is happening in some cases today."

But the negativity also reflects the stresses of ideological realignments, of which Clintonism may be the most visible sign. When Hillary Rodham was still an undergraduate, a friend and mentor of hers from home wrote her a letter questioning whether "someone can be a Burkean realist about history and human nature and at the same time have liberal sentiments and visions." Journalists have occasionally noted her response: "It is an interesting question you posed — can one be a mind conservative and a heart liberal?" The question these days is how to be a mind liberal and a heart conservative — how to be a technocrat with values. To judge from Hillary Clinton's pronouncements, you do that by reviving a tradition of civic republicanism which has been in partial eclipse for the past half century. In *It Takes a Village*, for example, she writes with sympathy about "character education," about William Bennett and C. DeLores Tucker's campaign against violent lyrics, about teenage abstinence, about civic responsibility and the virtues of voluntarism. In conversation too, many of her points of reference are social scientists whose findings tend to affirm civic culture as against rights-based liberalism. She'll talk, fluently, about the psychologist Claude Steele (and his theory of stereotype vulnerability) or the feminist educator Carol Gilligan (and her work on the gendered nature of moral epistemology) or the political scientist Robert Putnam (and his neo-Tocquevillean research on "social capital" and democracy). So when Mrs. Clinton called herself a conservative in the true sense of the word, she wasn't necessarily playing word games. The Clinton Administration is often described as soft, floating, indistinct, unformed — predicates that do a rather good job of describing the amoeba, that protean creature which kills by engulfing and assimilating its prey. I'd guess that to its unicellular fellows the bloblike amoeba must seem a silly thing — until they discover they're inside it. This is the politics of preemption — and if you are its target you must find it profoundly unnerving. It's why the enmity among ideological disputants can escalate even as their political differences narrow (and its why the Administration's moves toward the right are experienced by Republicans not as conciliation but as coöptation: they see not an outstretched hand but the covetous pseudopod of an amoeba).

Still, there's no politics without people; and, wherever those broader trends are leading, this particular First Lady really does seem an especially inviting target as all those comments about her "air of moral superiority" suggest. It's true that she can sound sappily pious, but then her job wasn't supposed to be First Ironist; we have Letterman for that. When I raise, inevitably, the subject of coping, she touches on her developing spirituality, on the role of religion in her life. It's just the kind of talk that makes journalists groan inwardly; but I sympathize, since I'm religious, too, though I try to keep quiet about it. (In Cambridge, where I work, religiosity is accounted one of those conditions that suggest some lapse of hygiene on the part of those afflicted, as with worms or lice.) Still, few spectacles are more satisfying than paragons of sanctimony getting their comeuppance. And then that spectre of Mrs. Jellyby has followed her around like a ghostly afterimage on a cheap TV set.

It is often said that in ancient times a man who stood accused of breaking an urn that he'd borrowed from a neighbor was permitted to make the following tripartite defense: that it was already broken when he borrowed it, that it wasn't broken when he returned it, and that he never borrowed it in the first place. The popular prosecution of the First Lady's character has availed itself of a similar latitude. In the course of a single conversation, I have been assured that Hillary is cunning and manipulative but also crass, clueless, and stunningly impolitic; that she is a hopelessly woolly-headed do-gooder and, at heart, a hardball litigator; that she is a base opportunist and a zealot convinced that God is on her side. What emerges is a cultural inventory of villainy rather than a plausible depiction of an actual person. George Orwell once wrote, with some wisdom, "Saints should always be judged guilty until they are proven innocent." At times, it seems that Hillary Clinton has been labeled a saint in order that she may be found guilty. The cover of a recent newsweekly emblazoned "SAINT OR SINNER?" under her photograph. Are those really the choices?

"When we say, 'Tell me what So-and-So is really like,'" the literary critic Harold Bloom has observed, "what we generally mean is 'Tell me the worst that can he said of that person.'" It's a phenomenon that is easier to identify than to escape, and it suffuses not only journalism but the culture that journalism serves. And the journalist's profound fear of being gulled only confirms him in his dualist creed — his dark conviction that character is a matter of surfaces and depths, appearance and reality, and that the "deepest" layer flatters least. So he offers the skull beneath the skin and wonders why Americans blench and say they hate politics. In Thomas Mann's story "Felix Krull," there's an episode in which the young Felix is taken by his parents to see a famous actor perform on the stage. He's the perfect leading man — captivating, graceful, surpassingly handsome, an image of perfection — and the audience gazes upon him "rapt in self-forgetful absorption." Afterward, Felix is brought backstage to meet him. Without the artificial lighting and thick makeup, the actor turns out to be repulsive in every way — sweaty, charmless, and carpeted with "horrible pimples, red-rimmed, suppurating, some of them even bleeding." Felix is devastated. Then, mulling things over, he comes to realize his error in thinking that he has seen through the veil to the reality beneath. "For when you come to think about it," he muses, "which is the 'real' shape of the glowworm: the insignificant little creature crawling about on the flat of your hand, or the poetic spark that swims through the summer night? Who would presume to say?"

Granted, the First Lady neither sparkles nor suppurates, but why are we so certain that reality is always to be found behind her public persona, her stated political views, opinions, and values? Why are we so certain that the truth is what has been concealed, and not, like the purloined letter, what's in plain sight? "I don't think you can ever know anybody else," Hillary Clinton has said. "And I certainly don't think you can know anybody else through the crude instruments available to us of exposing bits and pieces of somebody's life." Indeed, is it so obvious that the wheeler-dealer (and breadwinner) at the Rose Law Firm is more authentic than the woman who spoke so movingly at the women's conference in Beijing this fall? Which better represents the content of her life?

If you fear and loathe the press, it will sense that and punish you for it. At the same time, good will as a mental discipline strikes me as little more plausible than gratitude as a mental discipline. Logan Pearsall Smith, the great Quaker aphorist, once declared, "If we treat people too long with that pretended liking called politeness, we shall find it hard not to like them in the end." To complete the thought you can then hope that the liking becomes reciprocal. It's advice that might have profited another Quaker aphorist, Richard Nixon. Work on appearances, and hope that the rest follows. I'm always brought up short when people talk about Hillary's feelings toward the press as a "mistake" — the implication being that affect, too, is just a matter of strategy.

Try putting yourself in her place. During the 1992 campaign, the mainstream press attends closely to the issue of "bimbo eruptions" while the supermarket tabloids cover the story of your husband's supposed black progeny and Gennifer Flowers discusses his sexual prowess in a magazine with a circulation considerably larger than this one's. Months after you become First Lady, you spend two weeks with your dying father, and television reporters stake out the hospital, turning a personal crisis into another media spectacle; a prominent political commentator calls colleagues to spread the rumor that you've been spotted in the White House making love with a female veterinarian; you appear on "20/20" to find yourself closely interrogated about whether you hurled a lamp, or possibly a Bible, at your husband; a best-selling roman à clef depicts the steely wife of a Clintonian candidate enjoying a one-night stand with a campaign aide. And that's just a sample. Wouldn't you entitled to wonder why your involvement in a mammogram initiative that will save many thousands of lives gets scant coverage, while, say your trading in cattle futures 15 years ago takes center stage? Hillary Clinton can't help sounding utterly self-serving when she tells me she'd like people to look at her "and say, you know, what really matters is that for 25 years she's cared about kids and that's been a consistent theme, and maybe I should learn about that, instead of 'Omigosh, she's changed her hairdo again.'" But she may well have a point.

"I'm heartsick about what I'm watching now," Jan Piercy tells me. "We achieved something that I will be proud of until the day I die, and I'm watching how quickly it comes apart. I know profoundly, in ways now that I will never forget, just how deeply divided we are." Piercy was struck by an argument Hillary made when the Gennifer Flowers scandal broke: "She was saying, 'There have got to be boundaries.' It's even harder now. We've got to talk about holding people in public life accountable but allowing them their private life. There have got to be boundaries, some standards, a civility."

The larger problem is that our political discourse contains a stark contradiction. We continue to regard symbolism as subterfuge, even while acknowledging it as an essential instrument of politics. We recognize that politicians, in part, govern by their utterances, the values they promulgate, the image they project. (In dim light, it's hard to distinguish between George Will's statecraft-as-soulcraft and Michael Lerner's polities of meaning.) At the same time, for us village explainers image is less to be seen than to be seen through. Politics is for other people.

"Some of the personal attack leveled against me is a not very veiled attempt to undermine the positions that I have worked on and stood for," Hillary says. "The people who hold the view of exalted individualism and think that the market can solve all our problems are not so confident in their position that they don't feel it necessary to attack anyone who has a contrary point of view. And then I've made mistakes and I've engendered some criticism, I think justifiably, for things that I said or did or didn't handle well. So it's a combination of all that." Her gaze drifts off toward the map, with its color-coded demarcation of the liberated zones and the Axis-controlled holdouts. "We're becoming, as a culture, very hard; very cold and sterile in lots of ways, partly because of technology and global competition. So, no matter how one defines one's political or ideological identity, I think all of us have to reach down and redefine our human identity first and foremost." The alternative, after all, is that others will define our human identity for us.

Elsewhere in the building, policy papers are being drafted and re-drafted, numbers are being crunched and massaged, speeches are being punched up or toned down, Here we sit in the gloom of the late afternoon, and Mrs. Clinton, by way of demonstration, is looking, with willed gratitude at the bowl of pink roses on the long mahogany table. The discipline of gratitude requires noticing things you normally wouldn't and not noticing things you normally would. "I don't even read what people mostly say about me," she maintains, in her best pack-up-your-troubles tone. "I figure that'll all wash out historically, and a lot of this kind of day-by-day stuff doesn't amount to very much. And, in fact, I look at each day's news and I try to think, What will be important in five years, or 50 years?" Not those roses, which, on close inspection, are already beginning to fade. History vindicates, of course, but it can equally condemn, ignore, equivocate. Much depends on who writes it.

— ***Henry Louis Gates, Jr.*** is the Chair of the Afro-American Studies Department and Director of the W. E. B. Du Bois Institute for Afro-American Studies at Harvard University. He is the author of many articles for magazines including *The New Yorker*, *Time* and *The New Republic*. His most recent book is *Wonders of the African World*, the companion book for the PBS series.

Remarks at the 150th Anniversary of the First Women's Rights Convention

Hillary Rodham Clinton

THANK YOU FOR GATHERING here in such numbers for this important celebration. I want to thank Governor Pataki and Congresswoman Slaughter and all the elected officials who are here with us today. I want to thank Mary Anne and her committee for helping to organize such a great celebration. I want to thank Bob Stanton and the entire Park Service staff for doing such an excellent job with the historic site. I want to thank our choirs. I thought the choirs really added; I want to thank our singers whom we've already heard from and will hear from because this is a celebration and we need to think about it in such terms.

But for a moment, I would like you to take your minds back a hundred and fifty years. Imagine if you will that you are Charlotte Woodward, a nineteen-year-old glove maker working and living in Waterloo. Everyday you sit for hours sewing gloves together, working for small wages you cannot even keep, with no hope of going on in school or owning property, knowing that if you marry, your children and even the clothes on your body will belong to your husband.

But then one day in July, 1848, you hear about a women's rights convention to be held in nearby Seneca Falls. It's a convention to discuss the social, civil, and religious conditions and rights of women. You run from house to house and you find other women who have heard the same news. Some are excited, others are amused or even shocked, and a few agree to come with you, for at least the first day.

When that day comes, July 19, 1848, you leave early in the morning in your horse-drawn wagon. You fear that no one else will come; and at first, the road is empty, except for you and your neighbors. But suddenly, as you reach a crossroads, you see a few more wagons and carriages, then more and more all going towards Wesleyan Chapel. Eventually you join the others to form one long procession on the road to equality.

Who were the others traveling that road to equality, traveling to that convention? Frederick Douglass, the former slave and great abolitionist, was on his way there and he described the participants as "few in numbers, moderate in resources, and very little known in the world. The most we had to connect us was a firm commitment that we were in the right and a firm faith that the right must ultimately prevail." In the wagons and carriages, on foot or horseback, were women like Rhoda Palmer. Seventy years later in 1918, at the age of one-hundred and two, she would cast her first ballot in a New York state election.

Also traveling down that road to equality was Susan Quinn, who at fifteen will become the youngest signer of the Declaration of Sentiments. Catharine F. Stebbins, a veteran of activism starting when she was only twelve going door to door collecting anti-slavery petitions. She also, by the way, kept an anti-tobacco pledge on the parlor table and asked all her young male friends to sign up. She was woman truly ahead of her time, as all the participants were.

I often wonder, when reflecting back on the Seneca Falls Convention, who of us — men and women — would have left our homes, our families, our work to make that journey one hundred and fifty years ago. Think about the incredible courage it must have taken to join that procession. Ordinary men and women, mothers and fathers, sisters and brothers, husbands and wives, friends and neighbors. And just like those who have embarked on other journeys throughout American history, seeking freedom or escaping religious or political persecution, speaking out against slavery, working for labor rights. These men and women were motivated by dreams of better lives and more just societies.

At the end of the two-day convention, one hundred people, sixty-eight women and thirty-two men, signed the Declaration of Sentiments that you can now read on the wall at Wesleyan Chapel. Among the signers were some of the names we remember today: Elizabeth Cady Stanton and Lucretia Mott, Martha Wright and Frederick Douglass and young Charlotte Woodward. The "Seneca Falls 100," as I like to call them, shared the radical idea that America fell far short of her ideals stated in our founding documents, denying citizenship to women and slaves.

Elizabeth Cady Stanton, who is frequently credited with originating the idea for the Convention, knew that women were not only denied legal citizenship, but that society's cultural values and social structures conspired to assign women only one occupation and role, that of wife and mother. Of course, the reality was always far different. Women have always worked, and worked both in the home and outside the home for as long as history can record. And even though Stanton herself had a comfortable life and valued deeply her husband and seven children, she knew that she and all other women were not truly free if they could not keep wages they earned, divorce an abusive husband, own property, or vote for the political leaders who governed them. Stanton was inspired, along with the others who met, to rewrite our Declaration of Independence, and they boldly asserted, "We hold these truths to be self-evident that all men and women are created equal."

"All men and all women." It was the shout heard around the world, and if we listen, we can still hear its echoes today. We can hear it in the voices of women demanding their full civil and political rights anywhere in the world. I've heard such voices and their echoes from women, around the world, from Belfast to Bosnia to Beijing, as they work to change the conditions for women and girls and improve their lives and the lives of their families. We can even hear those echoes today in Seneca Falls. We come together this time not by carriage, but by car or plane, by train or foot, and yes, in my case, by bus. We come together not to hold a convention, but to celebrate those who met here one hundred and fifty years ago, to commemorate how far we have traveled since then, and to challenge ourselves to persevere on the journey that was begun all those many years ago.

We are, as one can see looking around this great crowd, men and women, old and young, different races, different backgrounds. We come to honor the past and imagine the future. That is the theme the President and I have chosen for the White House Millennium Council's efforts to remind and inspire Americans as we approach the year 2000. This is my last stop on the Millennium Council's tour to Save America's Treasures — those buildings, monuments, papers and sites — that define who we are as a nation. They include not only famous symbols like the Star Spangled Banner and not only great political leaders like George Washington's revolutionary headquarters, or creative inventors like Thomas Edison's invention factory, but they include also the women of America who wrote our nation's past and must write its future.

Women like the ones we honor here and, in fact, at the end of my tour yesterday, I learned that I was following literally in the footsteps of one of them, Lucretia Mott, who, on her way to Seneca Falls, stopped in Auburn to visit former slaves and went on to the Seneca Nations to meet with clan mothers, as I did.

Last evening, I visited the home of Mary Ann and Thomas M'Clintock in Waterloo, where the Declaration of Sentiments was drafted, and which the Park Service is planning to restore for visitors if the money needed can be raised. I certainly hope I can return here sometime in the next few years to visit that restoration.

Because we must tell and retell, learn and relearn, these women's stories, and we must make it our personal mission, in our everyday lives, to pass these stories on to our daughters and sons. Because we cannot — we must not — ever forget that the rights and opportunities that we enjoy as women today were not just bestowed upon us by some benevolent ruler. They were fought for, agonized over, marched for, jailed for and even died for by brave and persistent women and men who came before us.

Every time we buy or sell or inherit property in our own name — let us thank the pioneers who agitated to change the laws that made that possible.

Every time, every time we vote, let us thank the women and men of Seneca Falls, Susan B. Anthony and all the others, who tirelessly crossed our nation and withstood ridicule and the rest to bring about the 19th Amendment to the Constitution.

Every time we enter an occupation — a profession of our own choosing and receive a paycheck that reflect earnings equal to a male colleague, let us thank the signers and women like Kate Mullaney, who's house I visited yesterday, in Troy, New York

Every time we elect a woman to office — let us thank ground breaking leaders like Jeannette Rankin and Margaret Chase Smith, Hattie Caraway, Louise Slaughter, Bella Abzug, Shirley Chisholm — all of whom proved that a woman's place is truly in the House, and in the Senate, and one day, in the White House, as well.

And every time we take another step forward for justice in this nation — let us thank extraordinary women like Harriet Tubman, who's home in Auburn I visited yesterday, and who escaped herself from slavery, and, then risked her life, time and again, to bring at least two hundred other slaves to freedom as well.

Harriet Tubman's rule for all of her underground railroad missions was to keep going. Once you started — no matter how scared you got, how dangerous it became — you were not allowed to turn back. That's a pretty good rule for life. It not only describes the women who gathered in Wesleyan Chapel in 1848, but it could serve as our own motto for today. We, too, cannot turn back. We, too, must keep going in our commitment to the dignity of every individual — to women's rights as human rights. We are on that road of the pioneers to Seneca Falls, they started down it 150 years ago. But now, we too, must keep going.

We may not face the criticism and derision they did. They understood that the Declaration of Sentiments would create no small amount of misconception, or misrepresentation and ridicule; they were called mannish women, old maids, fanatics, attacked personally by those who disagreed with them. One paper said, "These rights for women would bring a monstrous injury to all mankind." If it sounds familiar, it's the same thing that's always said when women keep going for true equality and justice.

Those who came here also understood that the convention and the Declaration were only first steps down that road. What matters most is what happens when everyone packs up and goes back to their families and communities. What matters is whether sentiment and resolutions, once made, are fulfilled or forgotten. The Seneca Falls 100 pledged themselves to petition, and lit the pulpit and used every instrumentality within their power to affect their subjects. And they did. But they also knew they were not acting primarily for themselves. They knew they probably would not even see the changes they advocated in their own lifetime. In fact, only Charlotte Woodward lived long enough to see American women finally win the right to vote.

Those who signed that Declaration were doing it for the girls and women — for us — those of us in the twentieth century.

Elizabeth Cady Stanton wrote a letter to her daughters later in life enclosing a special gift and explaining why. "Dear Maggie and Hattie, this is my first speech," she wrote, "it contains all I knew at that time; I give this manuscript to my precious daughters in the hopes that they will finish the work that I have begun." And they have. Her daughter, Harriot Blatch, was the chief strategist of the suffrage movement in New York. Harriot's daughter, Nora Barney, was one of the first women to be a civil engineer. Nora's daughter, Rhoda Jenkins, became an architect. Rhoda's daughter, Colleen Jenkins-Sahlin is an elected official in Greenwich, Connecticut. And her daughter, Elizabeth is a thirteen-year-old, who wrote about the six generations of Stantons in a book called, *33 Things Every Girl Should Know.*

So, far into the twentieth century, the work is still being done; the journey goes on. Now, some might say that the only purpose of this celebration is to honor the past, that the work begun here is finished in America, that young women no longer face legal obstacles to whatever education or employment choices they choose to pursue. And I certainly believe and hope all of you agree that we should, everyday, count our blessings as American women.

I know how much change I have seen in my own life. When I was growing up back in the fifties and sixties, there were still barriers that Mrs. Stanton would have recognized — scholarships I couldn't apply for, schools I couldn't go to, jobs I couldn't have — just because of my sex. Thanks to federal laws like the Civil Rights Act of 1964 and Title 9, and the Equal Pay Act, legal barriers to equality have fallen.

But if all we do is honor the past, then I believe we will miss the central point of the Declaration of Sentiments, which was, above all, a document about the future. The drafters of the Declaration imagined a different future for women and men, in a society based on equality and mutual respect. It falls to every generation to imagine the future, and it our task to do so now.

We know that, just as the women 150 years ago knew, that what we imagine will be principally for our daughters and sons in the 21st century. Because the work of the Seneca Falls Convention is, just like the work of the nation itself, it's never finished, so long as there remain gaps between our ideals and reality. That is one of the great joys and beauties of the American experiment. We are always striving to build and move toward a more perfect union, that we on every occasion keep faith with our founding ideals, and translate them into reality. So what kind of future can we imagine together.

If we are to finish the work begun here — then no American should ever again face discrimination on the basis of gender, race or sexual orientation anywhere in our country.

If we are to finish the work begun here — then $0.76 in a woman's paycheck for every dollar in a man's is still not enough. Equal pay for equal work can once and for all be achieved.

If we are to finish the work begun here — then families need more help to balance their responsibilities at work and at home. In a letter to Susan B. Anthony, Elizabeth Cady Stanton writes, "Come here and I will do what I can to help you with your address, if you will hold the baby and make the pudding." Even then, women knew we had to have help with child care. All families should have access to safe, affordable, quality child care.

If we are to finish the work begun here — then women and children must be protected against what the Declaration called the "chastisement of women," namely domestic abuse and violence. We must take all steps necessary to end the scourge of violence against women and punish the perpetrator. And our country must join the rest of the world, as so eloquently Secretary Albright called for on Saturday night here in Seneca Falls, "Join the rest of the world and ratify the Convention on the Elimination of Discrimination Against Women."

If we are to finish the work begun here — we must do more than talk about family values, we must adopt polices that truly value families — policies like a universal system of health care insurance that guarantees every American's access to affordable, quality health care. Policies like taking all steps necessary to keep guns out of the hands of children and criminals. Policies like doing all that is necessary at all levels of our society to ensure high quality public education for every boy or girl no matter where that child lives.

If we are to finish the work begun here — we must ensure that women and men who work full-time earn a wage that lifts them out of poverty and all workers who retire have financial security in their later years through guaranteed Social Security and pensions.

If we are to finish the work begun here — we must be vigilant against the messages of a media-driven consumer culture that convinces our sons and daughters that what brand of sneakers they wear or cosmetics they use is more important that what they think, feel, know, or do.

And if we are to finish the work begun here — we must, above all else, take seriously the power of the vote and use it to make our voices heard. What the champions of suffrage understood was that the vote is not just a symbol of our equality, but that it can be, if used, a guarantee of results. It is the way we express our political views. It is the way we hold our leaders and governments accountable. It is the way we bridge the gap between what we want our nation to be and what it is.

But when will the majority of women voters of our country exercise their most fundamental political right? Can you imagine what any of the Declaration signers would say if they learned how many women fail to vote in elections? They would be amazed and outraged. They would agree with a poster I saw in 1996. On it, there is a picture of a woman with a piece of tape covering her mouth and under it, it says, "Most politicians think women should be seen and not heard. In the last election, 54 million women agreed with them."

One hundred and fifty years ago, the women at Seneca Falls were silenced by someone else. Today, women, we silence ourselves. We have a choice. We have a voice. And if we are going to finish the work begun here we must exercise our right to vote in every election we are eligible to vote in.

Much of who women are and what women do today can be traced to the courage, vision, and dedication of the pioneers who came together at Seneca Falls. Now it is our responsibility to finish the work they began. Let's ask ourselves, at the 200th anniversary of Seneca Falls, will they say that today's gathering also was a catalyst for action? Will they say that businesses, labor, religious organizations, the media, foundations, educators, every citizen in our society came to see the unfinished struggle of today as their struggle?

Will they say that we joined across lines of race and class, that we raised up those too often pushed down, and ultimately found strength in each other's differences and resolved in our common cause? Will we, like the champions at Seneca Falls, recognize that men must play a central role in this fight? How can we ever forget the impassioned plea of Frederick Douglass, issued in our defense of the right to vote?

How can we ever forget that young legislator from Tennessee by the name of Harry Burns, who was the deciding vote in ratifying the 19th Amendment. He was planning on voting "no," but then he got a letter from his mother with a simple message. The letter said, "Be a good boy Harry and do the right thing." And he did! Tennessee became the last state to ratify, proving that you can never ever overestimate the power of one person to alter the course of history, or the power of a little motherly advice.

Will we look back and see that we have finally joined the rest of the advanced economies by creating systems of education, employment, child care and health care that support and strengthen families and give all women real choices in their lives.

At the 200th anniversary celebration, will they say that women today supported each other in the choices we make? Will we admit once and for all there is no single cookie cutter model for being a successful and fulfilled woman today, that we have so many choices? We can choose full-time motherhood or no family at all or like most of us, seek to strike a balance between our family and our work, always trying to do what is right in our lives. Will we leave our children a world where it is self-evident that all men and women, boys and girls are created equal? These are some of the questions we can ask ourselves.

Help us imagine a future that keeps faith with the sentiments expressed here in 1848. The future, like the past and the present, will not and cannot be perfect. Our daughters and granddaughters will face new challenges which we today cannot even imagine. But each of us can help prepare for that future by doing what we can to speak out for justice and equality for women's rights and human rights, to be on the right side of history, no matter the risk or cost, knowing that eventually the sentiments we express and the causes we advocate will succeed because they are rooted in the conviction that all people are entitled by their creator and by the promise of America to the freedom, rights, responsibilities, and opportunity of full citizenship. That is what I imagine for the future. I invite you to imagine with me and then to work together to make that future a reality.

Thank you all very much.

— ***Mrs. Clinton*** delivered this speech on July 16, 1998 in Seneca Falls, New York.

Hillary Clinton as Threat to Gender Norms
Cartoon Images of the First Lady

Charlotte Templin

IT IS GENERALLY AGREED THAT CARTOONISTS have to be provocative —"the pit bulls of journalism"— according to cartoonist Michael Ramirez (Hemandez 1994). Cartoonists are not expected to be fair to the figures they choose to draw. The essence of the cartoon is satire, a distortion of the truth (Edwards 1995). Cartoonists routinely invoke stereotypes (Brotman 1996) and indulge in hyperbole and ad hominem attacks (Edwards 1995). They tend to consider any subject fair game (Riffe, Sneed, and Van Ommeren 1987) and, when criticized, often invoke generic criteria to defend themselves (Brotman 1996). They are generally represented as employing distortion to serve the cause of truth (McDonald 1977). But cartoonists also share fundamental biases with the societies they critique, and therefore cartooning has a heritage that has at times been racist and sexist.

Few public figures — and no other first ladies — have been targeted as frequently by cartoonists as Hillary Clinton, who has been the subject of hundreds of highly critical cartoons. The *Nation* was indeed on the mark when it referred, early in the Clinton presidency, to the "quasi-pornographic obsession" with Hillary (17 May 1993). Although Hillary should not be exempt from criticism any more than other public figures, an analysis of cartoons about her suggests that what she has been subjected to by cartoonists is not just criticism but sexism born of a backlash effect. When we consider the obsession with Hillary among cartoonists, the continual use of cliches and stereotypes, and the sexism inherent in the images and symbols used by the cartoonists to depict her, statements about the generic nature of cartoons hardly seem adequate to explain the virulence of the attacks.

As we know, the conservative discourse about Hillary Clinton is contested, and there are progressive voices raised in her defense. The public nature of Hillary's activities makes her a focal point for thinking and talking about gender norms, or, to put it another way, for the struggle over which gender norms shall prevail in the culture. That social struggle is a contest of discourses in which cartoons have figured importantly. Because of their pictorial nature, cartoons can present a message forthrightly that is often more masked in journalistic writings. The cartoon's use of metaphor and myth, cultural images and recognizable narratives, including fairy tales and recent historical events, has the capacity to code events or actors in a powerful way.

The contestatory nature of the discourse about Hillary Clinton signals the deep struggle still taking place in society over the role of women, and the attacks against her can be seen as part of the backlash against the professional woman. The conservative social formation that views Hillary's rise to prominence as a threat is attempting to use her to move the discourse of gender to the Right. Resentments of all kinds can be directed against women (e.g., the psychological threat resulting from male fear of being feminized and the economic displacement that has characterized late capitalism).

In *Backlash: The Undeclared War against American Women*, Susan Faludi (1991, 64) points out the connection between the psychological and the economic: male self-respect is based on the ability to be a good provider, according to surveys on social attitudes. The backlash of the 1980s emerged in a time of economic stress and was voiced by two groups in particular: blue-collar workers and younger baby boomers who had "missed the gravy train" (p. 65).[1] According to Faludi, these two groups are, however, best characterized as receptors of backlash theory. Faludi notes the role of a white-collar elite in backlash dynamics: "the backlash's public agenda has been framed and promoted by men of far more influence. . . men at the helm in media, business, and politics" (p. 66).[2] By characterizing Hillary as a monster of sorts, the cartoonists work with others in positions of influence to reposition women in subordinate roles. Hillary is the target of backlash politics, and the violence and magnitude of the attack can be accounted for by the fact that different social formations can unite around the issue of the need to preserve male power.[3]

The many hundreds of cartoons about Hillary Clinton make the point that, to borrow a phrase from Judith Butler (1990), Hillary is "not doing gender right." She has strayed from important gender norms and is being punished accordingly by the cartoonists representing a mainstream social formation. The cartoons of Hillary illustrate dramatically the culture's understanding of gender as a binary system. Essential to the meaning of the cartoons is the notion of gender asymmetry — a system built on oppositions and naturalizing heterosexuality. According to Butler, "the institution of a compulsory and naturalized heterosexuality requires and regulates gender as a binary function" (p.22). In Butler's formulation, gender is viewed not just as the reflection of a binary but is itself the means by which a sexual binary is constructed. If men are to be masculine, women must be feminine.[4]

Butler explains how naturalized and reified notions of gender support masculine hegemony and heterosexist power. Women's function is essential: women must reflect male power and assure it of "the reality of its illusory autonomy" (p.45). For Butler, gender is not an essence or a fact, but "performative, that is, constituting the identity it is purported to be" (p.33). Cartooning can be seen as one of what Butler refers to as the "regulatory practices" that bring about heterosexist subordination.

Germaine Greer's (1996) analysis of the institution of First Lady helps to focus and extend Butler's claim, as applied to Hillary Clinton. Greer points out that one of the primary functions of the First Lady is to convey the strong and active heterosexuality of the president, who is supposed to be, in general, not just sexually, a powerhouse or superhuman — one who can take on the rigors and challenges of running the country.

Some of Hillary Clinton's troubles may be attributed to the fact that the role of First Lady is very rigidly defined in the United States. Greer points out that the American First Lady is expected to play the role of "virtuoso housekeeper," to run the residence and entertain visiting dignitaries. The First Lady is not a queen, distant and formal; rather, she is expected to give press conferences, to make public appearances for charitable or public causes, and to stand beside her husband and show her appreciation for him — Greer says to lead the appreciation for him. However, among the most important of her functions, says Greer, is to "[reassure] us as to the head of state's active heterosexuality" (Greer 1996,22; see also Bostdorff 1998). The First Lady is supposed to have borne children by the president; she is supposed to convey that her greatest ambitions are as a wife and mother: "any indication that her husband and family are not in themselves sufficient to absorb all her energies is disadvantageous to her husband's prospects" (Greer 1996, 22). Giving the example of Nancy Reagan, whose pose as adoring wife facilitated her exercise of power, Greer offers the view that "any consideration of the First Lady's role shows that the less power she claims, the more she wields" (p.27).

Discourse, as a means of making sense of the world, has the function of deploying power in social conditions. According to John Fiske (1996, 4), analysis of discursive practices can have a liberatory effect: "It must uncover the processes of discursive contestation by which discourses work to repress, marginalize, and invalidate others; by which they struggle for audibility and access to the technologies of social circulation; and by which they fight to promote and defend the interests of their respective social formations." Dominant discourses serve the interests of dominant groups and are a means of undergirding the power of majority interests. The cartoonists of major newspapers largely represent the mainstream, and they choose a repertoire of images and cultural symbols that articulate the actions of Hillary Clinton in a certain way, endowing them with particular meanings and values.

Cartooning is a male enclave of a male-dominated profession (Pollitt 1993). Among the many cartoonists for major newspapers, I have found only two women: Signe Wilkinson and Ann Telnaes. (They have been sympathetic to Hillary Clinton.) To gain access to the nation's major newspapers and to be represented by syndicates, one would expect cartoonists to follow a hegemonic ideological line. Although not monolithic, cartooning is in general narrowly representative of one mainstream formation, which I will discuss in terms of its beliefs about gender. However, it should be noted that the social formations I am concerned with here do not rigidly follow gender lines, since there are male cartoonists who defend Hillary.

GENDER REVERSALS

OF OVER 400 CARTOONS that appeared between November 1992 and July 1996, nearly half fall into a category that could be called "Hillary is taking over."[5] Instead of reflecting male power, the proper role of woman according to Butler, Hillary Clinton has usurped that power. The standard joke is that Hillary is running the country — or is, in effect, the president. The joke started early and has been repeated ad nauseam by cartoonists, as well as stand-up comedians, greeting card companies, and T-shirt manufacturers. Several cartoonists show Hillary as the one raising her hand to take the oath of office at the inauguration (MacNelly 1992).

A Stayskal (1993) cartoon shows two desks in the Oval Office marked "His" and "Hers." Other cartoons make graphic representations of Hillary's power: Hillary building up her wing of the White House (Marlette 1993) and Hillary sitting on a high stool behind the president's desk closely watching his every move (Ramirez 1994a). In a Britt (1994) cartoon, Lloyd Cutler explains that as White House counsel, it is his job to advise the president and asks where she is. In a Stahler (1994) cartoon, the president sits for his portrait while the painter paints his wife, presumably the real power, who is sitting at a desk in the background. In a Stephanos (1994) cartoon, Hillary is a puppeteer. With a diminutive Bill Clinton puppet on her lap, she says, "Me run for president? What for?" There are many cartoons about Hillary planning to run in 1996. One of these, a Ramirez (1995) cartoon picturing a huge campaign sign atop the White House promoting Hillary Rodham Clinton (with Rodham in huge letters) in 1996, was named cartoon of the week by the *Gallery of Cartoons*.[6]

Of course, the Clintons initiated the "two-for-one" talk during the campaign by suggesting that if the nation elected Bill Clinton, it would benefit from the abilities and energies of both Clintons. Such talk raised the specter of an unelected co-president, an idea that might legitimately put people off and thus might indeed be material for the cartoonist whose raison d'être is to point out the unseemly or improper. However, it is hard to accept that the hundreds of cartoons showing Hillary Clinton massively in charge can be explained as a response to this fear, especially in view of the fact that such cartoons continued to appear in 1996, long after the Clintons stopped the "two fer" talk (which was actually dropped fairly quickly). After virulent criticism from many sources, including cartoonists, Hillary sought a low profile, especially after the 1994 elections, but the nature of the jokes did not change.[7] Rather than legitimate concern that the country has an unelected president, the cartoons reveal unease with a powerful woman and anxiety about changing gender norms.

In various power-grabbing moves, Hillary Clinton is shown as trying to get in line for every position of power that becomes available: Supreme Court justice, Surgeon General (Deering 1996; Barnett 1995). Other cartoons use various ways of showing Hillary's dominant position. In a Bennett (1993) cartoon, two men walk by 1600 Pennsylvania Avenue, and one points his finger and comments, "Look, it's Hillary Clinton's husband." In a Bish (1995) cartoon, Bill Clinton is seated next to the podium. When introduced as "this nation's most powerful leader," he comments, "Hillary's here?"

HILLARY CLINTON AS RADICAL FEMINIST AND EMASCULATOR

THE CRUX OF THE MATTER is the belief that Hillary Clinton, a "failed woman," is not fulfilling the requirements of heterosexism, which, as Butler's analysis illustrates, is compulsory in our culture and, according to Greer, an obligatory requirement of the First Lady. Hillary is, it is suggested, a "radical feminist," constructed as a woman who completely overturns traditional gender roles by reversing the power structure within a heterosexual relationship or as a lesbian. Although rumors about Hillary's alleged lesbianism continue to circulate, there have been some seemingly contradictory allegations about Hillary's sexuality. Pollitt (1993) mentions the rumor that Hillary has some sort of extraordinary sexual power over the president, and it has also been claimed that she had an affair with Vincent Foster. Characterization of Hillary as a radical feminist was the theme of several speeches — Pat Buchanan, Pat Robertson, Marilyn Quayle — at the 1992 Republican Convention. Hillary's use of her birth name is seen as evidence of her radical feminist leanings. Rodham, used in a number of cartoons, is a shorthand way to refer to her extremism.

To actually portray Hillary Clinton as a lesbian in a cartoon would be more daring than a mainstream newspaper could allow and presumably would be libelous.[8] However, cartoonists have no problem with the suggestion that the relationship between Hillary and Bill Clinton does not conform to heterosexual norms. The Hillary-is-taking-over joke makes the point about Hillary's dominance in a fairly crude way, but some cartoons use images that are very explicit about the sexual dynamic of the first couple, including some blatant suggestions that Hillary is emasculating Bill. The most striking of cartoons in this category shows the president wearing a dress and carrying a purse: "What's with all these White House changes?" says Bill in the first panels with only his head visible. "McLarty, Panetta, Gergen, Rivlin? Who's next, Hillary?" Then a full image of Bill shows him in a dress and carrying a purse, while Hillary, who is seated behind a desk working on some documents, says, "I feel your pain" (Peters 1994). Gamer (1995a, 1995b) consistently foregrounds gender reversals in his cartoons. We see Hillary as gun moll (and a mild-appearing Bill as partner) in "Bonnie and Clod." In another cartoon, Hillary is a doctor with an evil-looking syringe and Bill is a nurse. Garner (1993) also drew the president standing behind three large female figures — Hillary, a towering Janet Reno, and a woman in military uniform — saying, "I'm behind women all the way."

It is not surprising that there is keen interest in the first bedroom and what goes on there. As Greer points out, there has always been interest in whether the First Lady shares the president's bed. A large number of cartoons show the Clintons in bed. Some cartoonists may be drawing on the literary convention of the curtain lecture, but the primary effect of the cartoons is to measure the Clintons against dominant heterosexual norms. What do the Clintons do in bed? According to the cartoons, they read policy-wonk documents, with Hillary being by far the more avid reader of the two. In a Borgman (1993) cartoon, the president is reading a file labeled "Revenue Enhancement Options" while Hillary is intensely focused on a tome titled "Health Care Proposals."[9] With two walls of the bedroom floor-to-ceiling file cabinets and the bed covered with papers, the message is clear that this bedroom is highly unusual. In a Szep (1994) cartoon, the president (newspapers with headlines about recent problems of the Clinton presidency scattered on the floor on his side of the bed) has turned away from Hillary with the comment, "I said I've got a headache," while Hillary, reading documents on health care, recites a definition of and treatment for headache (and presumably we understand why the president is not romantically inclined). Hillary is consumed with the technical aspects of policy and therefore not a desirable sexual partner. A Trever (1994) cartoon shows the Clintons in bed reading: Bill has a large tome titled "Budget," but inside it is a partially concealed *American Spectator* (known as a right-wing publication). He looks over with alarm at Hillary, who holds before her an equally large tome labeled "Health Care" partially covering a book titled *The Lorena Bobbitt Story*. Bill is charged with stealing ideas from Republicans, but Hillary is defined by her sexual destructiveness. Characteristically, the Clintons lie in bed back-to-back or side-by-side but focused on documents, a book — something other than each other. In a Peters (1996) cartoon, a sleeping Bill is pictured with a blissful smile on his face. Hillary, who is sitting up in bed, says, "I bet he's fantasizing about another woman." Indeed, he is, for above Bill's head is a picture of his dream: himself with his arm around Barbara Bush. Bush, figured as the traditional woman, is the shadow figure against whom Hillary was measured during the campaign and who continues to have a symbolic function.

The explicit references to the nature of Hillary Clinton's sexuality in cartoons make them a locus for the most socially acceptable conservative discourse and give us a way to track conservative discourse. I have found only one example of print journalism in a mainstream publication that compares in any way to the pictorial representations. Camille Paglia (1996), the poster woman of conservative discourse on gender, takes up the ploy of criticizing Hillary by suggesting that she is insufficiently feminine, an ice maiden. In a *New Republic* article ("Ice Queen, Drag Queen") highly critical of Hillary, Paglia refers to Hillary's "genderlessness," her difficulty with being a woman ("it did not come easily or naturally"), and her difficulty in integrating her intelligence with her sexuality. According to Paglia, Hillary's female role is an act grafted onto a "butch substrate." Paglia also charges Bill Clinton with a "hostility to conventional masculinity" (pp.25-26) and points to the particular family dynamics of the childhoods of each to explain their development. Let us note also that one way to defend Hillary is to construct her as strongly heterosexual and very much in love with her husband. In an article in *The New Yorker*, Henry Louis Gates (1996) portrays her as a devoted mother and a woman in love with her husband, quoting a close associate who says, "She's crazy-ass in love with him . . . and if you see them together, you know. She gets that goofy look on her face. She lights up around him" (pp.124-26).

DOMESTIC IMAGERY

IT IS COMMON FOR CARTOONISTS to draw on imagery associated with women and on a whole set of ideas about women's roles that are natural to them and probably to most of their readers. Cartoon representations of Geraldine Ferraro, Walter Mondale's running mate in 1984, portrayed her as cook, girlfriend, and hot little number in a way that was demeaning to her as a senator and attorney and aspirant to an important public office (Miller 1993). Hillary Clinton is the wife of a officeholder, so she is in a very different category, but still the operative idea behind the cartoons that employ the domestic imagery is to call attention to the disjuncture between expected and threatening roles for women. A woman is escaping the categories that usually confine her — wife, lover, cook, and so is unusual at the very least and, for some, troublesome and threatening. At worst, Hillary is abusing or perverting her role as wife. In a Bill De Ore (1994) cartoon, Hillary is shown cooking up a health care stew while Bill sniffs ecstatically (another pot, labeled NAFTA, simmers in the background). In a MacNelly (1993) cartoon, Hillary and Bill look in an oven at a turkey labeled "Health Care," and Bill asks, "Is it done yet?" Hillary gives a roundabout answer in terms of "dialogue with facilitators" and "impact in terms of the dynamic." Hillary's high visibility makes for a kind of in-your-face example of not only the liberated woman but the liberated wife.

One extremely revealing moment during the campaign was the response to Hillary Clinton's remark about her choice not to stay home and bake cookies. The remark has haunted her ever since and has been the impetus for dozens of cartoons. In March 1992, Jerry Brown charged that Hillary's law firm had benefited from the fact that she was the wife of the governor. She replied, "I suppose I could have stayed home, baked cookies, and had teas." She also added a few rarely quoted words: "The work I have done as a professional, a public advocate, has been aimed to assure that women can make the choice . . . whether it's full-time career, full-time motherhood, or some combination" (Carison 1992, 30). Hillary later released her recipe for chocolate chip cookies, but the damage had been done. She was cast as an overly ambitious career woman who had abdicated her wifely obligations and her womanly role. In a period when most women do work outside the home, a statement in defense of that choice is seen as somehow unwomanly, suggesting a disjuncture between the realities of American life and a backward looking emotional set that still dominates many people's outlook. A cartoon captioned "Great Moments in American Law," showing Hillary baking her first batch of cookies, appeared during the campaign (Danziger 1993). A number of cartoonists used the cookie theme to portray tensions in the First Lady's role between her chosen function of adviser to her husband and a traditional female role expected of her in the culture. Borgman (1992) shows a sprightly and feminine Hillary addressing her husband and a group of balding and dour old men, presumably the cabinet. She speaks authoritatively of budget deficits and revenues, and then says, "Now if you'll excuse me, my cookies are burning." With attacks on Hillary rampant in early 1994 in connection with Whitewater, Ohmann (1994) created a cartoon showing Hillary ready to pack it in and stay home and bake cookies. Similarly, in a Marlette (1994) cartoon, the president, with his advisers standing behind his desk, tells Hillary that they have found a new job for her in the administration: stay home and bake cookies.

WOMAN AS BODY

THERE IS ABUNDANT EVIDENCE in the cartoons of the long-standing equation of women with the body — the imprisonment of women in their bodies (and, of course, the implication that for women to claim to be more than bodies constitutes an absurdity). Butler (1990, 11) cites Simone de Beauvoir's discussion of women's corporeality in which the "subject" is "always already masculine, conflated with the universal, differentiating itself from a feminine 'Other' outside the universalizing norms of personhood, hopelessly 'particular,' embodied, condemned to immanence." The persistent images of Hillary Clinton in bed come to mind here. A woman is one who is slept with. Woman as body is also the basis for an Asay (1993) cartoon in which Hillary pushes a baby carriage labeled "Health Care" under the caption "Hillary's Baby." The many cartoons on Hillary's hair (Horsey 1993) should be mentioned also. Hillary has changed her hairstyle several times (presumably under the advice of her advisers), but is this fact really worth the attention it has received? In 1996, Hillary was quoted as saying that she would welcome another child and would consider adoption. This episode was the impetus for several cartoons about adopting Republican values (Ramsey 1996) or about the fact that having already adopted Whitewater, Hillary's hands were too full to adopt a child (Horsey 1996b). If she were a real woman, she would adopt a child; as a failed woman, she devotes her energies improperly in the public sphere.

THE PUBLIC WOMAN

HILLARY CLINTON HAS BEEN associated with several other themes, including Whitewater and cattle futures.[10] The sheer number of cartoons produced on these topics is, again, remarkable. Why have these matters produced such a response from cartoonists — and from journalists in general? To answer this question, we should consider Hillary's status as a woman with a public role. We have learned that Hillary was an attorney for an important firm in Arkansas while Bill was governor, and that she took over the responsibility for insuring the family's financial future in handling investments as well as earning the larger salary. Everything we learn about Hillary adds more to the picture of her as a public woman — a woman who has, in many ways, lived the life of a man. Hillary's greed has been made much of (Der 1995; Ramirez 1994b), and again it is *female* greed that is worthy of so much public attention. A $100,000 return on an investment is especially noteworthy if the investor is a woman in public life.

The cartoons on Whitewater often feature the Clintons in canoes about to go over rapids, or in bed or other locations surrounded by rising water. In a Brookins (1996) cartoon with the caption "Home to Roost," Hillary is surrounded by chickens labeled with the problems of the Clinton presidency (e.g., "Travelgate," "Webster Hubbell") while a chicken labeled "Whitewater" is perched on her head. In a Horsey (1996a) cartoon, Hillary, in a flood of water that reaches her waist, opens a door to the Clinton campaign headquarters while a donkey seated at a desk asks, "Say, Hillary, how are you guys fixed for flood insurance?" After the Senate-sponsored Whitewater investigation had dragged on for weeks under the leadership of Senator D'Amato, and especially after the release of the report of the Republican majority in 1996, the scapegoating of Hillary reached its zenith.[11] At this time, there was a trend more favorable to Hillary, at least by implication, among some cartoonists. Cartoons appeared suggesting that Whitewater was a political issue kept alive by Republicans, and Senator D'Amato became a popular target for cartoonists (Keefe 1996; Varvel 1996).

CHERCHEZ LA FEMME

ONE NOTEWORTHY ELEMENT of the Hillary Clinton story is the amount of blame that has been laid at her door — surely an extreme case of *cherchez la femme*. She has been the target of choice for health care, Whitewater, cattle futures, Travelgate, Filegate — in short, just about all of the problems that have dogged the Clinton administration.

Some cartoonists — clearly from a very different social formation — have lampooned the tendency to blame Hillary Clinton for everything.

More than one cartoonist used an allusion to the bloody glove in the O. J. Simpson trial — "More bad news. The bloody glove fits Hillary" (Luckovich 1996). Hillary on the grassy knoll (from the Kennedy assassination) is another theme (Smith 1996). Signe Wilkinson (1996) lampoons the various constructions of Hillary from the "pants in the family" to Whitewater witch.

It is common for Hillary Clinton to be drawn as a something unnatural, a monster of sorts. She is a shark (Szep 1996b), a bizarre figure with a Pinocchio nose (Szep 1996a), and a criminal in a mug shot with a number (Hunter 1996). She has been drawn as Nixon many times, a heavily jowled figure with arms raised and fingers spread (Luckovich 1994; Siers 1994).

A pervasive technique is the use of negative female stereotypes in the drawing of a female human figure. Hillary Clinton is the shrew par excellence. She is a vicious-looking Queen of Hearts in a Siers (1996) cartoon shouting "Off with his head!" She bellows, screams, and complains. In some cartoons (e.g., the Peters drawings), Hillary's head is all mouth. She is known to throw things in cartoons (Brookins 1996), and her facial expressions are almost invariably sour. She changes her hairstyle and her mind frequently, blames Bill for everything that goes wrong, and is a messy housekeeper (Bush 1994).

"TAKE MY WIFE, PLEASE"

THERE ARE MANY CARTOONS about what is assumed to be the president's natural wish: to get rid of Hillary. A couple of cartoonists picked up on Nelson Mandela's decision to remove his wife from office, suggesting that the president would like to fire Hillary (Deering 1996). Others used the Henny Youngman line "Take my wife, please" (Smith 1994). In a Horsey (1996b) cartoon, Hillary (while taking a shower) calls out to Bill: "Ignore all those liberals carping about your shift to the right, Bill. Don't let *anyone* stand in the way of your reelection!" Bill, holding a newspaper with headlines about Hillary and Whitewater, says to two policemen standing at the door, "Okay, fellas, take her away." In a Toles (1996) cartoon, Bill and Hillary are seated on the sofa watching television, Bill eating snacks while Hillary, surrounded by piles of documents, examines a paper labeled "Billing Records." The TV announcer says, "Bob Dole has divorced Washington to help his campaign. What can Bill Clinton do to top *that* one?" We know that the joke that a husband commonly wants to get rid of his wife is as old as written literature, at least. In this context, the recurring use of the joke helps to establish the stereotypical responses to Hillary.

SILENCING HILLARY CLINTON

IN TIMES OF BACKLASH, the silenced woman is a popular image. Numerous cartoons deal with silencing Hillary Clinton, starting during the campaign. A Wright (1992) cartoon shows a graph charting the dramatic rise in the fortunes of the Clinton-Gore ticket after Hillary's mouth is taped shut. A Wagner (1994) cartoon shows a talking Hillary doll telling a customer, "If you can wait, I believe we are going to be drastically reduced." Clearly, a doll woman should be of the most demure and retiring nature. That the fantasy of silencing Hillary has great power is seen in the many cartoons (which I do not have room to cite here) picturing a restrained and silenced Hillary — muzzled, a zipper for lips, in a box with air holes. The message is that the country would be better off if Hillary kept quiet — although the cartoonist is not always presenting this message but sometimes commenting on the fact that others feel this way.

Some have suggested that Hillary Clinton's manner is the problem. She should be softer, more conciliatory, more of a lady. MacNelly (1994) drew Bill outside a closed door saying to someone, "No, you tell her to lighten up." The proper woman is supposed to "lighten up," to be amusing, supportive, ornamental. Greer (1996,22) says that President Kennedy told Jackie to smile, not to talk — and if she had to talk, to talk about the children. Hillary's often-reported effort to keep Chelsea out of the limelight is in conflict with this advice.

CONCLUSION

HILLARY CLINTON IS A convenient symbol for much that conservatives loathe. She provides a site for discussion of the "family values" that seem to be largely about regulating female behavior. Held up as the representative feminist, Hillary can be used as a stick to beat feminism and to scapegoat feminism for various ills of the modern world. Some of the cartoons I have examined can be subsumed in conservative discourse on gender, even though some cartoonists are not commonly identified as conservatives. There are clearly some cartoonists — for example, those employed by the *Indianapolis Star/News* and the *Washington Times* — who align themselves with conservative discourse. There are also, however, others, some of whom are usually identified as liberal, whose cartoons are quite similar in content to those of the most conservative cartoonists.[12] An examination of cartoon representations of Hillary reveals how widely shared are fear and resentment resulting from the loss of female subordination.

Fiske (1996,36) notes the inevitability of backlash in the complex societies of late capitalism where "power is always exerted along multiple lines of force, and those lines can be intertwined or separated out according to the political objectives of the alliances formed around them." Analysis of cartoon images of Hillary Clinton reveal that the alliances formed to isolate the professional women's movement are widespread. Fear and resentment engendered by the political and economic successes of the movement cut across other political divides.

Media events are "sites of maximum visibility and turbulence" in the culture and make accessible "currents of meaning" that may not be so visible at other times (Fiske 1996, 7). The controversy swirling around Hillary Clinton can be characterized as a media event that has extended over several years or a series of media events focusing on Hillary and related to topical themes: cookie baking, cattle futures, Whitewater, Travel Office dismissals, and so on. Cartoons have had an important role in the controversy and have proven to be a highly eligible form of discourse to discredit Hillary. Cartoonists are granted a certain license to distort and attack. Simplifying, stereotyping, and using symbols and narratives common to the culture to code people and actions negatively allow cartoonists to exceed the bounds of what is fair criticism, even for cartoons. The number and the virulence of the cartoons, with excessive use of negatively coded images of Hillary, reveal the strength of the culture's reaction to a woman whose actions and style place her outside the accepted female paradigm.

— ***Charlotte Templin*** is a professor of English at the University of Indianapolis and the author of *Feminism and the Politics of Literary Reputation*.

NOTES

1. According to Rivers (1996), 47 percent of those affected by downsizing have been white males.

2. Wasserman (1995) has commented on the displacement of economic anxiety onto Hillary Clinton (or feminism) in a cartoon where two self-described "angry white men" complain about corporations "cutting our pay, exporting our jobs and laying us off." One speaker says, "So we're angry at corporations?" and the other replies, "No, Hillary Clinton."

3. Not surprisingly, as part of a backlash phenomenon, the cartoonists who have attacked Hillary Clinton have come almost exclusively from her own race and class.

4. Americans require of their male politicians a conformity to a culturally defined masculine imperative. President Clinton has sometimes been criticized for falling short in this regard. This criticism is summarized in North Carolina political scientist Ted Arrington's (1994, 33) remark quoted in *Newsweek*: "These people like manliness and guns. They don't like Clinton because he doesn't seem manly. He lets his wife do too much." Janis L. Edwards (1994) discusses this topic in a paper titled "Man and Superman: Clinton and the Masculine Imperative" presented at the Western States Communication Association in San Jose, California. I thank her for letting me read the paper.

5. The cartoons used in this study come from the *Washington Post* feature "Drawing Board," the *National Review* feature "Help," *USA Today,* the *Newsweek* feature "Perspectives," the bimonthly publication *Best Editorial Cartoons* (formerly *Gallery of Cartoons*), *Best Editorial Cartoons of the Year* for the years 1992–96, the *Indianapolis Star* and *Indianapolis News*, and cartoons from the electronic database Newspaper Abstracts. Although my collection is large, I know that there are probably many other cartoons I do not have.

6. Some Republicans were evidentially seriously concerned about Hillary Clinton running for president. Wills (1994, 8) quotes Paul Johnson of *Commentary* as saying that the intemperate attacks must be continued in order to prevent Hillary from running for president after Bill.

7. At this time, Hillary Clinton retreated from the limelight to write a book on child rearing, later released as *It Takes a Village*. After taking a tremendous beating for the public role she played in the health care initiative, she sought a lower profile and turned (or returned) to the subject of children. In a similar fashion, she had retreated on a previous occasion from the use of her birth name Rodham.

8. Nor are there any direct accusations of lesbianism in the mainstream press. However, on *60 Minutes* (31 March 1996), part of a Don Imus song about Hillary Clinton's lesbian friends was quoted. The line "She goes to state dinners with her

lesbian friends, makes big investments with high dividends" was quoted with the comment that the rest of the song was not suitable for broadcast.

9. Borgman (1996) has gone on record criticizing fellow cartoonists who have drawn Hillary Clinton as "lazy people doing easy, below-the-belt cartoons." He says he likes Hillary: "What rubs people so wrong about Hillary Clinton is that she's a strong person with strong opinions, and that's what makes me like her." Borgman's drawings have a whimsical quality that is not unflattering to the Clintons. The ideological bent of some cartoons is hard to gauge. The themes surrounding Hillary are so compelling in our culture — so piquant — that it seems sometimes cartoonists take up the subject of a new type of First Lady in a way that says "Isn't this an interesting moment in history?" without necessarily implying criticism. The mere fact that so many cartoonists have taken up the "powerful Hillary" theme, even if as a kind of exercise, testifies to its compelling resonance, and that resonance has to do with the sexism in the culture. Following the many cartoons portraying Hillary as a kind of oddity is a way of tracking the sexism still rampant in our society, even if, in some cases, the cartoonists would identify their intentions as benign.

10. Early in 1994, it became known that Hillary Clinton had made $100,000 on cattle futures with an investment of $10,000. In the episode termed Whitewater, the Clintons had speculated on a land development project and lost money. The charge was made that there might be a question of conspiracy, tax fraud, and obstruction of justice.

11. The report was released by the Senate Whitewater Committee in June 1996. Republicans charged that Hillary Clinton tried to cover up evidence of her role in illegal transactions.

12. *Liberal Opinion Week* claims the following cartoonists: Borgman, Szep, Luckovich, Marlette, Wright, Toles, Danziger, Peters, Trever, Rogers, Bennett, and Wasserman. A publication on the opposite end of the spectrum, *Conservative Chronicle,* claims Barnett, De Ore, MacNelly, Stayskal, Wright, Asay, Brookins, Ramirez, and Trever. As we see, some camps claim the same individuals. Classifying particular cartoonists as either liberal or conservative is not my project. My point is that cartoonists across a large part of the political spectrum have similar attitudes toward Hillary Clinton.

Softening Her Public Persona

IT CAN BE HARD TO PIN down Hillary Rodham Clinton; she alters her look and public persona often, seemingly to suit a given political moment. Her hair, her clothes, her policy interests — these and other aspects of her persona have metamorphosed since she first entered the public spotlight.

These changes are not new. When Bill Clinton lost the 1980 gubernatorial election in Arkansas, partly as a result of Hillary's appearance, she changed her name from Rodham to Clinton, dyed her hair blonde and switched to contact lenses. In the beginning of the 1992 campaign she was an outspoken campaigner and policy wonk. Responding to those who found her too aggressive, she appeared as a loving wife and mother, providing her chocolate cookie recipe for comparison with Barbara Bush's. During the first term, Hillary Rodham Clinton shifted from leading the government's aggressive effort to redesign health care to promoting the more traditionally feminine cause of child welfare.

Hillary Rodham Clinton's continual evolution irritates critics who believe the transformations reveal her to be superficial, manipulative, or both. The First Lady's ability to respond to criticism and change in order to deflect it makes her a moving target. When criticized, she adapts. While she risks appearing inconsistent, Hillary Rodham Clinton maintains her relevancy. As a result, she continues to be an effective political force almost a decade after critics first aimed their sights at her.

In this chapter, Scotland's KIRSTY SCOTT describes Hillary's incremental softening over time and decries indications that the "new and confused cardboard Hillary is what the American people seem to want." Playwright WENDY WASSERSTEIN suggests that Mrs. Clinton's transformations send younger women the message that, in fact, "you can't have it all."

A Pale Image of the Real Hillary

Kirsty Scott

IN THE LAND WHERE REINVENTION of oneself is a national pastime, few have been as comprehensively made over, or perhaps done over, as America's First Lady, Hillary Clinton. The quiet, almost introspective woman who arrived in the UK and Ireland this week bears no resemblance to the tough-talking, uncompromising Hillary Rodham Clinton who burst on to the presidential campaign trail in 1992, laughing at suggestions that she should stay home and bake cookies, and completely eclipsing her pliant and philandering spouse.

The Hillary of 1997 has become a walking compromise, squeezed and moulded by the events of the past five blistering Washington years: the disastrous failure of her health care reform measures, the Whitewater affair, and her appearance before a grand jury, the accusation that she was a congenital liar by the country's most respected columnist, the President's alleged indiscretions, the suicide of a close friend and aide, rumours that she used psychics to contact Mahatma Gandhi and Eleanor Roosevelt, and behind it all the heavy continued pressure of public disapproval.

In the early days she tried to weather the storm, changing her hair, if not her opinions, to try to please. But turning blonder and fluffier cut no ice and so her focus started to shift. Gone were the heavyweight, meaty issues and in their place she claimed a passion for the issues affecting women and children. She wrote a book on child-rearing with such cheesy chapter headings as: Kids Don't Come With Instructions, and hinted that she would like a sibling for daughter Chelsea. She then "admitted" publicly that she had been naive and dumb in her approach to national politics and questioned her own political savvy. She started holding briefings with female feature writers rather than the Washington press corps, she was filmed baking in a White House kitchen. The nicknames of Feminazi and Sister Frigidaire began to recede. She became the dutiful and unthreatening wife, the devoted mom, the pillar of society.

Around the time of the re-election campaign she started to withdraw from the spotlight altogether. There were no interviews and few sightings. If she spoke at all it was through her husband or aides. She effectively disappeared. This for a woman whose graduation speech from Yale Law School made it into the pages of the *Washington Post*, who was named as one of the top 100 lawyers in the US, whose fierce intellect and social conscience won her the accolade of Girl Most Likely to Succeed at high school, who refused to succumb to the redneck, sexist atmosphere of the Arkansas gubernatorial days; and who gave women everywhere the briefest glimmer of hope that a bright, strong, articulate woman might be allowed a position of substance and influence in the world's most powerful nation.

It was not to be and the Hillary who turned 50 this past week is now more Barbara Bush than Betty Friedan. She has been broken and re-trained.

Her birthday celebrations, which have dragged on for weeks with one fawning love-fest after another, culminated in an appearance on the Oprah Winfrey chat show where much of the conversation was taken up with her appearance and her parenting skills. "Don't you think you look better than ever?" said Winfrey. "I think you've found your place. I think the hair, it's there. It's there!" "We've finally found a haircut for me," Clinton added, as the audience roared their approval.

And this is the saddest thing of all. That this new confused and cardboard Hillary is what the American people seem to want. Her approval rating which slumped to around 45 percent during the Whitewater debacle has shot up to around 67 percent and she now outranks her husband in the popularity stakes.

White House officials talk with pride of the work they have done on the First Lady. Just last week a top aide told the *New York Times*: "Her team have done a really good job of repositioning her. This has been a disciplined and focused comeback, a result of a series of very careful choices. Instead of doing 50 things, she's chosen a few high-profile projects and foreign trips with children and women's issues as the central theme. They have picked their spots carefully and it has worked."

There is always the hope that this re-emergence, however skewed, may signal the start of a real Hillary comeback. That in a few years we might see the old fire returning and the powder and pastels consigned to the White House dustbin. Indeed, some US commentators have already written with some alarm that the visit to the UK and Ireland are feelers for a more high-profile role. However, officials on both sides of the Atlantic have been quick to point out that her talks with Tony Blair will cover child care and education and she will spend her time in Dublin and Belfast discussing the role of women and youth in democracy and the peace process. Hillary, too, has destroyed any such thoughts, sticking firmly to the party line and insisting she is only doing what she has always wanted to do. Working with women and small children.

But, for all her insistence, her own confusion about who she is supposed to be can sometimes break through. During yet another public celebration to mark her half-century Mrs Clinton told an audience at the Chicago Historical Society last week: "I feel like I'm sort of in this disembodied experience."

An even more telling moment came towards the end of the week when she was taken back to her old Elementary School in Park Ridge, Illinois. Sitting down with former classmates and teachers she was asked to reminisce about the trivialities of early childhood. As the group around her introduced themselves to the media, one schoolfriend turned jokingly to the First Lady, asking: "And who are you?" Mrs Clinton looked a little taken aback and thought for a moment before she responded. "That's the question we're trying to answer," she said.

— ***Kirsty Scott*** is a free-lance writer at *The Guardian* (Manchester). Previously, she was a reporter for *The Herald* (Glasgow). This article appeared in the *The Herald* (October 31, 1997).

Hillary Clinton's Muddled Legacy

Wendy Wasserstein

HILLARY RODHAM, IN HER 1969 Wellesley College commencement address, eloquently summed up the hopes of her generation: "We're searching for more immediate, ecstatic and penetrating modes of living. . . . Every protest, every dissent, is unabashedly an attempt to forge an identity in this particular age."

That idealistic, forthright Hillary is gone — one of the saddest and most destructive consequences of the Monica Lewinsky scandal. In her place is a new Hillary, loyal wife. And, according to a recent *New York Times*/CBS News poll, 73 percent of Americans now approve of her. Her approval rating is at a record high, even as her actual achievements are at a record low.

As a 1971 graduate of Mount Holyoke College, I have always been struck by the fact that the three most recent First Ladies had all attended women's colleges. Both Barbara Bush and Nancy Reagan did a stint at Smith, and Hillary Rodham graduated from her alma mater with flying colors. Like their Seven Sisters classmates, all three women were trained to develop an independent intellect as well as the grace to serve living room teas.

Though I am not a close friend of Mrs. Clinton, I have had the pleasure of making her acquaintance on several occasions, including a dinner at my brother's house two weeks ago. In 1993, at an intimate supper for 100 (the guests included Toni Morrison and Julia Roberts), I watched in awe as the newly installed First Lady confidently whispered to the head waiter when to begin serving dessert.

I had no idea where this graduate of Yale Law School and children's rights advocate could possibly have picked up such a skill. But then I remembered dressing for "Gracious Living," a semi-weekly ritual at Mount Holyoke that consisted of formal dinners, complete with waitresses and folded cloth napkins. I'm sure Wellesley had its equivalent when Hillary Rodham was a student, too.

But the times were changing. When I entered college in 1967, the First Lady's junior year, it was not uncommon for students to describe themselves as "hoping to marry Harvard." By 1970, women's history was being taught at Mount Holyoke with a syllabus that included books by Betty Friedan and Germaine Greer.

Women like Hillary Rodham suddenly had the same career opportunities as the men they were supposed to wed. Marriage would be for love or companionship, but would no longer be a substitute for individual destiny.

If anyone's life would have been transformed by the burgeoning women's movement, it should have been hers. Ask any Yale Law School graduate of that era and he or she will remember the brilliance and ambition of Hillary Rodham. She was an activist, a student leader, someone with a great sense of civic responsibility. She was the hope for a new definition of professional women.

Not that anyone thought it would be easy. My college classmate Harriet Sachs, who started a women's law firm in Toronto, told me recently, "Hillary is a transitional figure." In fact, Mrs. Clinton has used those very words herself to describe her role in America's political landscape. Sadly, however, her current popularity seems a bridge to the past rather than the future.

The wife of the Presidential candidate who told a CBS interviewer in 1992 that "I'm not some little woman standing by my man like Tammy Wynette" is now being applauded for doing precisely that. The First Lady who dared to take on health care reform has now been diminished to a popular soap opera heroine. Maintaining the dignity of her marriage, difficult as that may be, is now seen as her greatest professional triumph.

Of course, she may have had no choice — what else would anyone have done in such a situation? But the truth is, long before anyone had ever heard of Monica Lewinsky, Hillary Rodham Clinton was hardly a feminist icon. She has always sent confusing signals.

She has flip-flopped on so many issues of image that her behavior can justifiably be called erratic. First she defiantly wasn't baking cookies, then suddenly we were barraged with her recipes for Christmas cookies. Initially, she sandwiched "Rodham" within her name, and then it magically disappeared. When the coast was clear, it slinked back out again. Her husband implied she'd be co-president, a first rate two-for-one bargain. Then her health care reform package failed, and she retreated.

Now, the impressive personal qualities — idealism, strength and poise under pressure — that she once directed toward influencing social policy are being used to maintain domestic tranquillity.

Sadly, the messages being sent to the younger generation of women are that "you can't have it all" and "don't expect too much." The name Hillary Rodham Clinton no longer stands for self-determination, but for the loyal, betrayed wife. She is moving further and further away from her role model, Eleanor Roosevelt, who used her perch as First Lady to be an independent advocate.

Indeed, Mrs. Clinton's high approval ratings means she's currently appealing to a constituency — older, more conservative women — that had never supported her. Those who were threatened by a First Lady who was aggressive and professional are impressed by her ability to keep the home fires burning in dire circumstance. Pity and admiration have become synonymous.

One hopes this will not be the end result. It's certainly not what all the feminists who have stood by Bill Clinton intended. One instinctively knows this is not what Hillary Clinton intended.

Personally, I wish the talented Hillary Rodham Clinton would stand up and sign in please. We women of her generation had hoped she would break new ground. Yet what seemed initially so positive is becoming a very unsavory parable.

— ***Wendy Wasserstein*** is a Pulitzer Prize and Tony Award-winning playwright whose works include *The Heidi Chronicles* and *An American Daughter*. (August 25, 1998.)

International Development &
Women's Rights

HILLARY RODHAM CLINTON'S commitment to women's rights has changed the face of U.S. international assistance. Her fact-finding and diplomatic trips have taken her all over the world, and she is described as the most traveled First Lady. By 1996, Mrs. Clinton had visited over 25 foreign countries. Her message has been consistent: women's lives matter, women are vitally important to their communities, women must be equal partners in their nations' growth and development.

Hillary Rodham Clinton used her trips to focus public attention on international development and assistance. She often highlighted the condition of women's lives and programs for improving their social and economic power. In 1997, PETER BAKER accompanied Mrs. Clinton to Africa — her ninth solo international trip — and describes how she flourishes away from the pressure and stress of Washington. THOMAS LIPPMAN looks at Mrs. Clinton's efforts to expand public and political support for foreign aid, pointing out that U.S. spends less than any other industrialized country on international assistance.

This section begins with MRS. CLINTON's highly regarded speech at the 1995 United Nations' Fourth World Conference on Women held in Beijing, China. Her remarks provide an example not only of Mrs. Clinton's power of oration (even critic William Safire has praised her speeches), but also the strength of her convictions about the importance of women's social and economic development.

Women's Rights are Human Rights

When families flourish, communities and nations will flourish

Hillary Rodham Clinton

MRS. MONGELLA, DISTINGUISHED DELEGATES and guests: I would like to thank the Secretary General of the United Nations for inviting me to be a part of the United Nations Fourth World Conference on Women. This is truly a celebration — a celebration of the contributions women make in every aspect of life: in the home, on the job, in their communities, as mothers, wives, sisters, daughters, learners, workers, citizens and leaders.

It is also a coming together, much the way women come together every day in every country. We come together in fields and in factories. In village markets and supermarkets. In living rooms and board rooms.

Whether it is while playing with our children in the park, or washing clothes in a river, or taking a break at the office water cooler, we come together and talk about our aspirations and concerns. And time and again, our talk turns to our children and our families.

However different we may be, there is far more that unites us than divides us. We share a common future. And we are here to find common ground so that we may help bring new dignity and respect to women and girls all over the world — and in so doing, bring new strength and stability to families as well.

By gathering in Beijing, we are focusing world attention on issues that matter most in the lives of women and their families, access to education, health care, jobs, and credit, the chance to enjoy basic legal and human rights and participate fully in the political life of their countries.

There are some who question the reason for this conference. Let them listen to the voices of women in their homes, neighborhoods, and workplaces. There are some who wonder whether the lives of women and girls matter to economic and political progress around the globe. Let them look at the women gathered here and at Hairou . . . the homemakers, nurses, teachers, lawyers, policymakers, and women who run their own businesses.

It is conferences like this that compel governments and peoples everywhere to listen, look and face the world's most pressing problems.

Wasn't it after the women's conference in Nairobi ten years ago that the world focused for the first time on the crisis of domestic violence?

Earlier today, I participated in a World Health Organization forum, where government officials, NGOs [non-governmental organizations], and individual citizens are working on ways to address the health problems of women and girls.

Tomorrow, I will attend a gathering of the United Nations Development Fund for Women. There, the discussion will focus on local — and highly successful — programs that give hard-working women access to credit so they can improve their own lives and the lives of their families.

What we are learning around the world is that, if women are healthy and educated, their families will flourish. If women are free from violence, their families will flourish. If women have a chance to work and earn as full and equal partners in society, their families will flourish.

And when families flourish, communities and nations will flourish.

That is why every woman, every man, every child, every family, and every nation on our planet has a stake in the discussion that takes place here.

Over the past 25 years, I have worked persistently on issues relating to women, children and families. Over the past two-and-a-half years, I have had the opportunity to learn more about the challenges facing women in my own country and around the world.

I have met new mothers in Jojakarta, Indonesia, who come together regularly in their village to discuss nutrition, family planning, and baby care.

I have met working parents in Denmark who talk about the comfort they feel in knowing that their children can be cared for in creative, safe, and nurturing after-school centers.

I have met women in South Africa who helped lead the struggle to end apartheid and are now helping build a new democracy.

I have met with the leading women of the Western Hemisphere who are working every day to promote literacy and better health care for the children of their countries.

I have met women in India and Bangladesh who are taking out small loans to buy milk cows, rickshaws, thread and other materials to create a livelihood for themselves and their families.

I have met doctors and nurses in Belarus and Ukraine who are trying to keep children alive in the aftermath of Chernobyl.

The great challenge of this conference is to give voice to women everywhere whose experiences go unnoticed, whose words go unheard.

Women comprise more than half the world's population. Women are 70 percent of the world's poor, and two-thirds of those who are not taught to read and write.

Women are the primary caretakers for most of the world's children and elderly. Yet much of the work we do is not valued — not by economists, not by historians, not by popular culture, not by government leaders.

At this very moment, as we sit here, women around the world are giving birth, raising children, cooking meals, washing clothes, cleaning houses, planting crops, working on assembly lines, running companies, and running countries.

Women also are dying from diseases that should have been prevented or treated; they are watching their children succumb to malnutrition caused by poverty and economic deprivation; they are being denied the right to go to school by their own fathers and brothers; they are being forced into prostitution, and they are being barred from the ballot box and the bank lending office.

Those of us who have the opportunity to be here have the responsibility to speak for those who could not.

As an American, I want to speak up for women in my own country — women who are raising children on the minimum wage, women who can't afford health care or child care, women whose lives are threatened by violence, including violence in their own homes.

I want to speak up for mothers who are fighting for good schools, safe neighborhoods, clean air and clean airwaves . . . for older women, some of them widows, who have raised their families and now find that their skills and life experiences are not valued in the workplace . . . for women who are working all night as nurses, hotel clerks, and fast food chefs so that they can be at home during the day with their kids . . . and for women everywhere who simply don't have time to do everything they are called upon to do each day.

Speaking to you today, I speak for them, just as each of us speak for women around the world who are denied the chance to go to school, or see a doctor, or own property, or have a say about the direction of their lives, simply because they are women.

The truth is that most women around the world work both inside and outside the home, usually by necessity.

We need to understand that there is no formula for how women should lead their lives. That is why we must respect the choices that each woman makes for herself and her family. Every woman deserves the chance to realize her God-given potential.

We also must recognize that women will never gain full dignity until their human rights are respected and protected.

Our goals for this conference, to strengthen families and societies by empowering women to take greater control over their own destinies, cannot be fully achieved unless all governments — here and around the world — accept their responsibility to protect and promote internationally recognized human rights.

The international community has long acknowledged — and recently affirmed at Vienna — that both women and men are entitled to a range of protections and personal freedoms, from the right of personal security to the right to determine freely the number and spacing of the children they bear.

No one should be forced to remain silent for fear of religious or political persecution, arrest, abuse or torture.

Tragically, women are most often the ones whose human rights are violated. Even in the late 20th century, the rape of women continues to be used as an instrument of armed conflict. Women and children make up a large majority of the world's refugees. And when women are excluded from the political process, they become even more vulnerable to abuse.

I believe that, on the eve of a new millennium, it is time to break our silence. It is time for us to say here in Beijing, and the world to hear, that it is no longer acceptable to discuss women's rights as separate from human rights.

These abuses have continued because, for too long, the history of women has been a history of silence. Even today, there are those who are trying to silence our words.

The voices of this conference and of the women at Hairou must be heard loud and clear.

It is a violation of human rights when babies are denied food, or drowned, or suffocated, or their spines broken, simply because they are born girls.

It is a violation of human rights when women and girls are sold into the slavery of prostitution.

It is a violation of human rights when women are doused with gasoline, set on fire and burned to death because their marriage dowries are deemed too small.

It is a violation of human rights when individual women are raped in their own communities and when thousands of women are subjected to rape as a tactic or prize of war.

It is a violation of human rights when a leading cause of death worldwide among women ages 14 to 44 is the violence they are subjected to in their own homes.

It is a violation of human rights when young girls are brutalized by the painful and degrading practice of genital mutilation.

It is a violation of human rights when women are denied the right to plan their own families, and that includes being forced to have abortions or being sterilized against their will.

If there is one message that echoes forth from this conference, it is that human rights are women's rights .... And women's rights are human rights. Let us not forget that among those rights are the right to speak freely. And the right to be heard.

Women must enjoy the right to participate fully in the social and political lives of their countries if we want freedom and democracy to thrive and endure. It is indefensible that many women in non-governmental organizations who wished to participate in this conference have not been able to attend — or have been prohibited from fully taking part.

Let me be clear. Freedom means the right of people to assemble, organize, and debate openly. It means respecting the views of those who may disagree with the views of their governments. It means not taking citizens away from their loved ones and jailing them, mistreating them, or denying them their freedom or dignity because of the peaceful expression of their ideas and opinions.

In my country, we recently celebrated the 75th anniversary of women's suffrage. It took 150 years after the signing of our Declaration of Independence for women to win the right to vote. It took 72 years of organized struggle on the part of many courageous women and men.

It was one of America's most divisive philosophical wars. But it was also a bloodless war. Suffrage was achieved without a shot fired.

We have also been reminded, in V-J Day observances last weekend, of the good that comes when men and women join together to combat the forces of tyranny and build a better world.

We have seen peace prevail in most places for a half century. We have avoided another world war.

But we have not solved older, deeply-rooted problems that continue to diminish the potential of half the world's population.

Now is the time to act on behalf of women everywhere.

If we take bold steps to better the lives of women, we will be taking bold steps to better the lives of children and families too. Families rely on mothers and wives for emotional support and care; families rely on women for labor in the home, and increasingly, families rely on women for income needed to raise healthy children and care for other relatives.

As long as discrimination and inequities remain so commonplace around the world — as long as girls and women are valued less, fed less, fed last, overworked, underpaid, not schooled and subjected to violence in and out of their homes — the potential of the human family to create a peaceful, prosperous world will not be realized.

Let this conference be our — and the world's — call to action.

And let us heed the call so that we can create a world in which every woman is treated with respect and dignity, every boy and girl is loved and cared for equally, and every family has the hope of a strong and stable future.

Thank you very much.

God's blessings on you, your work and all who will benefit from it.

— ***Hillary Rodham Clinton*** delivered this speech at the United Nations' Fourth World Conference on Women, held in Beijing, China, 1995.

The Woman Behind the Mask
Away from Washington, Hillary Clinton Shows a Different Face

Peter Baker

THE MARIMBA MUSICIANS and young dancing girls had already gone through three or four numbers by the time Hillary Rodham Clinton and her entourage arrived. As unobtrusively as possible, Clinton and daughter Chelsea slipped into the second row and took their seats on a bench in the small dirt-floor theater surrounded by thatched huts.

The first lady was glad to be in the second row. That way when the dancers tried to entice someone in the crowd to get up and sway with them to the African drums, she figured she would be safe while some unfortunate soul in the front row would be the one subjected to that public ordeal.

Sure enough, one of the aides on her goodwill trip through Africa, Steve Cohen, fell victim. A barefoot tribesman with an elaborate feather headdress had just picked up an 88-pound iron bar with his teeth and danced with it. Luckily for his dental plan, Cohen wasn't asked to duplicate this Simbi tradition, but merely to verify the weight of the bar by lifting it — with his hands. It took both of them just to get it to his knees.

Clinton took great delight in this, as she did in the Shangaan war dancing and the Makishi circumcision rituals and the small children in a giant crocodile costume who pretended to attack the television reporter sitting in front of her. But it was one of the last acts of the evening that elicited an audible response.

"Oh, look at the masks!" she exclaimed with a tone of almost child-like wonderment as another group of performers entered the stage. Their intricately carved masks were as large as the people they adorned — massive red-white-and-black faces, some appearing happy, some severe and others simply inscrutable.

Even with all of the remarkable sights and sounds she had witnessed this day — from the mist-shrouded rainbows over the world's largest waterfall to the long-tusked wild elephants rumbling along the shoreline during a Zambezi riverboat cruise — perhaps it should come as no surprise that the masks seemed to get Hillary Clinton's attention. In this land of many faces, she fits right in.

A two-week journey through Africa with the first lady provides ample opportunities to view all of Hillary Clinton's intricately carved masks — the happy, the severe, the inscrutable. Most of these are the faces she chooses to show: the empathetic presidential spouse visiting blind children in the Zimbabwean capital of Harare; the children's advocate greeted by a round of "We Are the World" at a Senegalese girls' school named after Martin Luther King Jr.; the goodwill ambassador paying courtesy calls on foreign potentates and announcing tiny dollops of U.S. financial assistance. There is also the face of the social activist conducting rambling round-table discussions with local leaders and inspecting innovative self-help programs for the downtrodden.

And then, every once in a while, the mask slips ever so slightly. In these rare moments, those around her get a glimpse of the anxious mother traveling on spring break with her only child, who at 17 is due to leave for college all too soon. Or the international feminist momentarily freed from the shackles of domestic politics, urging "solidarity" among the women of the world.

"These are all the same Hillary," said Melanne Verveer, her confidante and deputy chief of staff who is traveling with her through Africa. "You have to look at the totality of her life. This is who she is . . . . But they're not indivisible. They're all facets of who she is."

LIKE A SISTER

WHEREVER HER AIR FORCE plane has touched down in capitals across the continent over the past 11 days, the locals invariably have rolled out the red carpet for Hillary Clinton. Literally a red carpet, however frayed from use or damp with rain.

"Sister Hillary," as she was called in Dakar, Senegal, has been welcomed like visiting royalty. Half-naked dancers meet her on the tarmac. Singers compose lyrics in her honor. Women ululate in the distinctive high-pitched African warble that sounds strangely like an Indian war cry from an old cowboy movie.

Little wonder, then, that the woman who feels she has been treated so harshly by her many critics at home has ventured out of the country so often. This is her ninth solo trip abroad since moving into the White House, making her the most traveled first lady in history, according to the military officials in charge of transporting the presidential family. She has been to so many places, she has left her name behind. In Managua, they named a small-loan project after her, in Bucharest a school, in Prague an orphanage and in Bangladesh a whole village.

This trip to Africa is something of a landmark as well, the first time a president's wife embarked on her own for such an extensive tour of the sub-Saharan continent. And next week after she returns, her staff can begin nailing down her next destination, most likely the former Soviet republics later this year.

Overseas, she is "getting over her limited boundaries," said Gertrude Mongella, an activist in Tanzania who served as secretary-general of the United Nations Fourth World Conference on Women in Beijing in 1995. "She's more and more opening up her talents and skills. With the role she's playing now, she has just opened up like a pack of flowers."

Yet as bracing as it is to be admired abroad, Clinton still seems painfully uncomfortable at times in her role as a public figure.

In the South African township of Soweto, where the struggle against the system of racial oppression known as apartheid sparked a bloody student uprising more than two decades ago, Clinton stopped by a memorial to its first victim, a teenager named Hector Peterson. As the event ended, she saw a cheering crowd of hundreds of local residents who had been awaiting her for hours. Bill Clinton would have immediately headed over and shaken every hand he could. But for Hillary, a simple wave and smile would do.

Before the first lady could get into her car, though, Tokyo Sexwale, a leading anti-apartheid figure who now serves as provincial premier, implored her to go meet the masses. Given little choice, she turned and headed down the patch of grass, setting off a frenzy among surprised photographers and Secret Service agents rushing to catch her, unaccustomed to such spontaneity.

At the metal gate, her admirers seemed to turn into an uncontrolled mob, practically pushing over the barrier separating them, grasping her hands and arms and not letting go. Security guards began pushing back. Bodies were jostled, including hers. So with that, after perhaps 30 seconds of hand-shaking, Clinton turned on her heel and retreated to the safety of the car.

THE TEACHER

PRIMROSE SISHI RUNS A small school in South Africa where Zulu children are taught English. It's an out-of-the-way place, far from the world stage. So word that the wife of the American president would visit "gave me a lot of panic," Sishi admitted.

But that evaporated when Hillary Clinton showed up last week and glided into a classroom, easily slipping into the role of guest teacher, gently drilling the students on the difference between "inside" and "outside." This wasn't some exalted dignitary, Sishi decided; this was another woman with a passion for children and education.

"I felt so relaxed, especially when I first met her, finding that she was so warm, loving, understanding," said Sishi, wearing bright orange native-style garb and a black headdress.

Pauline Mukurazano, a 36-year-old widow and mother of four from Chitungwiza, Zimbabwe, had never really heard of Clinton, but decided after seeing her speak at a rural church that the first lady is actually an approachable person. Mukurazano said through an interpreter that she believed she "could just walk up and start a conversation" with Clinton.

It's hard to reconcile those impressions with the ones held by so many back home. She also has her share of fans in the United States, but in some quarters, Clinton is perceived as chilly and self-righteous, responsible for all manner of sins from the failed health care plan to Whitewater to the travel office firings. She is anything but approachable.

Once outside of the 200-mile territorial waters, though, the first lady can seem like a different person, more relaxed, liberated even. Out on the road, aides say, she can show more of the likable human side they see behind closed doors.

She occasionally strolls to the back of her plane to banter with the same reporters she spends so much time avoiding in Washington; while in Africa she has invited the press corps to lunch at a South African winery and several dinners in Tanzanian restaurants. After hugging local embassy officials during a departure ceremony a few days ago, she became caught up in the moment and suddenly turned to the news photographers hovering nearby and hugged them, too.

At these rare unscripted moments, she seems like a different person than the public speaker who carefully enunciates every word as if considering the weight of each before it comes out. She's chatty and engaging as she talks about her husband's knee injury and her daughter's college choices.

Still, Clinton gives the illusion of access while revealing quite little. The meals and airplane visits are kept strictly off the record. Formal interview requests are rebuffed. The only opportunities for any public dialogue come in highly controlled settings, at the end of photo opportunities when she entertains a question or two with her public mask firmly on.

Does she view herself as "the co-pilot" of the United States, as Mongella described her? How does she see her role in the international arena? Is she freer to raise issues while traveling than at home? She is asked to ponder such questions after being shown a 1.75-million-year-old partial human skull in a museum in Dar es Salaam, the Tanzanian capital. But introspection rarely visits a small, sweaty museum vault packed with dozens of people.

"I don't think about that," she said before lapsing into the official line about her hopes for the trip. "I want more Americans to know more about what is going on in Africa beyond what is often in the headlines," she said, "so if my coming here can bring more attention to the continent . . . I hope that will help Americans have a broader understanding of Africa and understand more fully the real stake we can have in a successful, prosperous, stable Africa in the future."

TAKING THE PLUNGE

NOT FAR FROM PICTURESQUE Victoria Falls, where the spray from millions of gallons of plummeting water is so powerful that it produces billowing, smokelike clouds that can be seen from miles away, entrepreneurs offer the opportunity to plunge from a bridge at what they claim is the highest bungee-jumping site in the world.

Watching as a pair of customers were hauled back up to the bridge earlier this week, Clinton encountered a shaggy-haired tourist who didn't appear to recognize her.

"They say that after sex it's the best thing that could happen to you," the man told the first lady.

"Is that right?" Clinton replied, trying to sound matter-of-fact.

The first lady politely declined entreaties to find out for herself, but in a political sense, she is no stranger to bungee jumping. And she still takes a leap every once in a while.

As in her other trips, she has convened round-table discussions at nearly every stop in Africa to talk with local women's leaders about the challenges facing them in their home countries, from family planning to education and economic advancement to domestic violence.

In Johannesburg, she listened as Adelaide Tambo, a member of the South African Parliament and widow of the late anti-apartheid leader Oliver Tambo, described abused women who felt so exasperated by the legal system that they took it upon themselves to cut off the penis of one batterer. In Harare, Clinton was told that some men believe women deserve to be beaten because they "have no manners" or were "wearing the pants and therefore . . . trying to usurp the man's position."

Through it all, the first lady nodded sympathetically and expressed the desire that, as she put it during one discussion, "women would engage in more solidarity to present more of a united front."

She sounded similar themes during an appearance at the University of Cape Town. In response to questions from students, the first lady touted the benefits of girls-only schools, predicted that a female president would be elected in the United States within 20 years and warned that women should not be "tricked or seduced into undermining" each other.

The reason women have been elected to the highest office in other countries and not the United States, she speculated, might be due to parliamentary systems of government in which the prime minister is the leader of the majority party and not elected directly. "They do not have to go out and sell themselves to the entire country and face all the required questions that we in public life have to deal with," she said. "It's very difficult for women to answer many of the perceptions and stereotypes the public holds about them."

For one brief moment, she seemed to be talking about herself — the mask slipping, but never fully falling away.

— ***Peter Baker*** is a staff writer at *The Washington Post*. He covered President Clinton's re-election and second term, and was the *Post's* lead reporter on the Lewinsky scandal. He is currently writing a book about the impeachment proceedings. (March 27, 1997.)

Hillary Clinton Urges Public to Support Foreign Aid

Thomas Lippman

IT WAS ONE OF THOSE WASHINGTON events where what was said was less arresting than who was saying it.

The message: Foreign aid is beneficial not just to the recipients but to the donors, and the United States should give more of it. The messenger: first lady Hillary Rodham Clinton.

She invited reporters to the Map Room of the official residence yesterday to hear her and a team of senior administration officials make a pitch for public support of U.S. assistance to developing countries and to the countries of the former Soviet Union struggling to make the transition to democracy and free markets.

The conversation, she said, was "aimed at the American public," which she said needs to be convinced that aid is a valuable tool for stabilizing troubled societies, addressing problems such as disease and overpopulation that threaten U.S. national security, and protecting the environment.

Sipping tea from an oversized CNN mug as she presided over the hour-long session, Clinton spoke more in philosophical terms than in specifics, stressing her personal commitment to maintaining and expanding the U.S. role in global affairs.

The meeting was the fourth this year in a series she said she plans to conduct on issues "that we believe to be important but don't have time to discuss at any depth."

She said she will "continue to speak out" on the importance of partnerships between government and private industry, and between the United States and its allies, in addressing global problems that could become security threats.

The percentage of the U.S. budget devoted to foreign assistance has declined steadily for years, and the United States ranks last among industrialized nations in the percentage of economic output devoted to aid.

But the aid budget appears to have bottomed out, and Congress seems likely to give President Clinton nearly all of the $7.7 billion he sought for bilateral and multinational development programs for fiscal 1998.

Hillary Clinton attributed that turnabout to a growing recognition in the Republican-controlled Congress of the value of assistance programs, many of which involve government purchase of goods manufactured in this country.

"I'm not sure as to the exact numbers," Hillary Clinton said, "but I was told by several people who are old hands in foreign affairs that a very large proportion of the Congress as constituted after the 1994 election had never held a passport, had never traveled outside the United States.

"The numbers that were quoted to me were shockingly high," she said, without specifying them. "As people have become more familiar with what the United States has done for the past 50 years, and as people have traveled and had briefings and shaken hands with and talked with not only people representing the administration but business leaders here and abroad, there has been a real learning experience," she said.

Hillary Clinton acknowledged that she was expressing views that the administration has espoused from the beginning of her husband's first term, not offering anything new.

But she said three events made it appropriate to restate the argument yesterday: the recent celebration of the 50th anniversary of the Marshall Plan, the president's planned unveiling today of a trade and investment initiative for sub-Saharan Africa and the 500th humanitarian flight of "Operation Provide Hope," a joint State Department-Defense Department program to provide medical assistance — including entire hospitals — to the former Soviet Union.

Hillary Clinton, who visited Africa earlier this year, said news media attention to African crises has obscured the fact that there are promising developments in many parts of the continent. Just as it would have been misleading in the 1980s for Europeans to say North America was in turmoil because of violence in Central America, she said, it is inaccurate today to depict all of Africa as mired in backwardness.

"There are bright spots in Africa," she said, just as "Cambodia and Singapore are not the same" in assessments of progress in Southeast Asia.

Asked about the apparent anomaly of promoting an increase in U.S. government aid activity while the administration is stressing the global importance of the free market, Hillary Clinton said her husband is always seeking the proper balance, "always looking for the third way, the consensus."

Much of Europe is going through a similar search for the proper balance between government and private responsibility, she said, "and I think that's a very healthy position to be in. Because if you put all your eggs in the government basket, we know the results of that. If you put all your eggs in the free market basket, we know that inequalities can become severe and threaten democratic institutions."

—***Thomas Lippman*** was a staff writer for *The Washington Post* for over 30 years. He retired in 1999 and is now the Vice President for Communications for the World Wildlife Fund. He is the author, most recently, of *Madeline Albright and the New American Diplomacy*. (June 17, 1997.)

It Takes A Village & Children's Development

MRS. CLINTON'S LONG-STANDING commitment to children and her advocacy on their behalf are well known. Eight months before the 1996 presidential elections, she published *It Takes a Village and Other Lessons Children Teach Us*. The book, which mingles Mrs. Clinton's views on child development with down-home stories about her childhood and marriage, was a best-seller. That year, Mrs. Clinton won a Grammy Award for best "Spoken Word" recording.

Some people (like LASCELLE ANDERSON) loved the book, praising its dedication to the idea that the nation has a social duty to invest in our youngest and most vulnerable members. Others hated it, either because they confused its message of collective responsibility with Communism, or because (like KATHA POLLIT) they thought it didn't go far enough in presenting workable solutions to the serious problems confronting American society.

This chapter also contains one of MRS. CLINTON's syndicated columns on the subject of raising healthy children. Since 1995, Mrs. Clinton (like Mrs. Roosevelt before her) has written a weekly column that appears in newspapers all across the country. Often using the lives of ordinary Americans to illustrate issues being debated by Congress or the public, her columns are one example of the way the First Lady has learned to use her position to promote the policies and agendas in which she believes.

It Takes A Village: and Other Lessons Children Teach Us

Book Review

Lascelles Anderson

THE CONDITIONS THAT DESCRIBE the typical circumstances of the nation's urban poor children are so well known as not to require repetition. However, for the sake of setting the context for this book by the First Lady of the United States, just a few of the conditions that can be cited include the following: the alarming and increasing levels of poverty experienced by urban children and their families, the difficulties associated with living in predominantly single-parent homes, the high levels of teen pregnancy, and the alarming number of acts of violence these children have either experienced themselves or witnessed within their homes, neighborhoods, and communities.

These risk factors, along with a host of other life-threatening circumstances and experiences, are just some of the conditions that impelled Hillary Clinton to write *It Takes a Village*. The calamitous social and economic predicaments facing growing numbers of the nation's most vulnerable citizens are the targets her book inveighs so strongly against. In Clinton's view, "village" is a powerful metaphor for "always being there" for children, whether those children are members of one's own family, children from other communities, or children in far away places.

Thus, this book emerges as a call for action to American parents — indeed, to all adults everywhere — to consider their obligations to all children differently.

It Takes a Village is simultaneously both a deeply personal treatise as well as a spirited defense of public policy in defense of children and an argument for a richer understanding of collective responsibility for the young. Each chapter issues from Mrs. Clinton's personal experiences as a mother and children's rights advocate, but then goes on to generalize from those experiences to identify public policy initiatives that have or can bring services to children in more coherent and person-friendly ways. Notably, she also draws plentiful examples of practices in other countries, countries that may be thought of as "less developed" than the United States, which richly exemplify the principles supporting the idea of the nation as a "village" united in the service of children. Indeed, her chapter headings are themselves statements of these principles.

The fundamental proposition of *It Takes a Village* is that there is an organic reality to the relationships that hold communities together, whether these be the near communities of our immediate families or the larger communities that hold groups of families together so that they may each pursue their separate objectives. Clinton argues that understanding of this essential organicity of social life must be constantly nurtured. Moreover, because children are the most tangible representation of the future, our obligations to the future are therefore obligations to the children who are here now. We adults, she attests, must take those obligations seriously to support the objective of the fullest development of all children. We must also come to understand the need for rich, dense, and smart approaches to assure this outcome. Our public policies must undergird the realization of this goal in everyday life.

Another important contribution of this book is the skillful way in which Clinton uses common experiences to communicate meaning about Americans' collective responsibility to their near and distant communities, and to link policy implications to our understanding of this responsibility. By so doing, she advances readers' appreciation for a more reflective practice of parenting and, even more importantly, for a deeper understanding of the importance of a norm of caring to the sustainability of community.

A commanding sense of justice denied pervades the pages of this book, but it is balanced by a hopefulness that much can be accomplished to right the situation. To her credit, Clinton's empirical referents are many and compelling, and they are buttressed by anecdotal stories that coherently support her arguments. In drawing attention to the factors that contextualize and structure children's lives, Clinton shares important insights on how concerned adults can and must act to enrich those contexts and structures. In stating and supporting her fundamental arguments, she displays a substantial command of the scientific and policy literatures from physics to psychology to systems dynamics. She imports concepts from economics in her call for adults to view their obligations to children as an investment in our collective futures, prodding us to be early rather than late in addressing children's needs.

Noting that human capacities that are not renewed or actively sustained atrophy over time, Clinton admonishes us to realize that the longer we delay in addressing the risk factors influencing our children's health and well-being, the more difficult it becomes to successfully challenge the impact of those factors, especially when they operate jointly with other negative effects.

To some, *It Takes a Village* may appear "soft" and overly concerned with collective rather than personal responsibility. But such a perception would be a mistake, for what we now know about what constitutes the elements of a successful life supports the strong assertion of the need for supportive networks of one kind or another (and, in some cases, of many kinds of supports simultaneously) to foster the growth of resilient, confident responses to the many risk factors that increasingly characterize the conditions of our children's lives.

Powerfully argued and richly documented, although not in the typical style of a scholarly book, *It Takes a Village* performs an outstanding service on behalf of children everywhere. The book is clearly a success, and well worth reading at least twice to fully digest the very useful — and yes, hopeful — messages contained between its covers.

— ***Lascelle Anderson***, an economist, is a Professor of Education and Director of the Center for Urban Educational Research at the University of Illinois at Chicago. He is the co-editor of Education and Development: Issues in the Analysis and Planning of Post-Colonial Studies. Reprinted by permission of Dr. Anderson and the *Journal of Negro Education,* 65 (1996), 92-93.

Village Idiot

Katha Pollitt

"SAINT OR SINNER?" asks the cover of *Newsweek* about Hillary Clinton. On the *New York Times* Op-Ed page, Maureen Dowd calls her a hybrid of Earth Mother and Mommie Dearest. I must say, I don't see what all the fuss is about. Don't countless politicians (and their relatives) use their positions to make profitable contacts and advance their friends? And don't they all talk about family, morals, responsibility, children and God? Even if the First Lady is guilty of the worst that is alleged against her — and if you can explain exactly what that is, you've probably been up to no good yourself — there's nothing new or exceptional about it: See the careers of Newt Gingrich, Al D'Amato, Bob Dole et al. This is what politics is all about, especially in places like Arkansas, aka The Heartland. "The people you read about in the papers? They all live next door to each other," an Italian journalist told me after a visit to Little Rock. "It's just like Italy!"

Well, there is one new thing: the gender issue. A lot of people still expect the wives of politicians to concentrate on the Kinder-Kirche-Kueche side of life, while their husbands go after the bright lights and boodle. H.R.C. has failed to observe this division of labor in her own marriage, for which tradition-minded folk like William Safire cannot forgive her. Now the First Lady has written a book, *It Takes a Village: And Other Lessons Children Teach Us*, only to land herself in more hot water. In yet another column criticizing H.R.C., Maureen Dowd took her to task for not acknowledging the ghostly pen of Barbara Feinman, a former researcher and editor for Ben Bradlee, Bob Woodward and Sally Quinn, all now apparently up in arms at this slight to their beloved assistant. Between Whitewater, Madison Guaranty, Travelgate and now Thankyougate, H.R.C. isn't likely to get much time to talk about her book, and since I know how painful that can be, I sat down and read the whole thing. Who knows? I may be the only columnist in America who can make that claim.

The ostensible thesis of *It Takes a Village* is that the well-being of children depends on the whole society. The real message is that H.R.C. is for family values. She prays a lot, alone and en famille. She's a good mom. She thinks young people should abstain from sex until they are 21. She opposes divorce: "My strong feelings about divorce and its effects on children have caused me to bite my tongue more than a few times during my own marriage" — I'll bet — "and to think instead about what I could do to be a better wife and partner. My husband has done the same."

I know I'm not supposed to take these notions seriously, any more than I'm meant to gag at the weirdly Pollyannaish tone of the prose, or wonder if Sunday school could really have been her formative intellectual experience.

Like her disapproval of television talk shows — thanks to which "we are saturated with stories about priests who molest children" and have become "skeptical of organized religion" — they're just campaign theater, nods to the cultural conservatives that are balanced by other nods, to flexible gender roles, legal abortion (a very small nod), a "modest" rise in the minimum wage. There's no attempt to think anything through: the damage to organized religion versus the damage to children left at risk of molestation, for example, or the kinds of social pressures that would be necessary to produce that bumper crop of 21-year-old virgins. Her opposition to divorce is left characteristically vague: She's "ambivalent" about no-fault divorce (the pet peeve of former White House aide and communitarian William Galston, who proposed abolishing it for couples with children recently on the *Times* Op-Ed page), but she says nothing about what it would really mean to return to the old system, in which spouses, lawyers and judges colluded in perjury, and wives who strayed could be denied custody and support. It's easy for her to talk: Her husband has obligingly provided her with grounds that would withstand even the most Savonarolaesque reforms.

What else? The First Lady is for sex ed that has both an abstinence and, for those youths determined to ruin their lives, a birth-control component; a free market that's also socially responsible; government that's both smaller and more social-worky. For every problem she identifies, a study, a foundation, a church, a business or a government-funded pilot project is already on the case: teaching poor young mothers how to improve their babies' cognitive abilities, encouraging fathers to spend time with their families, involving parents in their children's school. Some of these programs sound terrific, but none of them are on remotely the same scale as the problems they confront. If parents are too poor to afford school uniforms, they've got problems much graver than the community recycling of hand-me-downs can solve. The First Lady is thus a kind of center-liberal version of Arianna Huffington, who claims that "spirituality" and volunteerism can replace the welfare state. For H.R.C. the state itself becomes a kind of pilot project, full of innovation but short on cash, and ever on the lookout for spongers.

The real irony, of course, is that at the same time H.R.C. is conceptualizing society as a "village" united in its concern for and responsibility toward children, her husband is panting to sign the original Senate welfare bill, which his own Administration's figures say would plunge 1.2 million more children into poverty and render more desperate the condition of those already poor. How can a self-described child advocate, who goes on and on about the importance of providing children with enriched parental attention and quality care from their earliest moments of life, square herself with policies that would force low-skilled mothers of small children into full-time subminimum-wage jobs, with warehouse care for their kids? Exactly how will permitting states to deny benefits to children born on welfare further those kids' development? And what about the kids at the end of the line when the block grants run out?

After the media figure out Whitewater and insure proper recognition of Ms. Feinman's labors, some enterprising reporter might consider asking the First Lady about that.

— ***Katha Pollitt*** is a columnist for *The Nation* and a poet whose work has appeared in *The New Yorker*, *The Atlantic* and *The New Republic*. She has also written for *The Atlantic*, *Harper's*, *Mother Jones* and *The New York Times*. She is the author of *Reasonable Creatures: Essays on Women and Feminism*. Reprinted with permission from the February 5, 1996 issue of *The Nation*.

Talking It Over

Hillary Rodham Clinton

SHORTLY AFTER MIDNIGHT on the morning of March 25, when my husband and I were in Uganda, we were awakened with tragic news. For the fourth time since October, American children had opened fire on classmates at school.

This time, these tragic events happened in a town we knew well, Jonesboro, Ark. Four young girls and a teacher were dead. Bill and I were heartsick at this senseless loss of life.

Across the country and around the world, the questions were the same: "How could this happen?" and "What does it mean?" On talk shows, in newspaper columns and at kitchen tables, people sought explanations for this outbreak of child violence. The President called on the Attorney General and the Secretary of Education to convene national experts to study the tragedy.

But as the shock recedes, we are left with more questions than answers about how to prevent children from harming other children. Despite our inability ever to understand fully, we have to analyze why two young boys turned to violence if we are to find any help for the next child who might choose a gun to deal with his pain and problems.

We must not let ourselves off the hook by talking about "bad children" and "good children." We, the adults, have choices, and we know that the choices we make — as individuals and as a society — will affect how our children develop.

Everywhere we look, children are under assault, not just from violence but from neglect, from the breakup of families, from the temptations of alcohol, tobacco, sex and drug abuse, and from greed, materialism and spiritual emptiness. One in five American children lives in poverty. One in four is born to an unmarried mother.

This instability poses great risks to the healthy development and economic security of our children. The disappearance of fathers from children's daily lives has many consequences, including increased rates of violence and aggressiveness among boys. One of the ways to counter the absence of fathers is for adults — especially men — to step into the role of mentor and guide.

Clearly, children deserve safety and security at home. Yet, hundreds of thousands of children are victims of abuse and neglect. A recent study shows that children reported abused and neglected are 67 times more likely to be arrested between the ages of 9 and 12 than other children. Buffalo, N.Y.'s Police Commissioner Gil Kerlikowske sums it up this way: "We'll win the war on crime when we invest tax dollars in America's most vulnerable kids, instead of waiting until they become America's most wanted adults."

One of the best ways to combat juvenile crime is to give kids something positive to do after school. We should follow the example of Houston, Texas, where children play golf and soccer after school. Their mentors are coaches and teachers, not gang leaders.

We also have a responsibility to protect our children at home. Guns are the fourth leading cause of accidental deaths among children ages 5 to 14. Almost half of American households have guns, but often, instead of being locked up, they are merely hidden or left in a drawer.

In addition, we must take weapons off the streets. This week, my husband blocked the import of 58 types of military-style assault weapons into this country. As was the case when he signed the Brady bill, the gun lobbyists and manufacturers assailed the move and threatened to sue.

It's a moral outrage that these lobbyists and manufacturers are fighting this measure while at the same time marketing their products to our children — just as the tobacco industry has for years. Every self-respecting gun owner should condemn this latest cynical move to turn children into targets of gun advertising before they are emotionally able to handle the responsibility.

And let's not overlook the importance of the mass media. Too many television shows, movies and rock lyrics romanticize and trivialize violence. And video games have managed to transform millions of television sets into scenes of violence that children not only watch but also participate in.

As I have suggested many times, it's time to turn the TV off and spend more time with our kids. Time, after all, is what every child wants and needs. We live in a fast world, where slowing down to spend time with our families is hard to do — unless we make it a priority.

Our children are our greatest gift, our greatest responsibility, our greatest test. Never again do I want to wake in the middle of the night to the news that another child has murdered a friend or classmate. It's time for us to look into our children's eyes and remember what's important.

We owe this to Shannon Wright, the courageous teacher who sacrificed her life for her students. Her 3-year-old son keeps asking, "Where's Mommy?" We owe this to Natalie Brooks, Paige Ann Herring, Stephanie Johnson, Brittheny Varner and all the other children who have died so tragically on our watch.

— ***Hillary Rodham Clinton*** is a lawyer and children's rights advocate. She is the first First Lady to run for the Senate. She is the author of *It Takes a Village, and Other Lessons Children Teach Us*, as well as "Talking It Over," a syndicated weekly column drawing on her experience as First Lady. This article appeared on April 8, 1998.

Monica & Marriage

IN THE COURSE OF INVESTIGATING Whitewater, Independent Counsel Kenneth Starr discovered that President Clinton had had an affair with a young White House intern named Monica Lewinsky — and lied about it. The resulting scandal almost brought down the government.

In 1997, the Supreme Court ruled that a civil suit (Paula Jones' sexual harassment charges against then-Governor Clinton for activities that allegedly occurred in 1991) could be brought against the sitting president. In his January 1998, deposition in the Jones case, President Clinton denied having had a sexual relationship with Monica Lewinsky. Lewinsky, under oath, also denied the relationship. That same month, Starr received several hours of taped phone conversations from Linda Tripp, in which Lewinsky detailed her illicit relationship with the president.

In late January, news reports broke the story that Starr was expanding his investigation to examine whether Clinton had encouraged Lewinsky to lie about their affair in her Jones deposition. Starr believed Clinton may have lied under oath about the relationship and asked Lewinsky to do likewise. Starr therefore wanted to investigate whether Clinton was trying to hamper the on-going Whitewater investigation by obstructing justice, committing perjury and/or tampering with witnesses.

President Clinton vigorously denied the rumors with the now infamous remark that he "did not have sex with that woman, Miss Lewinsky." In this chapter, BRONWEN MADDOX describes Mrs. Clinton's fierceness in rallying to his defense against what she called a "vast right wing conspiracy" and looks at how Hillary's reaction was grounded not only in their 22-year marriage but also in her childhood.

After forensic evidence proved the allegations, Bill Clinton admitted the affair in a televised speech in August, and apologized. The First Lady released a statement saying that she "is committed to her marriage and loves her husband and daughter very much . . . she believes in the president, and her love for him is compassionate and steadfast." MARGARET CARLSON de-

scribes Mrs. Clinton's devastation at being "misled" by her husband.

The Independent Counsel delivered its findings to Congress in September, 1998. *The Starr Report* ran thousands of pages, included graphic descriptions of sexual acts between Lewinsky and Clinton and related evidence on the possible grounds for impeachment. In December, Bill Clinton became the second president ever to be impeached by Congress, for the "High Crimes and Misdemeanors" of lying under oath and obstructing justice to cover up the affair. The Senate trial ended in acquittal in February 1999, but the damage to Clinton's legacy may be irredeemable.

This section explores the Lewinsky scandal and, particularly, its effects on the Clinton's. JOE KLEIN looks at the state of the Clinton's marriage, while LOIS ROMANO examines how Mrs. Clinton's popularity skyrocketed as she nobly stood by her wayward husband. In 1999, Hillary Rodham Clinton granted a rare interview for the premiere issue of *Talk*. In her comments, Mrs. Clinton for the first time publicly discussed her husband's affair with Monica Lewinsky saying, "I don't believe in denying things. I believe in working through it. Is he ashamed? Yes. Is he sorry? Yes. But does this negate everything he's done as a husband, a father, a president?" MARY DEJEVSKY provides an overview of her remarks.

When the First Lady Took the Gloves Off

Bronwen Maddox

HILLARY CLINTON HAS COME OUT fighting for her man this week. But will she drop him if he falls?

In turning to nationwide television to mount her poised and passionate defence of her husband this week, Hillary Clinton told Americans: "I'm not only here because I love and believe in my husband." She added a banal elaboration — "I'm also here because I love and believe in my country." But her phrase was seized on as a reminder that in these uniquely troubled times for the Clinton presidency, Hillary Rodham Clinton has her own agenda.

The past extraordinary ten days in American politics have reopened perpetually intriguing questions about the First Lady. Will the woman who is a model for many American feminists continue to stand by her wayward man? Is she, as many believe, the power behind the throne, guiding a man who has repeatedly turned to strong women to fight his battles? And, as even her aides are now asking privately, when her husband's term in the White House ends in November 2000, will she quit their 22-year marriage and choose finally to start her own political career?

The President has vigorously denied allegations that he had an affair with 24-year-old Monica Lewinsky and tried to cover it up. But even if entirely unfounded, the claims have given the country cause to revisit the repeated humiliations he has inflicted on his family and political supporters.

Ms. Lewinsky's dresses and trouser suits are under forensic examination by the FBI for traces of Bill Clinton's semen. Mr. Clinton is said to have admitted on oath an affair with the Arkansas cabaret singer Gennifer Flowers, which he denied vehemently in his 1992 election campaign. And former adviser Dick Morris, who was himself disgraced after giving presidential secrets to a prostitute, pondered on national radio whether the President had been prompted to stray by "Hillary not necessarily being into regular sex with men," although he added he did not mean to suggest she was gay.

Hillary's reaction to this kaleidoscope of marital embarrassments has been to come out fighting. In two fluent breakfast television interviews this week, she attacked "the vast right-wing conspiracy that has been conspiring against my husband since the day he announced for President."

In contrast, her husband's 54-word denial, scripted by lawyers, when he denounced "that woman, Ms. Lewinsky," sounded persecuted and tense.

Hillary's breakfast show interviews were a public relations masterpiece, not least for the timing, which guaranteed that they would be repeated throughout the day. Television is a brutally honest medium, but in her case this was to her advantage, revealing her intelligence and self-discipline.

She is, as those who work with her testify, very, very bright. She has the voice of a lawyer, not a politician — clear, educated, with an edge to it, and uninhibited in attributing blame where she determines it is due.

Her account acknowledged no doubt of her husband or ambivalence in herself. The allegations "are not going to be proven true," she said. "We know everything there is to know about each other and we understand and accept and love each other."

Although she denied that "I am...running any kind of strategy or being his chief defender," she added: "I probably know him better than anybody alive in the world. So I would hope that I'd be the most credible defender." Many would agree with that, but would also ask why one of the most brilliant law students of her generation chose Clinton as the main beneficiary of her lifelong advocacy.

The answer to that lies partly in her Midwestern Methodist upbringing, which instilled a commitment to moral improvement in oneself, and to transformation of society through hard work.

Hillary Diane Rodham was born on October 26, 1947, and grew up in the all-white, serene Park Ridge suburb of Chicago. Her father Hugh, a Republican, was a tobacco-chewing, small-time curtain manufacturer who told his children that rewards came only through hard work.

Her mother Dorothy, who married before finishing college, was equally ambitious for her children; she spoke for a generation of postwar housewives in declaring "no daughter of mine was going to have to go through the agony of being afraid to say what she had on her mind." In a now famous episode when Hillary was four, her mother scolded her for allowing herself to be bullied by a neighbour's daughter. "There's no room in this house for cowards," her mother told her. "The next time she hits you, I want you to hit her back." The instruction obediently executed, to an audience of admiring boys, Hillary ran home to tell her mother "I can play with boys now."

The lesson Hillary learnt was that "you win one day, you lose the next day, you don't take it personally. You get up every day and you go on." She did not take it personally at 14 when NASA told her that she need not, as a woman, hold those hopes of being an astronaut. She was voted "most likely to succeed" in her high-school class.

It took Wellesley College in 1965 to politicise her. According to David Maraniss, *Washington Post* reporter and author of *First in His Class*, one of the most thoughtful biographies of Clinton, "her politics changed each semester at Wellesley, which is to say the years 1965–69 transformed her as they did millions of others of her generation."

Over three years, Hillary and her boyfriend Geoffrey Shields "underwent similar evolutions from Midwestern conservatives to northeastern liberals," Maraniss says.

In Hillary's case, this led to a deep conviction that government could radically improve people's lives, particularly through education.

In debates she was a pragmatist, known for arguing "you can't accomplish anything in government unless you win." But her speech at the "commencement" graduation ceremony in 1969 earned her national publicity for striking what was seen to be the idealistic tone of her generation: "Our prevailing acquisitive and competitive corporate life...is not the way for us. We're searching for more immediate, ecstatic and penetrating modes of living."

When *Vanity Fair* magazine asked her, ahead of the 1992 presidential election, for the "most ecstatic" event of her twenties, she replied "falling in love with Bill Clinton." They met at Yale Law School, where she arrived, thanks to the Wellesley commencement speech, with a formidable reputation among other students as an intellectual and political star.

According to the account both give, he followed her for several weeks, unable to bring himself to start what he predicted would be "nothing but trouble" although he had concluded "she was interesting and deep." Finally, she marched up to him in the library, declaring: "If you're going to keep staring at me, then I'm going to keep looking back, and I think we ought to know each other's names." She was attracted, she says, by the fact that he was not frightened of her.

From the beginning they were political allies, partners in the law school mock trials where she was widely credited with bringing clarity and discipline to his unstructured speeches. Mack McLarty, a childhood friend of Bill's, is quoted as saying: "I married above myself in terms of intellect, like Bill did."

Hillary applied none of the same restraint to her clothes, however. Bill Clinton later recalled ruefully, in one debate which they lost, that it didn't help that "Hillary wore this bright orange outfit." She was a master of the Sixties uniform, with flowing hair, sandals and jeans or swirling paisley cotton slacks. In Maraniss's account, she constantly changed the design of her glasses; her friend Carolyn Ellis called it "her whimsy — just the way she would change her hairstyle later, she changed her glasses all the time then."

In contrast, Bill Clinton looked then eerily as he does now: soft-faced, with a big-toothed grin, mouth usually partly open, as if dragged down by the jutting chin, already puffy around the waist but eternally boyish.

Ironically, given Hillary's attack this week on the legal interrogation of the President, her first post after law school was a prestigious staff job on the House Judiciary Committee inquiry preparing the impeachment case against Richard Nixon. But in deciding to marry Clinton and move to Arkansas, she cut short an ascent which would, on many predictions, have made her one of the nation's top lawyers.

Her 1992 explanation to *Vanity Fair* is perhaps one of the most revealing she has ever given: "I just knew I wanted to be part of changing the world. Bill's desire to be in public life was much more specific than my desire to do good." Those who argue that she sacrificed her feminist principles in putting her man above her career should recognise that from the beginning, she saw Clinton as her passport to real politics, the person who would enable her to turn her theories into reality.

She did not have to wait long; they taught law at the University of Arkansas briefly together until Bill was elected Governor in 1978. There is a telling photograph of them at breakfast in the Governor's mansion the morning after his first inauguration.

Bill, shirtsleeved, tousled, holding a coffee cup, slouches on one elbow on the table, smirking into his plate with the expression of a teenager reliving the previous night's triumphs. Opposite, Hillary holds up the *Arkansas Democrat Gazette* to make a point to him, her heavy legs protruding below the newspaper, heavy glasses and scraped back hair above, doggedly maintaining the appearance which infuriated the women voters of Arkansas.

Voters did not like it either when Hillary used her own surname in 1980 in the formal announcement of Chelsea's birth and finally got their revenge two years later, in throwing the couple out of the Governor's mansion. His arrogance was thought largely to blame, but his wife's intransigence in the land of the Southern belle did not help.

Arkansas aides date problems in the Clinton marriage — and his politically reckless attention to other women — from this point, the first real setback in his career.

The shock of losing also prompted Hillary into a deliberate transformation of her appearance. The glasses were replaced by contact lenses, the heavy hair lightened to blonde and bobbed, the heavy skirts replaced with neat suits in the tertiary colours beloved by television anchorwomen: fuchsia, turquoise and ochre.

Carolyn Huber, Hillary's administrative supremo through the Little Rock days, has been reported as saying: "She wants to win as bad as he does. She's more clear about what she wants and the way she wants it done. I don't think there's ever been a time when Hillary set her mind to something she wanted to happen that it hasn't happened."

As in one of Hillary's father's moral lectures, her determination paid off, giving the Clintons nearly a decade as Little Rock's First Family. The professional side of their pact held good; Hillary was put in charge of reforming the state's abysmal schools, a cause which earned her hatred from the teachers' unions, but which was perceived as a dramatic success.

Although tales of Clinton's woman-chasing continued, Maraniss argues that the provincial incestuousness of the Little Rock years deepened their marriage, making them dependent on each other. But those years also tarnished Hillary — as a partner of the Rose Law Firm and the Clinton household's main financial contributor — with the seamier side of Arkansas's reputation, notably the failed Whitewater land deal.

Hillary's aides all speak of her determination to be a loving, attentive mother, despite the demands of the campaign trail. She would help Chelsea with homework by fax, and spend hours curled up in hotel rooms listening to her daughter's tales of the day.

The disaster of the first two years of the Clinton presidency can be blamed on both. The ascent to Washington brought out the couple's worst flaws: his undisciplined enthusiasm and her theoretical grandiosity, leading to the fiasco of her health care reform proposals that were scrapped before going to Congress. Four years later, her analysis appears sound, her former political naivete scarcely credible.

In 1995, in a further transformation required to restore her husband's popularity, Hillary softened her image and shelved her hopes of spearheading real social change. After Bill Clinton's November 1996 re-election, she began to take a more active role, but as a supportive partner rather than a leader hoping to change the nation's hospitals.

However, the current turmoil may prove to be the battle of her life. Despite her self-deprecating account this week of her role, she is widely thought to be the main strategist behind the counter-attack, which has partly swung opinion back in her husband's favour. As many have pointed out, Bill Clinton, who grew up fatherless, has frequently turned to strong women to fight his battles, such as his Little Rock campaign manager Betsey Wright.

Clearly, at this point, Hillary's interests coincide with his; both would be devastated were he forced to resign. But will their paths now diverge?

The Clintons' friends have long argued "no." Five years ago, television producer Linda Bloodworth-Thomason, one of Hillary's closest friends, said: "Hillary doesn't have to stay with Bill Clinton. She could get to the Senate or possibly the White House on her own — and she knows it. But these two people are intertwined on every level, as a man and woman, as friends, as lovers, as parents, as politicians. This is a love story."

The caricature that the Clinton marriage is a purely political bargain clearly does no justice to the complexity of the relationship. White House staff deny that this month's surreptitiously snapped picture of the couple dancing on the beach was posed; Hillary has also retorted: "What 50-year-old woman . . . would choose to be photographed in a bathing suit with her back to the camera?"

She now looks more groomed than ever: she has perfected the authoritative inelegance of Washington, with her Oscar de la Renta evening dresses, cut to minimise the hips by over-emphasising the shoulders. She has a taste for fierce necklaces and trouser suits, even though they still irritate the heartland.

Yet a marriage so plagued by infidelity is hardly as simple as the Clintons would have the world believe. In none of Hillary's makeovers does she remotely resemble the parade of girls associated with her husband, with their big hair, high colouring and prominent mouths.

There is no need to conclude that it is a loveless marriage to observe that Hillary married a man with a genius for compartmentalising his life, and his women. Both Clintons said this week that they "boxed off" their troubles, as they appear to have done for 22 years. When the constraints of politics break open in 2000, they need do so no longer.

It is easier to sketch a professional future for her than for him, beyond the university sinecures available to both. The only suggestion to which White House spokesman Mike McCurry has responded politely is that Clinton might take over a Supreme Court chair, an appointment which would depend on Vice-President Al Gore's victory in 2000.

For Hillary Clinton, however, the possibilities seem more plentiful — most obviously a bid for the Senate or a state governorship. Despite her chameleon-like willingness to change her physical appearance, her political ideology was clearer than her husband's at the start and she has amended it less. Bill Clinton has tugged his party to a muddled centre under the New Democrat label; Hillary is still recognisably an old-fashioned liberal.

It is hard to see a future that will offer them a joint project of the kind which has provided the glue to their marriage. That is why, even taking the warmest picture of their alliance, this week's scandals may prove a turning point.

At moments of political triumph, Bill Clinton has been heard to launch into his favourite hymn, Amazing Grace, his Southern vowels stretching out the cadences: "How sweet the sound, that saved a wretch like me. I once was lost, but now am found, was blind but now I see."

The question facing Hillary Clinton is whether that anthem of redemption should still grace her husband. Even taking her word that she has not been blind to his failings, she may still have chosen to ignore the pain which undoubtedly followed. When the guillotine comes down in 2000 on their joint political project of a quarter-century, there must be some doubt whether she will continue to choose to stay.

— ***Bronwen Maddox*** is *The Times* of London's Foreign Editor. Previously, she was the U.S. Editor and the Washington Bureau Chief. She has also worked at the *Financial Times* as an editorial writer and award-winning investigative reporter.

An American Marriage

How to Explain Bill & Hillary Clinton?

Joe Klein

In early December of 1997, Diane Blair, who is one of Hillary Rodham Clinton's oldest and closest friends, visited the First Lady in her White House study. During a rambling conversation, the two women came to the subject of the global-warming treaty then being negotiated in Japan. Blair observed that "even intelligent people have trouble understanding what this is all about," and the First Lady agreed. The President then dropped in, joined the conversation, and soon, much to Blair's surprise, was enmeshed in a heated argument with his wife. "They were arguing about whether it does any good to do the right thing on a controversial issue if no one has a clue you're doing it," Blair recalled. "It was a high-pitched argument. It would not have seemed, to most people, a picture of loveliness. They were really, really angry with each other. And then, suddenly, the President took her in his arms and began kissing her all over her face and he said, 'God, what would I do without you?' I felt kind of embarrassed being there — I wanted to leave the room. But I just don't think you can fake that sort of thing."

There are several plausible ways to react to this story One is: Oh, yuck. Another is: Oh, come on. A cynic might say that Blair is an old

Clinton friend — the wife of Jim Blair; the Tyson Foods lawyer who helped Mrs. Clinton with her controversial commodities trading — cleverly perpetuating the party line that this is a solid loving marriage: a real relationship, not a political arrangement. There is also a third possible reaction: Blair's story conforms to the recollections of a great many people who know the Clintons well, even of some who left their employ feeling betrayed and disheartened. (And of some independent observers, too: early in the 1992 Presidential campaign, I accidentally witnessed the Clintons in a serious snuggle on a dark pathway after a speech in Columbia, South Carolina.)

The quality and texture of the Clinton marriage has always been the great unanswered question of this Presidency. Unlike most inquiries into the private lives of politicians, this one seems legitimate — because of the First Lady's deep and obvious involvement in the formulation of public policy (and, less so, because of the President's apparent weakness for involvements of other sorts.) Much of the speculation has been vapid tabloidy stuff: if he strays so egregiously and she sticks around, this must be cold, political partnership. Other strands of speculation are woven into psycho-babble about "enablers" and "addicts" and "denial." But even the best marriages are tangled and contradictory affairs, their psychological terrain unknowable to all but the immediate participants. "The only people who count in any marriage are the two that are in it," the First Lady said on NBC's "Today" program last week, an echo of comments she first made on "60 Minutes" in the mid of the Gennifer Flowers episode. "We know everything there is to know about each other; and we understand and accept and love each other."

When it comes to Clinton-marriage scenarios, the wisest course may be to remain indiscriminately credulous: He is chronically unfaithful. They fight like harpies. They are political partners. They are best friends. They love each other madly. None of these are mutually exclusive. The recent photograph of them dancing, in bathing suits, on the beach in St. Thomas, in the Virgin Islands, is a metaphor of sorts: no doubt they were aware of the cameras — the White House's later protests about the invasion of privacy are laughable — and they probably knew that the image might serve as a mild antidote to the embarrassment that would accompany the Paula Jones lawsuit. But it is also not impossible — and not at all contradictory — that the Clintons were besotted with each other at that moment. The President's problem has never been a deficiency of affection. And, as for the First Lady, a friend says, "I think she's goofy about him."

Which is not to say that this isn't a stupefyingly weird relationship. There are public aspects of it that mystify. Why, for example, does Hillary Clinton always look so radiant in the midst of a sex scandal? The canary-yellow suit she wore at her husband's third semiofficial White House denial ceremony (the vehement one, last Monday) was perfectly crisp and cheery; her face was composed and untroubled; even her hair style seemed less temporary than usual. Staff members remember a similar moment in the 1992 campaign, when the Gennifer Flowers and draft scandals broke during the New Hampshire primary. "We were all completely depressed and totally scruffy, the hotel where we were staying was a mess," Mandy Grunwald, a media adviser in that campaign, recalls, "and she walks in one morning just dressed to the nines. It was a dark pants suit with brass buttons, I think. She had her makeup on, her hair done meticulously. She had done all this intentionally, to send us a message: 'Stop moping. We are going to be professionals. The worse you feel, the better you should look.' It was her way of getting us going again."

Another explanation for the First Lady's radiance is less charitable: she looks good at such times because she is invigorated. Her husband needs her desperately; she is the essential element in his defense. Some Clinton acquaintances see this as a matter of love and insecurity: the First Lady is eager to win the President's affection whenever; and however; she can. A less friendly interpretation is that it may be a matter of power: if he's in her debt for defending him, she has more leverage to pursue her staffing and her policy objectives. Certainly the darkest periods for Hillary Rodham Clinton over the past six years have had nothing to do with any of the "bimbo eruptions." One was in late 1994, after her health-insurance-reform plan seemed a major factor in losing control of Congress to the Republicans; another was in early 1996, friends say, after her Rose Law Firm billing records suddenly, and very suspiciously, materialized in the White House. "You have to realize that the President always saw her as magic politically" a former staff member says. "He thought she had the magic touch." Several people remember a meeting in early July of 1992, when the Clinton team was brainstorming his Democratic National Convention acceptance speech. Mrs. Clinton was the one who came up with the last line — "I still believe in a place called Hope" — and "the look Clinton gave her when that happened was unforgettable," one recalls. "It was like, 'You always know the right thing.'"

But then, after her team's clunky performance on health-care reform, and her own refusal to take the Whitewater inquiry seriously at first, it seemed the First Lady had lost track of "the right thing" and become a political liability. (At that point, too, the President seemed convinced that the consultant Dick Morris had the magic touch.) That was a rough time, some friends say, which was relieved only when the First Lady went off on her worldwide travels, especially the spring vacations she took with her daughter, Chelsea.

When I accompanied Mrs. Clinton on her first big overseas trip — to South Asia, in the spring of 1995 — she seemed to be actively reassessing her political philosophy after the health care debacle. She was clearly impressed by the creativity of the non-governmental programs she visited, and she had lengthy discussions with her staff and with friends about the limits of government, about whether poor women and their children — her lifelong obsession — might possibly best be served through programs that circumvented traditional bureaucracies (programs that Republicans like Newt Gingrich, about whom she was quite curious, might agree to spend money on). "The health care fight — and Whitewater, of course — taught her a lot about herself and people and politics in Washington," Lisa Caputo, her former press secretary, says. "She definitely changed after that. Her sense of what her 'zone of privacy' was changed. As she said in her Whitewater press conference, she 'rezoned' herself."

The South Asia trip also gave many of the reporters who went along a chance to get a closer look at Mrs. Clinton's relationship with her daughter. Its normality was remarkable, given the circumstances. Chelsea seemed poised and smart; she had no reluctance about interrupting her mother — correcting her at times — when the two chatted with reporters about the day's events. "What I remember about that trip was the First Lady and Chelsea getting on the phone with the President and talking his ear off about what we were seeing," Melanne Verveer, the First Lady's chief of staff, says. "It's a constant thing with her when we're away. She's always saying, 'I can't wait to tell Bill about this.'"

While stories of intense battles between the President and the First Lady — always involving disputes about policy or political strategy, never about personal matters (at least, not in front of the help) — are common, former staff members are adamant about the closeness of the Clintons' bond. "When I think about them," Neel Lattimore, the First Lady's former deputy press secretary says, "I think about the two of them sitting on a couch on Air Force One, holding hands, telling some old political story and arguing about who's going to tell which part —and finishing each other's sentences. The chemistry is just out there — they're such great friends."

STILL, ONE WONDERS HOW Hillary Rodham Clinton actually does it — how she can defend her husband so staunchly and with such a straight face. Her closest friends say that the subject of his dalliances is one she never talks about. "I think she literally decides that she believes him," a former staff member says. "She focuses all her anger on the outside threat, on the enemies who want to bring him down." Several friends say that Mrs. Clinton makes a conscious effort not to get caught up in the media frenzy. She doesn't watch television or read the newspapers; she assumes that most of the pundits are opponents in any case. It doesn't hurt that she has, by nature, a more extreme sensibility than her husband. She is very much a Methodist of the moralizing, nineteenth-century sort; in another time, she might have been a founding member of the Women's Christian Temperance Union. ("She is more likely to see things in black-and-white than he is," a close friend says.) This seems to be a matter of personal style rather than of political ideology; her liberalism is more pragmatic than flaming (although when she ran the health care task force she was known to rail against the evils of "incrementalism"). She does have a weakness for fervent, all-or-nothing friends — Susan Thomases and Sidney Blumenthal are two — who tend to see the world severely divided between friends and enemies, and encourage her to see things the same way. (*Time* reported last week that Blumenthal "created a gigantic diagram inside his office outlining with circles and arrows the byzantine Republican conspiracy surrounding the [Monica Lewinsky] tapes.")

"Hillary taught me how to think in situations like these," one Clintonite says. "For example, a story suddenly appears in the *Dallas Morning News* that a Secret Service agent has witnessed Clinton and Lewinsky in a 'compromising' act in the White House. The *Dallas Morning News*? That's immediately suspicious. Dallas is where Paula Jones's lawyers are. Dallas is where Gennifer Flowers hangs out. And even more suspicious is the timing: the story appears on the very day that Monica Lewinsky is trying to make up her mind about what sort of deal to make with Ken Starr. It's a leak that is very much to Starr's tactical advantage — I'm sure that's how Hillary would see it. And then the story disappears within twenty-four hours. The *Dallas Morning News* simply retracts it. When the First Lady talks about a conspiracy, I think that's the sort of thing she means."

If so, she could be a lot more precise about it. Her wild claim on "Today" that a "vast right-wing conspiracy . . . has been conspiring against my husband" was absurd, but not quite counterproductive. It was, in fact, very smart politics: "It was a diversion," a former Clinton staff member told me. "It gave the press something to write about other than Monica Lewinsky."

Indeed, right-wing ideologues have long marveled at the Clintons' ability to do many of the same things the First Lady accuses Kenneth Starr of: the controlled leaks, diversionary tactics, smear campaigns against their opponents. Certainly they are masters of political theatre, as the President's State of the Union performance and the First Lady's television interviews proved once again. The day of the State of the Union Message began well before dawn for Mrs. Clinton, with preparations for the "Today" appearance, and ended well after midnight, with a jubilant party for staff and friends at the White House. She was up early the next morning for her interview on ABC's "Good Morning America," while the President headed out to press the flesh in the Midwest, accompanied by approval polls that rose with astounding speed as tragedy seemed to turn into farce. (Who, for example, could have guessed that a former teacher would call Lewinsky a stalker? Who could have guessed that Dick Morris would sound like a cad on a Los Angeles call-in program?) By week's end, the Clintons were triumphant.

There was, though, a quality to Mrs. Clinton's performance — the composed feverishness of it — that recalled a Victorian medical phenomenon called "the hectic flush," a roseate glow that women dying of consumption took on just before the bitter end. But the paranoid tinge had served her political purposes well. The sense of impending danger and implacable enemies had reinforced her belief that she and the President are doing important, historic things, and also reinforced her ability to reject even the most plausible claims against her husband. "I'm amazed by the political naivete — the good-versus-evil quality — of her whole operation," a White House aide told me several months ago. "It has enormous influence over the way things are done in this Administration, and I don't think it has been a particularly positive influence."

ON THE EVENING BEFORE her "Today" interview, Hillary Rodham Clinton attended a fund-raising dinner for UNICEF, where she received a sustained and emotional standing ovation. Her remarks were eloquent and brief. She was at home. This was her political family — the Eleanor Roosevelt wing of the Democratic Party. It represents a decided personal advantage that she has over her husband, and one that may become more apparent if the Lewinsky siege ends badly. There will always he a solid wedge of the Democratic Party that will admire Hillary Clinton and identify with her, no matter what happens.

The President has no such home. Indeed, in the unlikely event that Bill Clinton is forced out of office he will have no obvious place to go — no San Clemente, no Plains. He has lived in public housing for nearly two decades. A career's worth of often inspired ideological improvisation has left him politically homeless as well, without a devoted uncritical constituency. Except for her.

—***Joe Klein*** is the Washington correspondent for *The New Yorker*. He has also written for *Newsweek*, and commented on American politics for CBS News. He is the author, among other works, of *Primary Colors*. "An American Marriage: How to Explain Bill and Hillary Clinton," Copyright 1998 by Joe Klein, originally appeared in *The New Yorker*, February 9, 1998. Reprinted by permission of the author.

Reflections of a Woman
Whatever Her Reasons, Hillary Clinton Stands by Her Man. And the Public Approves

Lois Romano

MARGOT SAGE-EL IS CO-OWNER of a small bookstore in Montclair, N.J., where she describes her clientele as mostly "highly educated women with high-powered careers." Like many others around the country, her customers have spent their fair share of time chattering about the latest sex scandal in Washington — but not about the tawdry details.

"We don't even care about the dress — get over it," Sage-El, 42, declares from her home.

What her customers do want to talk about, she says, is Hillary Clinton.

"I just don't know what drives her," muses the small business owner, who has clearly given the first lady some thought.

"She's maintaining her own dignity — not so much standing behind her man — she's maintaining her own self-respect with this dog she's married to. It's her choice to stay with him — for whatever reason, I can't figure out why. . . . I don't know what she's going to get out of it."

Hillary Rodham Clinton is inarguably the most analyzed woman in America today, in part because she has not allowed herself to be pigeonholed into any neat little packages. She has eschewed the traditional images of the political wife — keeping her maiden name for years and refusing to exploit her daughter for the pages of *People*. She has even avoided the trappings of physical consistency: She has had more dramatically different hair styles in the past six years than most woman have in a lifetime.

The right has long tried — with some success — to define her as a left-wing feminist out of step with the traditional American woman — whomever that is. But for the average Jane, the fascination has been much more basic: What does drive her? Why, people wonder, would a smart, successful woman stay with an admittedly unfaithful husband?

The speculative answers have always been too simplistic, often political and sometimes just plain mean-spirited. She's crazy about him, some of her loyalists suggest, and so she looks the other way. She stays in it strictly for the power, her political detractors flatly state. She lives her own life, others sniff.

Answers or insights about the first lady are no clearer today than they were when she arrived at the White House. Yet the American public seems to be rallying to her side these days, giving clear approval of the job she is doing and how she has conducted herself in the midst of the scandal. She is no more translucent or less complex than before. But perhaps that is the point. In her, they say, are many things. In her, they are seeing themselves.

"I identify with her because she really is a woman of my generation, and here she is in this traditional role, first lady, she didn't fit into," says Sage-El. "She tried to make it work the way she envisioned it, and the public slapped her down. . . . She's still trying to find her place. And with marriage, too — we all know that marriage isn't perfect and you do have to let some things go to make the whole picture work."

As President Clinton's troubles have escalated, and as he prepares to testify about his relationship with Monica Lewinsky on Monday, Hillary Clinton seems to have risen above it all in the eyes of many American women. Recent public opinion surveys, in fact, show that more Americans than ever — women in particular — say they have a favorable view of her.

"She may not be behaving as a first wife should behave, but women believe she is behaving like a first lady should behave — loyal and dignified," says Myrna Blyth, editor in chief of *Ladies' Home Journal*.

"Women may be saying, 'I would throw the bum out,' but they don't want to see the first lady behaving like that."

Partisan skeptics caution that public opinion could still shift as the facts continue to unfold. "If it comes out that the president lied and Hillary knew he lied, the American public would be disenchanted," says Republican pollster Ed Goeas. "She would no longer be a victim. She would be a co-conspirator."

But for now, women tend to be looking at Hillary Clinton in a different light. Few see her as a victim or a dupe. To the contrary, some say they see the 50-year-old first lady as a totally modern woman, who is not standing tall merely to protect her husband and cling to their relationship, but to protect the dignity of her own role — as first lady, mother and professional woman.

"People are watching her for different things now . . . how she's able to compose herself under this barrage of bad press directed at her husband," suggests Mia Levy, 22, a recent graduate of the University of Pennsylvania. "She is the first lady and, granted, nobody elected her to be, but it is a position. . . . It's a role. [She's] not just a wife or a mother."

Indeed, Hillary Clinton is the first presidential spouse with her own full-time career, plucked from a generation of women struggling to have it all yet guilty about giving up their traditional homemaker roles. She believed, friends say, that if she openly took the lead on issues she cared about, like health care, there would be less speculation about her hidden power. Instead, many seemed uneasy with her cards-on-the-table approach.

But over time some say they came to appreciate her consistent commitment to her causes and the commendable job she did raising her only child, Chelsea. And there is something else. Even in 1998, American women are still grappling with their own ever-changing roles — in relationships and in the work force. Clinton, some women point out, reflects those universal struggles.

"I think it's simply that all of a sudden Hillary has become more human," says Ruth Fine, 70, a leader in philanthropic causes in Boston.

"I don't think it's pity. I think this is what happens to lots of relationships, and you live with it. Probably more people than we know live with such relationships. Forget what we think of the man, it's the relationship thing, and I suspect it's the way life is for lots of people. I think people see it that way, and they empathize."

Kelly Oakleas, 21, a University of Kansas senior who has barely begun to examine her own choices in life, says she admires Clinton for balancing her roles — something to which Oakleas aspires.

"Women are put in such hard positions. You never know what to do," says Oakleas, who describes herself as a conservative and a Christian. "You can be like a family woman, and be kind of like in back of your man. Or you can have your own career and do your own thing and be independent. And I think it's really hard for women to go to the middle. I just think we have it rough."

Experts add that part of Clinton's approval could be coming from the fact that in the past decade women have become less judgmental about adultery. Isaiah Zimmerman, a Washington clinical psychologist and marriage therapist, says that many of the women he sees today are more tolerant about infidelity because they appreciate the complexities of maintaining long-term relationships.

"They want to forgive and save the marriage, and they see the first lady as trying to do this in the face of forces trying to destroy the marriage," Zimmerman says.

Ellen Levine, the editor in chief of *Good Housekeeping*, says she too has seen a marked change in women's attitudes toward adultery in recent years.

"When the whole Gary Hart episode happened, American women were mad at Lee Hart. They wanted her to leave him," says Levine, who conducted surveys on the subject while editor of *Woman's Day*. Today, *Good Housekeeping*'s 4.5 million readers are largely supportive of the first lady, she says, admiring Clinton "for her dignity."

A poll to be published in *Ladies' Home Journal*'s September issue shows that as many women today — 46 percent — would forgive their husbands for being unfaithful than would not. A similar poll conducted by the magazine seven years ago indicated that only 12 percent would forgive men who who cheated on them.

Blyth and Levine also say they believe there is another reason their readers have been overwhelmingly pro-Hillary. "The public today is very wary of issues that cross the line between public and private," Levine says. "They are sending a clear message that this is none of our business."

Most of those interviewed agreed that by actions and words Clinton herself has sent a very clear message that this is strictly a personal matter — that she has it under control and that, if she is okay with it, why should others judge her.

"She has made a decision not to air her dirty laundry in public," says Betty Hung, a 27-year-old San Francisco investment banker. "I don't buy into this victim stuff. I tend to think she knows everything that is going on."

Hung, like others, expresses a great deal of admiration for Clinton because she is "trying to move beyond the sordid stuff and get on with her job."

Women also seem to be giving Clinton the benefit of the doubt — that however things appear, perhaps she is making the right choices for her and her family, and that when all the facts come out, she will ultimately come to the right conclusions about her marriage and her life.

Christine Strauss, a 45-year-old elementary school librarian in Colorado and mother of two daughters, says Clinton is appropriately "defending her husband."

"That's the thing that a courageous person does," says Strauss. "But I'll be very interested to see what happens after he is out of the White House. I think she should divorce him."

"I am sure she has addressed it in her way and in the appropriate place," says Blanche Lambert Lincoln, 37, a former House Democrat from Arkansas who is running for the Senate. "But I don't know that it is her responsibility to answer to the American public about what is happening in her private life."

— ***Lois Romano*** is a reporter for *The Washington Post*, for whom she is covering the 2000 presidential elections. She has also written for *Playboy*, *Good Houskeeping* and *Redbook*. She has been nominated for the Pulitzer Prize. Staff writers Libby Ingrid Copeland, Tom Kenworthy and Dale Russakoff contributed to this report. (August 15, 1998.)

The Shadow of Her Smile

Margaret Carlson

IT WAS NEARING MIDNIGHT in the solarium, the informal room on the third floor of the White House. The Mexican food had been cleared away, and a few dinner guests were hanging out waiting for the President to come back from taking a phone call. Just as he was returning, the First Lady noticed out of the corner of her eye that the TV was on, tuned to the David Letterman show. Casually, she leaned over, picked up the remote control and switched the set off before the President could hear a barrage of scandal jokes.

It's hard to believe she would need to protect him from the Top 10 Reasons Monica Is a Babe. But Hillary's gut response is always to defend the President against incoming fire. What's different this past month is her failure to go on the offense. For the first time, she hasn't scraped the staff off the floor, quarter-backed the Hail Mary pass or given her own statements. And when she said, just before the worst performance of his life on August 17, "It's his speech. Let him say what he wants," it wasn't helpful, nor meant to be.

What a time for a work slowdown. The First Lady may not be able to save the President the way she saved the candidate, but she surely will hurt him if she doesn't stand by him once again, and not like some potted plant. Within days after the Lewinsky scandal broke, Hillary was on the "Today" show shouting her husband's praises. But for weeks now, there have been only perfunctory remarks during icy cameo appearances, bad body language and her failure to refer to the President with her usual "my husband" at a Moscow event.

Like so much coming out of the White House, Hillary's anger could be one more piece of spin, which makes it hard to interpret her switch to a hyper-smiley face during a flurry of public appearances at the end of last week. If Hillary had been faking anger because that's what any normal person would feel, she did it well. Rather than say anything herself, she issued a chilly statement of forgiveness through an aide. The Administration seemed eager to disclose that the Martha's Vineyard vacation was a time for "healing." It certainly wasn't a time for fun. She sulked behind sunglasses, stared straight ahead and answered in monosyllables. There were no late evenings singing around the piano with Carly Simon and Beverly Sills, no going out every night till all hours, no golf. The guest house where the President spent most of his time alone was akin to the woodshed.

Like most marriages, the Clintons' is a mystery, only more so. How can she stand his repeated betrayals? Does she yearn for power that much, or does she, in the words of Sara Ehrman, the friend who reluctantly drove her across the country from a promising legal career in Washington to instant obscurity practicing law in Arkansas, still "love him something awful"? The Clintons nearly separated in the late '80s, after the then Governor had an affair. But several years ago, a friend noticed that the marriage was much improved. "Hillary liked living above the store. He was under a kind of White House arrest, almost always home for dinner with her and Chelsea."

It's just this proximity that fuels the current Capitol parlor game: What did Hillary know, and when did she know it? Writer and television producer Linda Bloodworth-Thomason says it's ludicrous to think that Hillary knew her husband had been involved with Lewinsky in her very own house but defended him anyway. "Anyone who thinks Hillary knew what happened before the two of them had their conversation wasn't there that weekend. The second floor of the White House was a somber place." Until then, the President had told Hillary that he had befriended Monica and that she had taken his attentions the wrong way.

In the face of so many awful rumors, including one that the Clintons murdered Vince Foster, the Monica accusation was just more gunk from the sewer.

The aftermath of the confession was brutal. Hillary spent several days in her room, talking only to her mother who was staying at a cabin in Pennsylvania, going to church and then meeting, along with Chelsea, with Jesse Jackson. One friend says the First Lady will rally to keep Kenneth Starr from prevailing but won't be out there waving the flag. "That old feeling has really suffered. She won't be getting over this for a very long time." Hillary has also taken to vigorous workouts. "She's so enthused about her state-of-the-art exercise equipment," says a former aide, "that she talks about it as if she's hosting an infomercial." When you've lost control of so much around you, you can at least get thin.

By Friday, a friend says, Hillary had "reconnected the President's oxygen tube" and rallied to help absorb the incoming fire from Starr. She had resumed the "my husband" business in her introductions and adopted a modified Nancy Reagan gaze as she listened to the President at Friday's prayer breakfast, although a friend jokes that if the President apologizes one more time, Hillary *will* kill him. Sensing an opening, aides are pushing her hard to go on TV to shore up the President. But if she reads the report and has any feelings left at all, the only honest reaction will be to let him this time twist slowly in the wind.

— ***Margaret Carlson*** is a columnist for *Tine*, the first woman columnist in the magazine's history. She has covered the last three presidential campaigns and serves as a panelist on CNN's weekly programs "Inside Politics" and "The Capital Gang." (September 21, 1998.)

"I Still Love Bill Despite his Weaknesses," Says Hillary

Mary Dejevsky

MUSING AT LENGTH FOR the first time on her chequered marriage, Hillary Clinton blamed her husband's serial infidelity on his disturbed childhood and described his White House dalliance with Monica Lewinsky as "a sin of weakness" not "a sin of malice." Given his background, Mrs Clinton said stoically, it is remarkable he turned out as well as he did — and anyway, they still love each other.

"Yes, he has weaknesses. Yes, he needs to be more disciplined, but it is remarkable, given his background, that he turned out to be the kind of person he is, capable of such leadership," she said.

Talking of his childhood in Arkansas, where his presumed father died before he was born and his step-father was a wife-beating alcoholic, Mrs. Clinton said: "He was so young, barely four, when he was scarred by abuse. There was terrible conflict between his mother and grandmother." Hinting at the therapy sessions she and her husband are supposed to have undergone, she explained: "A psychologist once told me that for a boy being in the middle of a conflict between two women is the worst possible situation. There is always a desire to please each one."

The US First Lady was interviewed by Lucinda Franks for the inaugural issue of *Talk* magazine, the new venture of the British-born editor, Tina Brown, which is underwritten by the Disney Corporation. The attention-grabbing look at the world's most scrutinised marriage was the latest volley in *Talk*'s publicity campaign.

Equally, though, it may be seen as a gamble by Mrs Clinton, who is still deciding whether to run for the Senate for New York, to give sceptical voters answers to some of their more insistent questions before her campaign starts in earnest — questions such as "why does she stay with him?," "might she not be a little to blame?" and the widely circulating theory that there was a political payback for her in a share of his power.

Of the genuineness of their marriage, Mrs Clinton revealed with a tinge of regret, that until the Lewinsky scandal, she believed he had overcome his womanising. "I thought this was resolved 10 years ago," she said. "I thought he had conquered it; I thought he had understood it; but he didn't go deep enough or work hard enough."

And in an attempt to counter the impression that the marriage was just a succession of infidelities, she said of the period after his affair with the Arkansas nightclub singer, Gennifer Flowers, and before his relationship with Monica Lewinsky: "You know we did have a very good stretch — years and years of nothing."

Of her decision to stay, Mrs Clinton said he needed her to help him through his "dysfunction" and because, "we have love." She went on: "There has been enormous pain, enormous anger, but I have been with him half my life and he is a very, very good man. We just have a deep connection that transcends whatever happens."

She traced his affair to an accumulation of stresses and strains for both of them: the suicide of their mutual friend and White House official, Vince Foster, and the deaths of her father and his mother. But she also insisted that his prime motive in lying about the affair — it was the lying rather than the adultery that put his job on the line — was to protect her.

— ***Mary Dejevsky*** is *The Independent*'s Washington bureau chief. A former editor with the BBC Monitoring Service and World Service, she contributes to CNN, MSNBC, and international radio and television programs. (August 2, 1999.)

1998 Elections

PUBLIC DISSATISFACTION with the Lewinsky scandal and investigation may have helped the Democrats in the 1998 elections. The Starr investigation and House consideration dragged on throughout the year, until most Americans were heartily sick of what was often perceived to be a partisan vendetta. Many Americans took their cue about the Lewinsky scandal from the First Lady: if she's forgiven him, shouldn't we? Her popularity went through the roof as people marveled in her dignity throughout the grueling year.

MARY MCGRORY describes the effects of Hillary Rodham Clinton's tireless campaigning in the 1998 midterm elections. Mrs. Clinton visited at least 20 states, nine in the week before the election alone, and raised million of dollars for Democrats.

On Election Day, Democrats made significant gains, winning five additional House seats and the governor's races in Alabama, California, Georgia, Iowa and South Carolina. They held their Senate losses to a minimum, maintaining Barbara Boxer's seat and defeating conservative stalwart Lauch Faircloth. In the highly contested New York Senate race, Hillary helped Democrat Charles Schumer defeat Al D'Amato, an outspoken Clinton critic and leader of Senate Whitewater investigations.

Republicans were left with the narrowest Congressional majority in 33 years. Exit polling of voters revealed that "almost 60 percent approved of Clinton's job performance, said he shouldn't resign and wanted Congress to drop the impeachment inquiry altogether."

In the wake of Republican losses, Newt Gingrich announced he would not seek reelection as Speaker of the House and would leave Congress at the year's end. On the same day Clinton was impeached, Gingrich's replacement — Bob Livingston — stepped out of the Speaker's race and resigned from Congress in the wake of revelations about his marital infidelity. Mrs. Clinton, meanwhile, became the first First Lady to appear on the cover of *Vogue*.

Mr. & Mrs. Comeback Kid

Mary McGrory

IT'S RESURRECTION CITY at the White House in both East and West Wings. Not only did the master find love and vindication after being treated for weeks as a pariah by Democrats, but the first lady found a new role and a new image for herself as a one-woman rescue squad for her party.

Hillary Clinton was considered a woman wronged, and the object of some baffled sympathy from people who thought she should leave the brute. Now she's an avenging angel who answered last-minute 911 calls from close-call candidates.

She was everywhere, and often — eight times in New York where Democratic challenger Chuck Schumer was in a cliffhanger with Clinton critic Al D'Amato. She went back for a finishing touch on the day before the election. In California, where her kin by marriage was struggling against an Asian-American opponent, she made six appearances.

She took hopeless cases, like Buddy McKay in Florida, who was battling Jeb, of the surging Bush brothers. She went to Georgia for cookie-maker Michael Coles, who unexpectedly ended up giving Republican Sen. Paul Coverdell a good scare. She did fund-raising. She did voter turnout. She went to coffees and box lunches.

Women turned out by the thousands to salute her. They seem to have suspended speculation about her mysterious marriage.

Hillary Clinton is finally being seen as the political force she has always dreamed of being. After years on the road, she knows the ins and outs of local politics. In Iowa, where Democratic State Sen. Tom Vilsack astonishingly won for governor, she was there, exhibiting her cozy acquaintance with all the players.

While the president was doing things only a president can do — jousting with Republicans over the real meaning of the budget and meeting with foreign leaders — Hillary Clinton was being the perfect surrogate. She brought White House glamour to the provinces without any of the president's scandal baggage.

Relations between the First Couple are strained, according to the president, who makes periodic attempts to convince the country that his extra-marital fling has been, on balance, salutary because it forced him to work harder at his job in the hope of being forgiven by the nation and by his wife. She can put up with infidelity but not, it seems, with the career-wrecking stupidity exhibited by her reckless mate. The leader of the Western world is still in the doghouse, he hints, but confident of release. He can be expected to try to turn last Tuesday's surprising outcome into a public pardon. He and the first lady were sharing binoculars at the Glenn space launch, so maybe private redemption is just around the corner.

Hillary Clinton's message to women with wandering husbands is not easy to parse. Is she saying just grin and bear it? Or is she implicitly urging them to find out what is good in the marriage — such as a unique opportunity to make a difference. Women in less-than-perfect unions can see that although she was humiliated by her husband's public admission of adultery and lying, she was not humbled by it.

The angry white males who are such a force in places like Texas and Georgia have relented, polls show. Yes, she is still a feminist who defends partial-birth abortion, a Wellesley graduate with cast-iron self-confidence. But she took it on the chin and came up smiling. They like her better for that.

The Clintons may be reconciled — if they need to be — just because they have so much to talk about. Surely, they must want to congratulate each other on the stunning turn of events, and to cackle over the fact that the subject in Washington has changed so decisively from "Will Clinton Be Impeached?" to "How Did Gingrich and the GOP Go Wrong?"

Some people think that Hillary Clinton is auditioning for a post-White House job. She has demonstrated beyond dispute that she can handle anything that requires inexhaustible energy. Her speaking skills and zest for travel are in a class with her husband's. Will she walk away in the millennium, or keep up the career, the political partnership on her own? She hasn't been able to be Eleanor Roosevelt, as she once hoped, but she sure can be Bill Clinton.

— ***Mary McGrory*** is a syndicated columnist with *The Washington Post* where her column runs twice a week. She received the Pulitzer Prize for reporting at *The Washington Star.* Taken from the MARY MCGRORY column by Mary McGrory. Copyright 1998 by The Washington Post. Distribution by Universal Press Syndicate. Reprinted by permission. All rights reserved. (November 8, 1998.)

Senate Race

WHAT DOES THE FUTURE HOLD? From the moment President Clinton won the 1996 elections, there was widespread speculation about what the First Lady would do when his term ended in 2001. When New York Senator Daniel Patrick Moynihan announced his retirement in November, 1998, Hillary Rodham Clinton's name was immediately floated as a possible successor. In 1999, Mrs. Clinton fueled speculation about her intentions by embarking on a "listening tour" of the state. At the beginning of the new year, Mrs. Clinton moved into a house in upscale Chappaqua, NY and, in February, announced her candidacy for the U.S. Senate against New York City Mayor Rudolph Giuliani.

In this chapter, various authors weigh in on Hillary's Senate race. DEE DEE MYERS, who worked on Clinton's first campaign and was his Press Secretary during the first term, sets the campaign in context and suggests that Mrs. Clinton is seeking "the imprimatur of institutional power."

CHRISTOPHER HITCHENS suggests that there may be little to choose from when comparing Clinton and Giuliani, and envisions the two as a power couple for the new millennium. ELLEN CHESLER defends the First Lady's efforts, noting that she is a welcome addition to the long history of New York's progressive reformers. Finally, former Congresswoman PATRICIA SCHROEDER looks back at her relationship with the First Lady and cheers Mrs. Clinton's efforts to gain the Senate seat and a political position that she has well and truly earned as her own.

In Pursuit of Traditional Power

Dee Dee Myers

WHEN NEW YORK DEMOCRATS began urging Hillary Rodham Clinton to run for the U.S. Senate, most people didn't take it seriously. Not that she wouldn't be a good candidate. But after all she has been through, it seemed a safe bet she'd rather invite independent counsel Kenneth W. Starr to a state dinner than spend a year doing battle with the New York press corps for the honor of being one of 100.

But the truth is, Clinton would love to be a senator. Ending months of speculation, she announced Friday that she would set up her exploratory committee. The fact that she really, really wants to enter the race says a lot about who she is and how she sees the world.

In a phrase: She's old-fashioned. That may seem ironic, since Clinton has become the far right's poster child for the assault on "traditional values." But in truth, she is uncomfortable with many modern ideas and prefers the security of an orderly world in which public service is the highest calling and power derives from respected institutions.

Of course, it's no longer that simple. In the information age, big corporations, the federal government and wealthy individuals no longer hold a monopoly on power. It's portable; it attaches to individuals and ideas, not just institutions. No one denies that Colin L. Powell and Oprah Winfrey have power. They make things happen just by weighing in. Powell hosts a summit and creates enthusiasm for volunteering. Winfrey urges people to read, and her suggested titles become bestsellers. They pick their topics, make their rules — and get results.

Think what Clinton could accomplish if she leveraged her celebrity, experience and passion on behalf of a few favorite causes. But that's not what she wants, at least not now. For her, the bully pulpit isn't enough; she wants the imprimatur of institutional power. Like the U.S. Senate.

Perhaps her view was shaped, at least in part, by her bruising experience in the 1994 battle to reform health care. Though she doesn't say so publicly, she seems to have concluded that her role as head of the health care task force was part of the problem. The public was anxious about her unelected status. Her opponents used that to attack her credibility. When push came to shove in Congress, she was part of the problem, but she couldn't be part of the solution. She needed a seat at the table.

The failure of health care, and the ups and downs of her years in the White House, have done nothing to shake Clinton's faith in government. If anything, they've strengthened it. Only government can make the kind of sweeping changes that improve people's lives. But for her husband, she probably would have run for elective office years ago.

As an advocate and the wife of a governor and president, she's always had juice. But without being sanctified by the voters, that influence has always seemed suspect, even to Hillary Clinton. So as she contemplates the next chapter of her life, she doesn't want to be a personality; she wants to be an inside player. So much so that she's on the verge of jumping into a brutal campaign that she might not win. As she told Dan Rather recently, the U.S. Senate is "probably the most important legislative body, I would argue, in the history of the world." If that's true, given all she believes, then it's worth the risk.

Clinton's old-fashioned sensibilities have roots in Park Ridge, Ill., the orderly Chicago suburb where she grew up, her conservative father's daughter, a Goldwater girl. She excelled in high school and attended Wellesley, one of the "Seven Sister" colleges considered the pinnacle of Eastern establishment education for women in the mid-1960s, a far cry from counterculture campuses like Berkeley. Even as her politics began to change — her support for the civil-rights movement and opposition to the Vietnam War led her to reregister as a Democrat — her methods didn't. While many kids her age were trying to tear down the establishment, Clinton was trying to get inside it, to use its power to achieve her goals.

After Yale Law School and a stint on Capitol Hill, she left a promising career in Washington to follow her boyfriend to Arkansas. Two years later, she married him and never looked back. As a friend of Clinton's recently told me, "When she said 'for better or for worse,' she meant it — and she got it." Even after everything she's been through, she's still there.

People have speculated that Clinton is running for the Senate so she can leave her husband without really leaving him. But it may be more her effort to stay. She has endured a lot of criticism and not just from feminists, for becoming something she said she would never be: a stand-by-her-man woman. But if she has her own career, and a power base independent of her husband, then she is less wife and more partner. Staying, one could argue, is an act of strength, not weakness.

Clinton's old-fashioned ideas about public service, power and the role of institutions seem out of place in Los Angeles — like a Model T rolling down the 405. After all, people came west to escape the bounds of traditional society, in which people were expected to accept the established order, embrace rules rigged against them and wait their turn. They also seem out of place for a progressive, even liberal, Democrat, a feminist, a path-breaker in her own right. But there they are. For better or worse, they are drawing her into a campaign for the Senate.

— ***Dee Dee Myers*** is a contributing editor to *Vanity Fair.* She worked on the 1992 Clinton campaign and served as President Clinton's press secretary from 1993-94. This article appeared in the *Los Angeles Times* (June 6, 1999).

Hillary
N.Y. Progressive

Ellen Chesler

LET'S GET BEYOND THE psychobabble that so often passes for informed political analysis these days and take Hillary Rodham Clinton at her word. Perhaps there is no agenda to her Senate candidacy deeper than the challenge she first set for herself and her generation thirty years ago in a Wellesley commencement address that made national headlines: To practice politics as the art of making possible what appears to be impossible.

From this point of view, Hillary Clinton can lay claim to the effective blend of idealism and tenacity that has characterized generations of progressive reformers in New York. And surely these ties should qualify her as a native as much as a lifetime of rooting for the Yankees.

Like Eleanor Roosevelt, with whom she likes to identify, Hillary Clinton has spent the better part of her years as First Lady schlepping around the country and the globe, meeting as often with the powerless as with the powerful. There is nothing really new about her much-publicized listening tour of New York except the several hundred reporters who are now part of her entourage. She has visited more schools, daycare centers, hospitals, family planning clinics, model factories, housing projects, parks, micro-enterprises, agricultural cooperatives and the like than her staff can tally. She has boundless energy and enthusiasm for this sort of thing, born of her understanding that what works, and what's therefore to be taken most seriously, is rarely the product of elegant social or economic planning but rather the less predictable outcome of the often messy process of democratic politics, where policy-makers are obligated to respond to myriad interests.

These encounters are reminiscent of those instigated by New York's most fabled progressive reformers, many of them women, who placed great emphasis on the value of individual case management of social welfare by competent, caring professionals. They too traveled extensively, pioneering the kind of firsthand observation and methodical survey research in factories and tenements that we now take for granted as the basis of informed public policy and yet do not always manage to achieve. They built voluntary civic institutions like settlement houses that in turn modeled innovative ways to provide public health care, safe water, food and drugs, more accountable institutions of criminal justice, decent housing, parks and recreation, and wage and hour protections, all of which they saw as necessary conditions for nurturing responsible citizenship.

As the tale is often told, these worthy arrangements created widespread public demand for activism by the federal government and helped to spawn the modern social welfare state with its more secure, if still inadequate, sources of funding and more exacting professional standards for dealing with the poor. But lost in modern efforts to create formal distance between the state and its clients in order to protect their rights was the idea of providing assistance aimed at building personal capacity and self-reliance. This shortcoming fueled the disenchantment that resulted in the compromised welfare reforms of the Clinton era.

Redressing those compromises, without going back to failed policies, is the challenge that must animate Hillary Clinton's bid to remain in public life. That she has a good chance at winning on such a platform is clear from election outcomes since 1996, which have suggested that women especially remain convinced of the need for federal interventions to help them in their own lives and to assist those less fortunate.

It will be important for Hillary Clinton to challenge the view that she is complicit in the abandonment by her husband's Administration of the welfare safety net that New Yorkers first wrote into the New Deal. She can point to the many ways she has worked in private and public to replace what had become a deeply flawed system of pitifully inadequate handouts with better integrated programs of economic subsidy and social support — programs that aim to help lift families out of poverty and to restore hope and opportunity where there was once dependency and despair.

MANY OF THESE INITIATIVES are already in place, if not yet adequate to the challenges before them. The Clinton Administration has had success in increasing the minimum wage, rewarding work through the earned-income tax credit and passing the Family and Medical Leave Act; widening opportunities for education and job training; expanding access to Head Start and daycare; and protecting reproductive choice. Incremental changes in health care provision have resulted in a substantial broadening of the population of working families eligible for insurance (though they are not necessarily yet enrolled). Among these advances is CHIP, the Children's Health Insurance Program, which covers young people through the age of 18. The Administration has also made low-income working families, not just welfare recipients, eligible for Medicaid, and it has enacted portability legislation that allows workers to hold on to health care when they lose their jobs.

Such measures are valuable, but they must be expanded and rigorously enforced. Given her demonstrated interests and commitments, it's easy to imagine that Senator Hillary Rodham Clinton would place such expansion and enforcement at the center of her policy agenda, advocating massive public education and outreach and an effective system of penalties for states and localities that do not enroll a higher percentage of eligible clients into programs like Medicaid. Her extensive knowledge of these issues will assure her a leadership opportunity when Congress reauthorizes the welfare bill in 2001 and 2002, as will her mastery of the minutiae of health care policy, now that her idea of building consumer protections into managed care is on the table again.

Legislative service is the logical culmination of Hillary Clinton's lifelong devotion to civic life. Voters should reward her for years of experience at trying, if not always succeeding, to address the widely acknowledged flaws of even the most well-intended of our public policies. And we should help sustain her conviction, in the face of so much evidence to the contrary, that political office is still a respectable platform for this commitment.

— ***Ellen Chesler*** directs the Open Society Institute's Program on Reproductive Health and Rights; her previous books include *Woman of Valor: Margaret Sanger and the Birth Control Movement in America*. "Hillary Clinton: NY Progressive" reprinted with permission from the August 9-16, 1999 issue of *The Nation*.

Twin Souls

Christopher Hitchens

CYNICAL ABOUT POLITICS I may be, and cynical about politics I'd be a fool not to be (since everyone else these days is suddenly a shellbacked cynic, too) but nothing prepared me for this deadpan report from Gail Collins in *The New York Times* last February 17. Crediting that old Harlem blowhard Charles Rangel with an original idea, Ms. Collins was almost lost for breath:

> Mr. Rangel proudly announced that the contentious and near-bankrupt New York Democratic Party had "pulled together an offer that the First Lady can't refuse," *including a guarantee that the nomination would be hers for the asking, without a primary.* Later he explained that the party's power to insure Mrs. Clinton a free ride was based on the theory that *"you can always promise no primary to an 800-pound gorilla."*

I barely know how to begin (and I need hardly add that the italics above did not appear in the original), but really . . . I step lightly over the question of what might have been said if the First Lady had recommended the distinguished Congressman in the same terms. I step with equal lightness over the Mobbed-up idiom (how would the *Times* have played it if someone with an Italian name had been made a Republican Party-machine offer that he "could not refuse"?) I even wonder if any-one but a timeserver from the Congressional Black Caucus would have gotten away with describing our own dear former co-president as any kind of primate, let alone an 800-pound specimen. This is a nonjudgmental age, after all, and why should anyone care about character while the economy booms? Unless that character is Rudolph Giuliani, the man with the cheese-grater handshake, who is widely suspected of being her likely opponent. No, what I ultimately thought, as I let the paper drop from my hands, was about my first sight of New York.

In 1970, I lurched out of the Port Authority terminal to discover that everything I had hoped for was true, only more so. I vaguely knew, of course, what New York looked like, because I'd been born in this century, but not what it sounded like, or what it felt like, or smelled like. Right across the street was a star-spangled campaign storefront for James Buckley, brother of the more celebrated William F., then the hero of "Firing Line." JOIN THE MARCH FOR AMERICA, the sign said. In that year, he ran as the Conservative Party nominee for Senate against Charles Goodell (Republican) and Richard Ottinger (Democrat), and won. Mr. Goodell held the seat only because Robert Kennedy had been murdered and Nelson Rockefeller had appointed him pro tem. There were rallies and arguments everywhere, about the war and civil rights and (yes, I recall distinctly) independence for Puerto Rico. I stayed with the subject of New York politics, and observed John Lindsay as Mayor, L.B.J.'s ex-attorney general Ramsey Clark going straight and running — as later did the floppy-hatted feminist Bella Abzug — for the Democratic Senate nomination (and being beaten by Jacob Javits in the main event), and James Buckley eventually coming up against Professor Daniel Patrick Moynihan and finishing second. Hell, this was a state in which Gore Vidal had done well in a congressional race in a conservative district in '96 — outpolling Jack Kennedy who was atop of the ticket — and in which Norman Mailer, Jimmy Breslin, and William F. Buckley, Jr., had been able to run at least in a city election and create some decent noise. There may not have been giants in those days, but there was some vivid and vivacious politics.

SADDENED BY THAT THOUGHT and affronted by a fatuous, money-driven applause machine aimed at a coronation, one might decently demand a return to the politics of division. Anything to save the honor of New York. And yet, and yet. The subhead of that ignoble *New York Times* report read, naively but suggestively: "Hillary Thinks, Rudy Waits, Pundits Yearn." I propose only a small revision: "Pundits Think and Wait, Rudy and Hillary Yearn." For what are we really gazing at if not the potential romance of the century? As they contemplate running, aren't they really seeking a mate?

Like so many lovers, Hillary and Rudy will — on some refulgent still-to-come day — look back and bashfully review the moment when each of them just knew. Was it, she will breathe into his indomitable ear, the time when she saw how right—how very right — he was about Jerusalem and the Puerto Ricans? How vapid and girlish she had been — how untutored and innocent — until she switched her positions to match his! No, he will grin alarmingly yet indulgently as he half turns on the masterful pillow. For him, everything became as crystalline as the first morning in Eden when she came out in favor of sexual abstinence for the under-21. "Oh, Rudy," she exhales. "Honey," comes his muffled yet decisive response as he buries his well-honed muzzle like a hatchet in her . . . block that metaphor. And at this point she becomes, truly becomes, what she has only faked all year. She becomes a woman on the verge.

Vogue and *Talk* can drivel all they like about strong womanhood, but one has to be able to recognize sexual and political magnetism when it's staring one right in the face. See the pair of them as they try and pretend to fight it during the photo op at the 1996 unveiling of the Eleanor Roosevelt memorial in Riverside Park. Attraction of opposites doesn't cover it, if only because they are more twins than opposites. This is real, and fierce, and animal. It's coupling, and it's doing what comes naturally. Here is the Montague-Capulet checklist.

1. She comes out for dairy-industry subsidies while on her "listening tour" of up-state dairy farms. *The Wall Street Journal* attacks her for putting special interests before milk-hungry schoolkids. Something stirs in Rudy's breast. Not only does he (belatedly) come out for the same subsidies, but he claims he did so in a much neglected speech that was delivered earlier than hers! This is more than mere gallantry.

2. She has herself photographed dancing on a beach with her grue-

some husband just before Ms. Lewinsky sends everything into the tank. He has himself photographed dancing at Gracie Mansion with his rarely spotted wife, some time later. Body language was still language when last I checked. "I feel your pain" would be an approximate translation of his semaphore.

3. They are both keen Yankee fans, but he can be her guide and (a phrase from a sad past) her "mentor." In fact — and this thought makes me perspire — he'll have to be her mentor. "Come my Cub, and let me kiss away those tears."

4. They have both, very extensively and very deliberately, betrayed their own parties. No going back.

5. They both believe, when it comes to other people, in the politics of personal destruction.

6. They were both publicly opposed to the impeachment of President Clinton.

7. They are both enthusiasts for capital punishment, mandatory sentances, and the war on drugs.

8. They both ban smoking materials anywhere they can ban them (Mrs. Clinton having failed with the use of cigars in the White House).

9. They have both had advice from Dick Morris: Mr. Giuliani's advice useful but free, Mrs. Clinton's advice bad but expensive.

ONE COULD GO ON AND ON. But at how many weddings could you have said half as much about twin souls? The "donor community" loves them both, if not equally, but Mrs. Clinton's deftness with cattle futures could help smooth the mayor's return passage to those downtown boardrooms whose occupants he so offended back when he was a brokerage-raiding perp-walking U.S. attorney. Mr. Giuliani doesn't have much time for pets; Mrs. Clinton edited a cringe-inducing book of kid's letters to Socks and Buddy. Where they don't make a perfect fit, they have gaps that truly suggest they need each other. I hesitate to mention it, but the very word "prosecutor" and "indictment" could at least keep a spark going at the dinner table for years to come.

But let's stay with the breakfast table for now. Recall the stupid and pointless battle that was going on while I was writing this. Some fool in some Brooklyn museum decides to mount yet another exhibition of tapped untalent that upsets the Catholics, or at least upsets their spokesmen or cardinals. Filth! Public money! (Write the ensuing dialogue yourself, or paint it by numbers, or indeed with elephant dung, as we now term it.) Says Rudy: Stay away from this vileness until I can have it torn from the taxpayers' wall. Says the wife of the leader of the Free World: I wouldn't grace the building with my own presence, and I'm quite sure without viewing the stuff that it's offensive, but I'm not certain that we should penalize the museum. Sensation in a slow season for the press! Hillary blasts Rudy and vice versa! Grow up, comrades. What is this but a low-cholesterol and bran-centered non-event? You can just picture it: Husband in Scarsdale throws down the newspaper and says that's it — he's never contributing another penny to a museum he's never supported, and he's never paying another visit to a gallery he's never heard of until this very morning. Wife says soothingly that he's probably quite right but that it might not be all the gallery's fault, and he's about to miss his train. Can't you just see and hear this Westchester idyll?

EVERYBODY KNOWS THAT WE are looking at two dead-battery marriages here. Yet in each expired partnership, there is always one who is secretly hungry for love. (Actually, there are probably four partners hungry for love, or at least affection, but the president and Donna Hanover just don't compute as a team.) What an awful waste it seems, that the two most viable survivors should be glaring at each other instead of stealthily smirking. Just ask yourself: What use would either one of them be in the Senate? Mrs. Clinton would have to be "collegial" and "bipartisan" with a "deliberative body" nearly half of whose members voted to convict her (first) husband. And she'd have to remember that one electrifying and armpit-igniting moment on the Hill when she pledged universal health care. Mr. Giuliani would be reminded, often not too gently, that he is only one hick in Hicksville, and he wouldn't have the scope (for the indulgence of micro-megalomania) that he had as mayor of the Big City.

In order to determine which one of them gets to waste away in this manner, they have to affect a few courtly and dull disputes about things such as school vouchers. Not really enough to keep the mind and soul alive, is it? Look how tepidly things are tending, and how disagreements more or less have to be confected. Trying to draw the sting from any mention of health care, Hillary patronizing says that she's now "from the school of smaller steps." What's Rudy to do — say that he feels the same way about jaywalkers? Or — even more of a joke issue when you think about it — her fans complain of the mayor's undue "abrasiveness" while she retains the services of the suave and gallant Harold Ickes. This sham fight has a huge boredom potential that is already beginning to manifest itself. And the dance of the 700 "exploratory" veils, in a race without declared candidates, would deserve to be called foreplay in any other connection.

But together! As a team. As a power couple. I imagine them (or "envision" them, as they would both prefer to say) as the joint stewards of the government of New York. Here is a large but essentially empty position — Mario Cuomo was only one of many to demonstrate how you can hold it and grasp it and yet leave it vacant — which cries out for the abolition of loneliness at the top. Together, the one-time Goldwater girl from Illinois and the subverter of Pataki could make the sweetest music since George and Lurleen Wallace formed their Alabama combo. Totally unfit for anything but public life, and extremely reluctant to go back to the practice of law, they could be content in pretending to govern the state, and New Yorkers — of all shades and conditions — could pretend to be governed by them. From Niagara to Viagara in one triumphant bound.

I say nothing about the children, because it's not my way to make war on the innocent, but we can at the very least be pretty sure that there wouldn't be any more of them. Also that the existent ones wouldn't be offered up, or would not consent to be offered up, very much in public. Do not say that this is a small mercy.

BACK IN THOSE DEAR LOST DAYS, there were two other New York political currents, swirling dankly below the surface of the mainstream. There was always some unpolished Italian law-and-order type — one Democratic mayoral candidate in particular I remember named Mario Procaccino — who thought that Frankie Rizzo's tough-guy Cop Land Philadelphia was the way for New York to go. And there was always some overwrought female-victim type who thought that the personal was the political. Now we have a law-and-order Italian who grabs the Democratic working class votes by the bagful, and an overwrought female victim who can't decide whether the personal is political or whether it isn't (and who prays to be given Al Sharpton's endorsement — but not yet, dear Lord, not yet, otherwise she would have mentioned the names of Abner Louima and Amadou Diallo by now).

The other great thing this pair holds in common is a fanatical attachment, at least in theory, to family values. Jake La Motta, on hearing how attractive his new opponent was, once growled, "I dunno. I got a problem: if I should fuck him or fight him." Fiddle with the gender a bit and this is a highly pertinent question for our own Italian stallion and his proud but pettish potential antagonist. How long can he ignore those demure, downcast, and essentially complicit glances? Is he a man or a mouse? Is she a strong woman or a mere flirt?

I see it now. A brave day in the New York spring. Onto the steps of City Hall emerge the blissed-out duo, blinking with astonishment at their own happiness. Snapping in the breeze atop the building are the flags of Illinois, Arkansas, New York and Palermo. Case-hardened newsmen and lensmen wipe away many tears. *The New York Post* runs a headline: HEARTLESS COUPLE IN BOTTOMLESS LOVE. Both bride and groom, with snarling grins, affect to see, and share, the joke. Just to think of this scene is to realize how every, truly, madly, deeply *right* it is. Come on, come through, New York, New York.

— ***Christopher Hitchens*** is a columnist for *The Nation* and a frequent contributor to *Vanity Fair* and the *Times Literary Supplement*. He has been Washington editor of *Harper's* and book critic for *Newsday*, and is the author of several books, including *No One Left to Lie To: The Triangulations of William Jefferson Clinton*. This article appeared in *Vanity Fair* (November 1999) and is reprinted by generous permission of the author.

You Go, Girl!

Patricia Schroeder

MY HUSBAND JIM and Hillary Clinton bonded instantly. I was so jealous. As soon as they met, they started reminiscing about their youth in Chicago and debating who was the biggest Cub fan. While they were chattering away about their favorite Chicago food and restaurants, I was finally able to wedge myself into the conversation. This was during the 1992 Presidential primary. Obviously, I changed the topic to the Family and Medical Leave Act and the Women's Health Equity Act, both having been vetoed by President Bush. I had put too many years of effort into those bills to miss my chance to lobby Hillary, even it if was rude. Of course, she was right up to speed on both issues. Her involvement and knowledge of public policy issues are total. She promised if they were elected, she would do everything she could to get these bills enacted into law. They were and she did!

Soon after the Inauguration, I got a call from her office that she would like to meet with the Congressional Caucus on Women's Issues, which I co-chaired with Olympia Snowe. We were doing back flips because we had tried to meet with the Reagan and Bush people for 12 years and only had a pile of rejection letters to show for our efforts.

What a joy all of us to have a First Lady so involved and willing to act. We firehosed her with all the issues we had been working on that had been vetoed or thwarted, Hillary took detailed notes and said she would go to work.

To be honest, I thought her heart was in the right place, but there would be so many demands on her time that we shouldn't count on instant action. I was wrong. The very first bill signing at the White House was my Family and Medical Leave bill. I was stunned. Over the next two years, I almost got bored with White House bill signings. The Women's Caucus agenda just kept rolling out for the President's signature. In between the bill signings for all of our bills that were previously bottled up, the President and Vice President asked to meet with the Congresswomen. They gave us so much more time than we expected, some Congresswomen had to leave for planes. What a difference an election makes and a very focused First Lady makes.

So I'm disclosing my bias; I'm a total fan. I went with Hillary when she went to the University of Michigan (my alma mater) to give a graduation speech. It was such fun to just catch up on our lives. Chelsea had just gone to her first formal dance. The President was in Russia at some big summit and very upset he was missing the big event. She laughed as she told how he kept sneaking out of the meeting to phone and find out how things were going. They finally had to tell him things weren't going to go well if he didn't stop calling, because Chelsea couldn't get ready for talking on the phone to dad!

Obviously, I'd love to be her best friend, but neither of us had time to wash our pantyhose, much less have coffee and chat. There were many political occasions where we got to spend time together and I was amazed at how fast she plugged into each of us, remembering our prior conversations and starting up where we stopped the last time. She came to Denver to do a health care forum for me when health care was the issue. She was mobbed by supporters; confronted with very nasty protesters; and we dragged her all over the city. We even took her to the Colorado National Guard tents that had been set up in the low-income areas of Denver. They were dispensing health care just like they do when they practice foreign deployments. Hillary was totally into it. She never complained about the expanded schedule, seeing it as the brain food we hoped it would be.

I could describe more events that we shared, but being in the public eye a little myself, I'm totally in awe of how she handled the floodlights that have focused on her life 24/7. Raising a teenage daughter in today's world seems to be a Herculean task for anyone. Imagine doing it in front of the world. Her rootedness in family and her ability to focus, no matter how high the political gale force winds are blowing, are amazing. It's very clear she has been the economic pillar of the Clinton family since they were married. We now also know she's been the emotional pillar of that family. No one should have to tough out what she has during the latest scandal.

I chuckle when people ask why she would run for Senate in New York. "Doesn't she know tough it will be?" they asked. Where have they been? Mars? Do they think she's been eating bon-bons and getting her hair done as First Lady? I think she figures it's time for the family to support her emotionally and financially! She always puts her whole self into whatever she takes on. She is not one who demands pampering. She really loves people and relates to them. And Hillary is one of the smartest women I've met. She is a great transitional model for women at the end of the century. She has protected her husband and child as a lioness. Now she is asking her husband to hold her purse while she does something she's always wanted to do.

I'm ready to stand up and shout, "You go, girl!" She has waited for her turn and it's here. Hillary Rodham Clinton is one classic American role model for the end of the century that has seen so much change in women's lives.

— ***Patricia Schroeder*** served in the House of Representatives from 1972-1995. She was a member of the House National Security Committee, the House Judiciary Committee and chaired the Select Committee on Children, Youth and Families. She is currently the President and Chief Executive Officer of the Association of American Publishers (AAP). "You Go, Girl!" was written for *Speaking of Hillary*. Copyright 2000 by Patricia Schroeder.